The Life and Lessons from a Warzone:
A Memoir of Dr. Robert Nyeko Obol

The Life and Lessons from a Warzone: A Memoir of Dr. Robert Nyeko Obol

Robert Obol

ISBN 978-1-300-06846-4

To the People of Pajule and Florence Pope

Table of Contents

Author's Note

The format in which I have written this book is intended to identify the significant and defining events in my life as a young boy, an adult, and a minister of God. The main focus of this book is about my work for three years in Pajule parish in the Archdiocese of Gulu, as an associate pastor and later pastor, which were marked by insecurity, war, violence, mistrust, fear, and uncertainty. Most of the events I speak of are from my own experiences, and I will always have a very vivid memory of them.

During the time I worked in Pajule, one of the things that always came to my mind whenever a significant event took place was that at some point in my life, I would have to tell the story. This is because while all people involved in a war experience its negative consequences, the experiences that individuals go through are unique from person to person, community to community. For example, my own personal experiences and perceptions were most of the time completely different from those of my next-door neighbor and unknown to him or her, unless I decided to share them.

In writing this book, I have several motivations. I want to communicate to readers who have not had an actual experience of war in their lives the feeling and nature of what daily life is like in politically unstable and volatile areas. I also intend to point out the misperception that many people have about an ongoing war. Many times those in the news media report inaccurately about a war. It is common for them to report that a country is at war, and yet most of the time it is only a section of the population, a region, or a few communities experiencing the brunt of the war.

In a warzone the tables are turned upside down. It is not stability or normalcy that defines people's lives, as we all take for granted, but violence and uncertainty. The goal of this book is to demonstrate how people learn to survive and adapt to this new reality. I also desire to mention the profound impact of war on a society and recognize actions that express resilience, human goodness, and excellence in a warzone—actions like kindness, forgiveness, reconciliation, dedication to duty, generosity, celebration, thanksgiving, faith, hope, and love.

I also want to talk about the lessons people learn living in a warzone. Living in a warzone is like being thrown into a fast-flowing river and told to swim or drown. People are constantly thrust into the unexpected and have to immediately make the best of it with little or no room for mistakes. They learn from what they see, what they hear, what their own feelings and their bodies tell them, their own mistakes and those of others, and above all their own personal reflections on what goes on in their own lives and in those around them.

In this book, I also demonstrate the unique understandings and insights that people in a warzone develop about words, concepts, and ideas that become daily realities they have to live with. For example, those who live in a warzone understand insecurity as a situation in which everything is up in the air, there is no one to turn to for reassurance, those who carry out wrongdoings are most of the time not held accountable for the crimes they commit since they cannot be traced, it is not possible to trust any person or institution, and the rules and norms that govern human conduct and human relations as we all know them do not apply.

A warzone is a place in which people constantly ask questions and most of them remain unanswered—questions like why is this happening? Who is responsible for what took place? When will this violence come to an end? Why doesn't God intervene? Why can't the adversaries talk to each other and resolve their differences amicably?

This book also shows the common bond that all people share, however different the context of their lives; that for people who live in warzones, just like the rest of society, it is family, faith, relationships, and the church community that provide meaning and strength to their lives.

I want to talk about my own faith journey as well. My work in a warzone made me ask myself many questions about my own safety and that of others. There were many times while traveling that I narrowly missed entering into deadly ambushes since the incident took place either before or immediately after I had passed. These narrow misses made me constantly worry about my own safety and at the same time ask myself why I had survived and others did not. This made me a strong believer in providence; that whatever happens in my life at any one moment is not by accident, and that it is God who is ultimately in charge. As a result I came to the theological conclusion that so long as God had a goal for me to accomplish, even if working in Pajule was filled with dangers like working in a minefield, I would be safe.

Further, I wish to explain some of the collaborative decisions I participated in that were filled with risk and adventure outside my expected role as a minister of God. That I now believe God's hand was in all of them. These decisions saved lives, protected the town, and strengthened the sense of community.

Finally, I desire to discuss the presence of mystery in a warzone. There so many things that take place in a warzone that we would desire to have a fuller grasp of, but many times even if they are explained, we have only partial information about or understanding of them. For example, we shall never have a complete understanding of why it is that individuals who claim to be spiritually motivated are not bothered by the shedding of the blood of the innocent. Or why people who look and sound normal constantly commit heinous crimes. Why human beings are very cruel to one another. Why adults who should know better force children to commit terrible crimes. And why families that have lost loved ones are willing to forgive without any reservation.

Chapter One

1985: A Chaotic and Consequential Year

It was a crisp October night in 1985 when a group of unknown gunmen attacked Buda—the town in eastern Uganda where my father worked and lived with his family. When the gunshots started at two in the morning, my father immediately got up from bed, dressed hurriedly, and ran from his room to the other end of the house where my cousin Jildo and I were sleeping. Fortunately, my mother and the rest of the family members were at the ancestral home at Madi Opei in northern Uganda.

My father found that my cousin, who was seventeen years old at the time, had been awakened by the barrage of gunfire from the town. However, I, his thirteen-year-old son, was deeply asleep. My father's first thought was that we should all get out of the house, but the fact that I was sleeping became a problem for both of them. They did not know what to do with me, and yet they had to act fast since the attack on the town was intensifying.

In the culture of the Acoli people, it is generally believed that when a person is asleep he is not to be awakened in the middle of a gunfight. There is a cultural assumption that it may be one's luck that a person sleeps through an exchange of gunfire. There is also the fear that awakening a person in the middle of one's sleep may make him disoriented, and if he were to fall into any danger or harm after being roused, the party who woke him up would be blamed for the injury or death. Because of this, most people do not wake up someone who is asleep because they would not like to live with the guilt of being responsible for any harm that was caused. Further, it is culturally presumed that an attacker in his right conscience will show decency and respect for a sleeping person, since he is harmless. So, my father and Jildo let me sleep.

My father asked Jildo to remain in the house and take care of me. He was afraid that if the attackers were to overrun the town, which was defended and protected by less than twelve policemen, he would be their primary target since he was the manager of the only bank in town. It was always presumed that the bank manager had the key for the repository where the money was kept. If the attackers were to overrun the police guard post, they would have come to seize him so he could take them to the money.

So, my father escaped out of the house through the back since the front entrance faced the direction of the town, where most of the gunfire was concentrated. The house had a four-meter wall around it. To get out of the house, he carefully opened the wooden door, trying not to agitate a rusty bolt that often made a lot of noise, and once he had made his silent exit, Jildo locked the door behind him.

Fortunately, there was no one waiting to either attack or snatch my father. However, as he stepped out of the compound, he was again seized by fear. Even though he was now free to move or run in more than one direction, he realized that he was more vulnerable to a physical attack while outside the enclosures of the house.

Another challenge was the night. There was no moonlight, and the house was surrounded by a banana plantation with plants almost seven meters high that completely blocked any vision of the skies. In addition, the hilly terrain made spotting an approaching attacker almost impossible. At this very moment, the safest thing for my father to do was to go into the banana plantation and lie down in the cover of the broad green leaves. However, he was afraid that one of the attackers might be lurking within, waiting for the moment the police guard post had been overrun to attack the house. Second, my father was terrified by the fact that banana plantations tended to be a home for insects, spiders, and, in some cases, killer snakes. Because of these concerns, instead he lay down in a deep hole shaped like a tunnel between the wall of the compound and the banana plantation. This was at a distance of about fifty meters from the house. While he was concerned about his safety, he also wanted to keep an eye on what was happening to us in the house.

As he lay still, the gunfight continued for the next two hours. As dawn approached, the temperature began to drop dramatically. Fortunately, he had been able to don the winter coat that he had last worn almost two years ago as a student in Milan, Italy, but had not touched since then because the weather was always warm in Buda.

At around five a.m., the guns fell silent. The few policemen had stood their ground and pushed back the attackers. To be certain all was safe, my father returned to the house at six a.m. He was shivering and exhausted and had not slept the entire night. My cousin was also fine; he had diligently kept watch at my bedside all night. On my part, I had slept throughout the night. It was only at breakfast that they told me how intense and frightful the night had been for them.

Such incidents were the norm at the end of 1985. As a young boy at the time, I recall that in the news coverage there was much chaos and violence in the country from the very beginning of the year. In the south-western parts of the country, the rebel army known as the National Resistance Army (NRA) was fighting the government of the Uganda People's Congress (UPC), led by President Milton Obote. It was common to hear news of attacks and ambushes in that part of the country and even of land mines being used to blow up civilian passenger vehicles.

There were also tribal and regional differences within the military that made them fight among themselves. The UPC government blamed these clashes and infighting on uncoordinated troop actions by their forces. By the middle of the year, the NRA had killed several prominent military officers and soldiers at lower levels during such attacks. At the end of July, some of the government soldiers led by Bazilio Olara Okello, an Acoli tribesman, overthrew the regime of Milton Obote, a Lango tribesman, on July 27, 1985; and the army commander, Tito Okello Lutwa, an Acoli, became president.

There were many factors behind the collapse of the Milton Obote government. In the first place, the NRA rebels were putting a lot of military pressure on the government soldiers by inflicting many casualties. Second, the internal tribal and regional differences among the government soldiers played a significant role. Third, there was war fatigue in the country. Most of the soldiers who overthrew the government of Milton Obote were tired of war. They had spent almost a decade in exile during the regime of Idi Amin and participated in the 1978–79 liberation war coming from Tanzania into Uganda that eventually removed Idi Amin from power. But in less than two years, the country was at war after the elections of 1980, and the UPC political leadership was unamenable to any compromise.

Most of the government soldiers who had been in exile for a decade had experienced the personal and painful side of political instability. Many suffered marriage and family breakups because they had no way to communicate with their wives and children to inform them that they were still alive. In fact, when most of these soldiers returned, they discovered that their wives had remarried and started a new life of their own. To these soldiers who were exhausted with war and who had overthrown the government of Milton Obote, peace talks with the NRA rebels were the logical option. Despite the fact that the peace talks had been initiated, fighting continued, and much of the south western part of the country fell under rebel control and was cut off from the rest of the country.

It is important to note that the undisciplined army, under the military government, also contributed to the political chaos and instability in the country. It was accused of rapes, lootings, and killings. This made the regime lose the political support and goodwill of most Ugandans, even if it was pursuing a dialogue to address the political challenges facing the country. By the end of 1985, it was a common occurrence for small groups of people with no military training to constitute themselves overnight into a rebel group under the leadership of an influential local politician or an ex–army officer in order to fight the military government in power.

In addition to the chaos caused by the overthrow of Milton Obote, the country was confronted by regional and ethnic differences. The rebels were seen as a Bantu group and were supported by most of the Bantu ethnic groups in the country. In Uganda, Bantu tribes are the dominant ethnic groups in most of the western, southern, and eastern parts of the country.

On the other hand, the military regime was taken as a government of the Northerners because the bulk of its soldiers came from the north, east, and west Nile regions of the country. The military regime was strongly supported by the west Nile region since it allowed the people that had gone into exile in the neighboring countries to return home after the overthrow of Idi Amin Dada. These regional and tribal differences between the North and South in Uganda have existed since colonial times; however, the UPC government had tried to minimize and suppress them since as a political party it had to get support from all over the country.

At the end of the year, we would always go home to the North for our Christmas and New Year celebrations. That November before our journey, I was to sit at Saint Austin Catholic parish in Mbale town for my seminary entrance examination for admission to St. James Preparatory Seminary in Achilet, Tororo. Saint Austin's Catholic parish was a thirty-minute drive away. From Buda, I was among the fifteen candidates selected who had met the requirements of the vocations committee in the parish.

The interview was to be in Mbale and was to last a full day, so my father brought me the day before. As people came to the end of their workday, we noticed most of them hurrying to leave the city center. It appeared that if one were to have a safe night, one would have to move as far as possible from the downtown area. This was strange to us because for many years we had spent a night in Mbale on our way home, since there were many more amenities and places to go for entertainment than in Buda. We always went out to watch a movie at one of the theaters in the city, but this time we had to be behind closed doors by seven p.m. for fear of attacks by armed thugs.

The following day, after I had a full day of oral and written interviews, we were ready to leave for Kitgum, which is in the North. Previously, we had traveled there by bus in a day, passing through the three major tribal regions of Teso, Kumam, and Lango, finally entering Acoliland. But this time we could not use the bus to travel directly to Kitgum because these areas had turned very hostile to the military regime in power, partly because they were very sympathetic to the Obote regime that the military had overthrown. And the government soldiers continued to abuse the rights of the people in these areas and the Teso region in particular, where on several occasions they stole cattle from the people.

So in order to travel to Kitgum, we had to use the train, since it was the only means of transport that was available and it passed through less-populated areas. Even traveling by train was not entirely safe, but it was the only option we had. We believed that with its speed it could pass safely through an ambush, as it would be difficult for the local people in the hostile spots to either stop it or unscrew its rails without technical knowledge and equipment.

There was no set time for the train to arrive, but we expected to board it between midnight and two a.m. However, we had to get to the railway station by six p.m. so we would not have to travel there when it was dark. At the railway station, we found many people who were also traveling to northern Uganda; the primary talk was of the growing level of insecurity in the country and the uncertainty about having a safe trip home. Some of the travelers who had come the day before from Gulu and were returning that evening shared stories about how attempts were being made by the local people living along the railway lines to place huge logs on the rails with the hope that the train would run over them and overturn.

As a young boy hearing stories of possible threats to the train, I really felt afraid of the journey ahead. This was also the first time I would travel on a train. However, the fact that I was traveling with my father gave me some peace of mind. I just felt within myself that as long as I was traveling with him, everything would be OK.

As we sat waiting for the train under the veranda of the main office at the railway station, a government soldier came and stood in front of us. He was about five feet tall with a slender build, and he began to look over my father very intently for almost ten minutes without saying a word. This made us very uncomfortable. At this time a government soldier taking a particular interest in a single citizen was not a good sign. It could mean that the military had been tracking him or the soldier was trying to remember someone suspicious who had been described to him. However, to break the uncomfortable silence between us, I greeted him, as I was convinced that he spoke the same ethnic dialect that we did. In fact, I was right. He was interested in talking to us and asking some questions, but he did not know how to begin a conversation.

It was then that he started to talk to my father. He said that he remembered him vaguely because in 1971, there was a young man who came from the neighboring village of Madi Opei to his village of Agoro and married one of its most beautiful ladies. In fact, this soldier was talking about the cultural wedding ceremony of my father to my mother. My father was able to confirm that indeed he was the one. This soldier told us that he was going home to the North, but he was not intending to return soon since there was, in his words, "a big war" coming from the southwestern part of the country. He was alluding to what was happening at the time, when the NRA rebels were engaging in peace talks with the Tito Okello regime and at the same time were arming themselves and capturing more territory. He could sense that the momentum was shifting in favor of the rebels.

By midnight, the train had not arrived. Since it had been a busy day for me, I soon fell asleep. At that moment gunfire broke out. There were a lot of shots from the direction of the military barracks in Mbale, known as Bugema. The travelers at the railway station suspected that it might be NRA rebels attacking it. The biggest challenge for most of them was where to go since they did not know the surroundings of the railway station and there was hardly any camouflage. Fortunately, many of them were able to hide in the tall grass nearby. My father and a few women with several young children remained sitting at the railway station. These mothers felt that they had nowhere to go, and on his part, my father could not leave because I was sound asleep on the cement floor. In fact, I slept through the entire exchange of gunfire.

The train finally arrived at around two a.m. making very loud sounds that woke me up. This was only a few minutes after the guns had fallen silent, and most of the travelers left their hideouts. As the train approached, I picked up my belongings and started to run toward it. My father shouted and stopped me, reminding me that I should not leave him since we were going to sit together. After we had taken our seats on the train and were about to begin our journey, he described the apprehension he'd gone through during the time I was asleep.

As we started to travel, I could feel the speed and force with which the train moved. The faster it went, the harsher the sounds became in my ears. It sounded like something was constantly being violently thrashed. I wondered if I could manage to tolerate these grinding sounds since our trip was going to be at least sixteen hours.

Once aboard, I could again feel the chaos in the country. After we had paid the transport fee at the railway station and boarded the train, we were on our own. There were no lights in the railroad car, and so it was completely dark. If we needed anything, there was no one to ask for assistance. I could see that when food or water spilled on the passengers, they would tear any remaining parts of seat covers to clean it up. It seemed as if one was free to do anything.

On the way to Gulu, the largest town in northern Uganda populated mainly by the Acoli people, we reached our first stopover in Teso. As was the case at all stopovers, there were soldiers at checkpoints looking for rebel infiltrators. At these checkpoints, the government soldiers would ask for identity cards and tax documents and focus on the physical features and dialect of the travelers. My father made sure that all his documents were in order, and since I was thirteen years old, his documents took care of mine.

However, one government soldier, about six feet tall, slender, and dark skinned with his gun strapped on his back, came over to us and asked my father to provide his identification. I thought he looked newly recruited. From his accent I could tell that he was a Northerner. My father politely and respectfully provided all that was asked for since he did not want any trouble. When he saw a new sandal in my hands, which my father had bought for me as a Christmas gift and was still in its package, he immediately asked for the receipt. Since we had just bought it, I immediately checked my bag for it. Unfortunately, I did not find it. It appears that I misplaced it or forgot to ask for it at the time we bought it. For about five minutes, the government soldier insisted that he wanted the receipt and began to raise his voice. Because of this, my father nodded to me to give the sandal to him to avoid any further problems. I believe that the soldier also noticed how frustrated my father had become. When I handed over my sandal to him, the soldier was surprised, embarrassed, and uneasy as well; he stared at both of us silently and then gave the sandal back to me. This incident once again demonstrated the high degree of lawlessness in the country at the time; a soldier at a checkpoint whose primary duty was to protect the citizens could make up rules and laws for the citizens to abide by.

We arrived in Gulu the following day around four thirty p.m. and were greatly relieved that we had been able to reach Acoliland while traveling under such conditions. We spent the night in Gulu and the following day left on a bus for Kitgum and eventually Madi Opei, my father's birthplace. That December, much of our time was spent listening to the radio in the hope that a peace agreement would be signed and there would be peace in the country. The peace agreement was later signed, but the war continued. Every day, the BBC reported that the NRA rebels were getting closer to the capital city, and innocent people continued to die across the country.

Chapter Two

The Beginning of My Seminary Training

When it came to January 1986, we were to leave Madi Opei and return to Buda in the Eastern part of the country where my father worked. We got to Kitgum town in a military lorry since this was the only means of transport available. There we got a military truck that was traveling from Kitgum to Mbale. The truck belonged to a high ranking military officer in the army and since the driver had armed escorts, we felt that we would be safe. On reaching Buda, I received news from a man called Naki who worked with my father at the local bank that I would begin my seminary training in a week's time.

On January 18, 1986, I started my final year of grade school/primary seven at St. James Preparatory Seminary in Achilet, Tororo. I traveled with my father, and eventually we arrived in Tororo City, where the seminary was located about four miles away from the city center. When I met the rector, Father Wet, he congratulated me on working so hard to qualify. I was excited to be admitted. When I saw some seminarians I was already acquainted with, I ran to them, and the first thing I asked them to do was take me to my place in the dormitory. The excitement made me forget my father, and in fact he returned home without us saying farewell to one another.

As I started my preparatory seminary training, the war between the government of Tito Okello and the NRA rebels was still raging. The rebels were getting closer and closer to Kampala, the capital city of Uganda. Even during our first week in the seminary, we were aware that the war was intensifying, but we had ceased following it keenly since none of us had a radio and we were young, being between the ages of twelve and fifteen years. So we relied on what we were told by the seminary authorities.

In the course of our first week of classes, we kept hearing rumors that Kampala had fallen into the hands of the rebels. On Friday it became apparent to us that something significant had happened in the country because in the middle of the night we heard a lot of gunshots from the direction of Tororo, in particular the military barracks of Rubongi that was along the road to Achilet Preparatory Seminary.

The following morning, our first Saturday in the seminary, we woke up to a lot of chaos. From the compound of the seminary, we could see government soldiers fleeing with their families in trucks filled with looted property and household items, while others searched for any vehicle that they could forcefully take from its owners to transport them to wherever their destination was.

On seeing the chaos, it became apparent to us that the NRA had overthrown the government of Tito Okello Lutwa. And that day would mark the beginning of the lack of peace for northern Uganda because most of the soldiers of the deposed military regime fled northwards and crossed the border of Uganda to camp in South Sudan. Later, when these former government soldiers were attacked in their Sudanese camps, most of them fled back to Uganda and started to fight on August 25, 1986, against the new government.

The year 1986 meant great change in the country. For most of the years since Uganda had gained independence in 1962, the country had been ruled by Northerners, and for the first time real political and military power had passed into the hands of Southerners. This change also gave an opportunity to the rest of the country to express their true feelings about Northerners, who are for the most part of Luo or Sudanic origins.

Achilet Preparatory Seminary was in the eastern part of Uganda, an area culturally dominated by the Jophadola, who are also of Luo ancestry. So, the Jophadola naturally made up a large part of the seminary, but the majority of the students were composed of the Bantu: Bagishu, Samia, Bagwere, Baganda, etc. The other ethnic groups were the Iteso, who were a sizable number, and the Sabiny, who were very few; and these were neither Luo nor Bantu.

In the whole school I was one of two seminarians who were Northerners. Personally, I was surprised by the level of hostility and prejudice we experienced as seminarians, even though we were just in our early teens. There was much resentment expressed toward me because of the fact that I was a Northerner and a person of Luo origin—and consequently I was one of the "killers" or someone cruel. It was difficult for me to have an argument or a discussion with a fellow seminarian without being reminded that I was a Northerner. Other students would mock me by mimicking a government soldier of the former regime breaking into a house speaking Swahili (the official language of the army) with a northern accent. This was often done to make me feel bad or to silence my point of view. This experience made me realize for the first time that there were very deep divisions in my country that I could not ignore.

While there was unanimous hostility to Northerners, occasionally tension would arise between the Bantu and the Jophadola, who were Luos. Statements like "Now is the time for the Bantu to rule this country" were explosive among the students. The Jophadola would get incensed, and then I would get caught up in the middle and not know what to say and with whom to side.

What I admired was the stand of most of our teachers, who were both priests and laymen. They may have had their own biases, but I never experienced any directed at me. In fact, as a Northerner I felt safe and protected by them. Normally no students tried to either justify or publicly propagate their inclinations, though they often came to the fore when there were outbursts and heated arguments among us. But more often they were subtle in demonstrating them.

At the end of 1986, I completed my preparatory seminary schooling at Achilet, and in March of the following year, 1987, I joined the seminary high school at St. Pius X Seminary, Nagongera, Tororo, which was about twelve miles away from Tororo. My education at the seminary high school would normally have taken six years, but I would study at the school for only four years.

At that point I was now eighteen years old and wanted to study in a school that was not a Catholic seminary. I was even willing to go to a public high school. I had four reasons for doing this:

First, I considered studying in a non-seminary environment to be an essential part of my process of discernment. I had joined the seminary when I was thirteen years old, and I felt that it was now time for me to make comparisons and contrasts between life inside and outside the seminary before making any final commitment.

Second, I also wanted to confirm my vocation. Within myself, I had always felt that God wanted me to be a priest. Though I knew that leaving the seminary would expose my vocation to many risks, I was convinced that the burning desire in me for the priesthood would weather all the storms that would come my way.

Third, I also believed that two years out of the seminary would give me the opportunity to return to my diocese. I had joined the seminary in Tororo because my father happened to be a civil servant, and I hoped that if I were still interested in the priesthood I would be able to join Gulu diocese, which was my home diocese.

Fourth, as a seminarian, I was required to have a parish that I belonged to, but it had become almost impossible to be part of a parish in the diocese of Tororo because my parents no longer lived there.

In May 1991, I joined a Catholic high school called Saint Charles Lwanga Kasasa in Masaka, which was run by the Brothers of Christian Instruction. This school was not a seminary, but the school rules were strictly enforced. Its dominant ethnic group was a Bantu tribe called the Baganda. At this school, I had to work hard to fit in and be like the rest of the students. I believe that at the end of two years I was like them in everything. But as the two years came to an end, it became very clear to me that God was calling me to be a priest. In the first place, my love and desire for the priesthood had increased, and second, when I thought about being a priest I experienced inner peace while anything else gave me restlessness and inner turbulence.

Saint Charles Lwanga Kasasa was located in the South. Even now, five years after the overthrow of the regime of Tito Okello, there was still a very strong prejudice against Northerners. In fact the first evening I reported to class, a student called Kibirige asked my name in the local language of Luganda, which I could understand but not speak. When I told him my name, it was obvious to him that it was not a Bantu name but that of a Northerner. He immediately turned to the class, which was majority Baganda, and began to complain in the local language: "I do not know why in all my classes as a student at Kasasa, there always has to be an Okello" (a common Northern name) "or a Northerner in it." He appeared agitated with my presence. The rest of the class listened without making any comments, like they had not heard what was said. I was surprised and frightened as well but was certain that he was not going to attack me. However, this student insisted before the class that he wanted to know what region I came from. To get him off my back, I told him that I was not from the northern part of the country but from the eastern region, and that I was a Jophadola by tribe. Since the Jophadola are Luo speakers and share some similar names with Northerners, I was certain that he would be unable to make distinctions.

After completing St. Charles Lwanga Kasasa, I returned to my home diocese and joined Alokolum Seminary in Gulu to begin my college years. Alokolum was in the Northern part of Uganda where I studied philosophy for three years. After completing Alokolum, I did one year of internship at Lacor Seminary High School, Gulu and then I joined Ggaba Seminary in Kampala. I was a student of theology in Ggaba for four years, which also marked the end of my training for the Catholic priesthood. The seminaries for both philosophy and theology were national seminaries and were made up of a multiplicity of tribes. Issues of ethnicity and regionalism would arise, but in a more subtle manner. However, my seminary training gave me the opportunity to learn new ideas from students who were from different parts of the country, and to see things through their eyes as well.

At a cultural level, this deepened my self-awareness, especially with regard to how people looked at my tribe and region. It was also a moment for me to reflect on my own cultural and tribal attitudes toward them as well. I came to discover that when it comes to the crime of tribal bias and prejudice, no one has clean hands, for we Northerners have our own biases and prejudices toward the Bantu tribes; for the most part we see them as cowards, liars, thieves, and incapable of being trusted. Above all, I believe that this awareness of my own cultural assumptions and prejudices toward others and my own awareness of their tribal and cultural prejudices toward me made me at ease in dealing with them, because I always believed that beyond the prejudices they were real people like me with good hearts and intentions.

My Final Journey and Ordination to the Catholic Priesthood

The high dropout rate from the seminary training in the diocese of Gulu throughout the decade of the nineties also weighed on me heavily. Most of the seminarians voluntarily abandoned their training for the Catholic priesthood at different stages of their formation for one reason or another. For example, at the end of August 1994, the beginning of the academic year 1994–1995, I was one of seventeen college seminarians who participated in the annual general meeting—and out of this number only two of us eventually became priests. Because of this priestly ordinations were rare in the diocese. Seeing my contemporaries constantly leave the seminary was depressing but also strengthened my resolve to continue to the end. I was convinced that even if I had many choices about what to do with my life, God still needed young men like me who were open to giving up other opportunities in life to serve Him; and I believed that I could do it.

The vocation crisis in the diocese of Gulu at the time worried everyone. The Christians wondered about whether they would have priests to serve them in the near future, and the priests worried about the continuity of their ministry and why young men were not being drawn to their vocation. For the seminarians in the diocesan seminary high school, it was equally devastating, because whenever a college seminarian left his training, they lost a role model or someone that they looked up to.

So I was firmly convinced that my choice to be a priest would contribute toward restoring faith, hope, and stability in a Church that was experiencing a crisis of self-confidence and self-doubt. In August of 1997, when I reported to Ggaba Seminary, I was the only student from my diocese; and yet, the neighboring diocese of Arua that was carved out of the diocese of Gulu had forty seminarians.

It was in June 1999, when I had two years left before my ordination to the priesthood, that I had a memorable encounter with one of my clansmen. We had gone to Madi Opei, my father's birthplace, to visit the gravesite of his elder brother, who had passed away two months before. By this time my home parish had not had a priest assigned to it for three years. Throughout the many years that I had been a seminarian, I'd had plenty of support from my family and my adopted parish of Christ the King, but almost no open encouragement from any members of my father's clan.

I remember that as the years went by and I was approaching the final stages of my priestly training, many of the paternal relatives kept asking me questions like "Robert, what are you still doing in the seminary?" "Why are you, a young, intelligent and handsome man, wasting yourself in that place?" "Can't you find something better to do with yourself?" "Why do you intend to kill the clan and tribe?"

I paid attention to their questions, and the ones that I could answer, I did. But I avoided as much as possible entering into any argument since I knew that I would not be able to convince them nor would they change my mind. I personally understood their ambivalence, indifference, and at times, their hostility to me becoming a priest since they placed married life above everything else. Because I was the firstborn in my family, they expected me to get married and raise children to keep the family line alive—and at a certain point be a leader of the clan as well. But if I became a priest, all these sacred cultural responsibilities and obligations would be in jeopardy.

So in the evening, as we were getting ready to leave for Kitgum, Onesimo, a crippled gentleman supporting himself with a walking stick, came to me. He told me that he had something important to discuss with me. I had not seen or met him before. I think he was in his early forties, but he looked much older. In my short dialogue with him, I could tell that he was not a regular churchgoer but he intensely loved the parish church of Madi Opei and the presence of a priest in the community. He told me that he had a request to make of me, and I promised him that I would consider it seriously if I were able to do something about it. He said:

"Robert, do us the honor of becoming a priest. See what is happening in our parish? We have not had a priest assigned here for almost four years; whenever we ask for one to be appointed here, we are always told that there are very few priests in the diocese. If you become a priest, it will be hard for them to always tell us that there is no priest to be assigned to our parish since we shall ask them to assign you to work here as our son. You never know; you might become our voice as well."

These words moved me deeply because they expressed the sentiment of a community that was experiencing a void. It needed a spiritual father and leader. At the same time, this request gave me some satisfaction because I could see how much progress the community had made in its values. In the past all that they had cared about was that one married.

When I was young, I was attracted to the life of the priest as one who gives personal attention to any person who comes to him, even if he does not know them. But as I got older, I became more attracted to the priesthood because of the humanity and self-offering of Jesus Christ. While the choice to be a priest is deeply personal, the thoughts and concerns of Onesimo served as an inspiration to me. It reinforced my conviction that if I were to become a priest, it would not be to benefit myself but to serve others. The following year, on July 15, 2000, I was ordained a deacon in Gulu cathedral. And one year later, on August 18, 2001, I was ordained a Catholic priest at Christ the King Parish in Kitgum, which is in Kitgum vicariate since Gulu diocese had been elevated to an archdiocese in 1999 and later subdivided into two vicariates, Kitgum and Gulu.

One day before my priestly ordination, I met my bishop; and in our discussion, he expressed his intention to appoint me to Pajule parish, which had been run by the Comboni missionaries for the last forty years. He informed me that the missionaries were soon leaving control of this parish to the local diocesan clergy. There was talk in the course of the preparations for my ordination that I might be assigned to teach in the diocesan seminary high school; but the bishop was of the idea that I needed to have a holistic experience, and that is why he was assigning me to start my priestly work in a parish setting.

My priestly ordination was an occasion of great joy for the people. Since the elevation of Gulu diocese to an archdiocese in 1999, and the arrival of a new bishop, no one from the diocese had been ordained a priest. The last ordination under the former bishop had taken place almost four years ago. And the venue for my ordination was Christ the King, my adopted parish where I had lived and grown up. The members of the parish had been supportive of me at each and every stage of my seminary training. Many of them saw their own dreams and imaginations fulfilled in my becoming a priest.

It was close to eleven years since a priestly ordination had taken place in Kitgum vicariate. Because of the insecurity, most ordinations were done in Gulu vicariate at the cathedral itself. Among the thousands who came to my priestly ordination, some were witnessing a priestly ordination for the first time in their lives, and this day would mean so much to them. It was a remarkable moment in the lives of the children and youth as well.

I remember that when the Mass was about to begin, my sister Palma sat next to me with the rest of my family, relatives, and clan members. They were all waiting for the moment when I would be presented by my parents to the bishop to be ordained. I recall a remark that I made to her: "Palma, in all my life, I have not seen you so colorfully and elegantly dressed as you are today." Her answer was the most surprising to me: "Robert, a few minutes from now, I am going to be substantially changed forever; I will no longer be called Palma only but the sister of a priest." Her response reflected the pride and joy that everyone had in my becoming a priest.

There was also a lot of elation in the Madi Opei parish because I was going to be the first priest from among them. The last person who had gone so far in his training was my father, who had left the seminary in 1970. Some of them told me this: "Father Robert, from now onward when the priests of the diocese are assembled for a liturgical celebration marching in procession, we shall be proud to point out that you are one of our very own."

My mother also told me of her unique experience at my ordination. When the prayer of consecration came to an end and it was announced that I was now a priest, she felt like a heavy weight was taken off her shoulders and breathed a huge sigh of relief. She then realized how stressed out she had been all the years I was studying to be a priest because I could have dropped out or been dismissed at any time.

With my ordination to the priesthood, a journey that had started almost sixteen years ago came to an end. It had begun with a few words to my father: "Daddy, I want to join the seminary." He had replied, "If that is what you feel, we shall discuss it with your mother in the evening." I remember on that very evening, after some discussion both parents gave me their blessing to join the seminary.

After my ordination, I had a vacation of two months that I termed "my honeymoon period." I spent this time visiting the different places where I had studied and grown up, and the many friends I had made in the course of my seminary training. On October 4, 2001, I reported to Pajule Parish to begin an eventful period of my life and work. Within very short time, the security situation completely deteriorated. Large groups of LRA rebels had crossed the borders of South Sudan into Uganda.

In the hands of my parents in 1972. The little child who would one day be a priest

At the Alokolum seminary chapel, I am seated third from the right. We are singing our hearts out because from an early age we were taught that one who sings prays twice.

A class photo at the end of our philosophical studies at Alokolum Seminary in May 1996. I am kneeling on the extreme right. We had real doubts if we would successfully complete our last semester. Gulu had become very insecure because of the LRA attacks.

The second year high school seminarians whom I taught Latin and religious education during my year of internship. I am seated on the right in a white cassock. As the old saying goes many are called but a few are chosen; a handful of them have become priests as well.

At one of the entrances to the chapel of Ggaba Seminary in 1999. This place of worship was located at the center of most of the seminary buildings as a sign that all the activities in the place were to lead us to God.

With the students of St. Paul's National Major Seminary, Kinyamasika when they came for a volley ball match at Ggaba National Major Seminary. I am kneeling on the extreme right. This was one of my final competitive volley ball matches as my seminary years were coming to an end. Volley ball helped me develop a sense of humor, since we always joked that playing volley ball was not only an art but a science.

I will forever remember the words of my seminary professor of pastoral theology who always said it was much harder to become a deacon than a priest because it involved raising a lay man to the level of a cleric. I am being ordained a transitional deacon on July 15, 2000.

15

Our final theology class photograph in May 2001 before my ordination to the priesthood. I am kneeling on the extreme left. A number of us here joined the seminary in our early teens. Definitely, we now looked like real men.

I am being presented by my parents and clan members to the bishop moments before my ordination to the priesthood.

The book of the gospel carried in majesty on a chair. A sign that Jesus is a king who speaks to his people whenever the gospel is proclaimed.

Lying down prostrate at my ordination to the priesthood surrounded by the altar boys, liturgical dancers and with the whole congregation kneeling and praying for me, it felt like I was in the company of the angels.

Before the end of my ordination Mass, my bishop asked me to bless him. I had received new powers as a priest through him and he wanted to be among the very first to experience their spiritual benefits.

The Mass for the ordination to the priesthood takes close to five hours or even more; that is why one of the altar boys at the end needed to rest his head on his hands.

After I had been ordained a priest before the final blessing my bishop with great excitement told the congregation that he had a brand new priest that he wanted to introduce to them. For the first time he referred to me as Reverend Father and told them that I would be the 61st priest serving in his diocese and he was giving me a personal name "Rubanga Mar" meaning God is love.

Soon after my ordination to the priesthood with my bishop, parents and the clergy who participated in the Mass.

At Christ the King parish with some of the Little Sisters of Mary Immaculate of Gulu immediately after my ordination. One of them was late and is caught trying to sneak in.

At my first Mass in front of the parish church in Madi Opei and standing next to me is the pastor of the parish Fr. Matthew Lagoro. There were so many people that the Mass could not be celebrated inside the Church.

Chapter Three

My First Days in Pajule

As a newly ordained priest in Pajule, I faced the challenge of loneliness. The missionary order that ran the place before had two or three priests in the parish most of the time. Their constitution required priests to live in a community. But this was not the case with the diocesan priests. When I reported to Pajule in October 2001, we were only two priests but were in charge of two parishes, Pajule and Puranga, which meant that often we would be alone for weeks.

After the first three days in Pajule parish with my pastor, he left for a full week to attend to the affairs of Puranga parish. This gave me a new experience. I could not believe the solitude and the loneliness that his absence brought in the evenings. At the end of the day, there was total silence in the whole parish locality. And, yet, during the day, the place was very busy since close to a thousand people were participating in different activities within the parish itself, the elementary school, nursery school, and tailoring school. In short, in the evenings, the place was like a ghost town. I really wondered within myself if this was the priestly life I had been preparing for and longing after.

At the seminary, while studying for the Catholic priesthood, I had become accustomed to living with several people since there were no less than one hundred students at any one moment. However, life as a priest was different, and Pajule parish had its own unique challenges as well; the parish was on a vast piece of land that was close to forty acres and the rectory was at its center. I felt like my only neighbors were the many buildings around the rectory. The nearest homes were those at the edges of the parish with the exception of the convent.

Fortunately, at the time I began my priestly ministry in Pajule, the place was experiencing a brief moment of peace and stability. However, since I had not lived there long enough to get to know the people, I was often afraid that someone could jump over the wall into the compound of the rectory to steal something or harm me. I felt I needed to have two dogs, both for security and for company. My father had a love for dogs and cats, and we always had both of them around the home when I was growing up. I got my love of dogs from him. In the culture of the people in Pajule and the surrounding areas, dogs are for hunting and security. They are not kept as pets. Since I was not the one in charge of the place, I asked my pastor if we could have two puppies to be raised in the parish. From our earlier conversations I knew that he did not like dogs, but he did not turn down my request since we were just starting to develop a working relationship, and above all he did not want to frustrate a newly ordained priest wanting to put his many theories about parish life into practice.

After a couple of weeks, my pastor went to Gulu and returned with the two little puppies, a mixture of an African local breed and a German shepherd. These puppies brought a comforting and reassuring presence to me in the parish when I was alone. And in the evening they would go around the compound and bring signs of life to the place. Since they were intended to be for security, I did not bring them into the rectory, but they had their own shelter outside where they stayed during the day. It was only in the evenings that they were released and allowed to move freely within the compound of the rectory, which was surrounded by the walls. I was always certain that even if they were very young, they were always safe because of the wall. But what surprised me most was the friendship and company and the love that I experienced from my two puppies. Even if the rectory was a very big house, they were able to figure out where my bedroom was and would sleep by my window.

After about twelve months, I gave the female puppy to one of the local hunters in the parish since I discovered that she found the walls of the parish too restrictive. She would jump over the wall, and I would have to look for her almost every morning. The male puppy that I had named Simba remained with me. Simba is a Swahili word for lion. I named my dog Simba because he was a big dog; he also had a color like that of a lion. In the evenings, he was tough and fierce and would not allow anyone who was not authorized to come inside the walls of the rectory.

However, Simba also had a soft and loving side; outside the compound of the rectory, he was a quiet and humble dog. If I had not returned to the parish by six p.m., he would go and sit in front of the church facing the town to wait for me, and when he saw me return home he ran toward me in excitement. As he ran toward the vehicle, he was never afraid that I might run over him, and when I stopped and opened the door, he would jump in. There were times when I would travel away from the parish for a couple of days, and the parish cook reported to me that every evening I was away Simba would go and sit in front of the church till late in the night waiting for me. He would only return when the parish cook led him back to the rectory. When the security situation deteriorated, Simba became like one of us. When we were scared and afraid, he was scared and afraid. When we fled for our lives and hid, Simba did the same. Gunshots frightened him like any of us. If there was danger, he could read the fright that we had from our eyes and actions. For all these reasons and more I count him to be among my truest and sincerest friends. I agree with the saying that in order to have a true friend get a dog.

Chapter Four

The LRA and Its Return

As I mentioned before, after the overthrow of the military regime of Tito Okello Lutwa in January 1986, most of the defeated government soldiers fled to the South Sudan and returned after a period of about eight months to fight the new government in power. There were groups like the Uganda People's Democratic Army, and the Holy Spirit Movement led by Alice Lakwena. But in the year 1988, a group called the Lord's Resistance Army (LRA) was started by a young man called Joseph Kony. He was a little known and yet charismatic individual who recruited hundreds of young men and women and adults to fight the government of Uganda.

Joseph Kony claimed that he had a prophetic mission to cleanse the Ugandan society and Ugandan government of moral and spiritual evils. His followers believed that he was filled with supernatural powers, and that the "spirits" gave him unique superhuman qualities since they believed these "spirits" warned him of impending dangers to his life coming from intriguers within the LRA and from foreign enemies. Second, they also believed that Joseph Kony could predict the fate of the LRA in a battle, for example, if they were going to be successful or defeated. Because of this presumed knowledge that Joseph Kony had, LRA commanders followed his instructions very scrupulously, and he enjoyed absolute authority and obedience within the LRA. This cultivated a culture of extreme fear and a mystique about him that was reinforced by the brutality with which dissent was dealt with in the LRA.

Joseph Kony claims that he is fighting the government of Uganda to implement a manifesto that ensures that Uganda as a country is ruled by the divine law of the Ten Commandments. Most Ugandans and many people outside the country believe that this is the reason why the LRA is fighting.

To an observer, the LRA's claim that it is led by supernatural goals is contradicted by its actions, which do not reflect any supernatural goodness or divinity. It has been responsible for hundreds of killings, and for sexual battery and violence against thousands of young girls who are abducted and in most cases turned into sex slaves.

Further, its methods of recruitment and self-sustenance as a force have also been very troubling. It has heavily relied on the abduction of children because it has found it difficult to voluntarily recruit adults—most adults tend to flee from the LRA. The civil society organizations that have been working in northern Uganda estimate that the LRA abducted about thirty thousand people as it waged war against the Ugandan government. And this brutality has not been limited to the people of northern Uganda but also extends to parts of eastern Uganda and the South Sudan and parts of the northeastern Democratic Republic of the Congo and the Central African Republic.

In the early 1990s, the LRA became more sophisticated militarily and more brutal in its war efforts against the government of Uganda when the Islamist Government in Khartoum began to arm them. The Sudanese government blamed the Ugandan government for aiding the Sudan People's Liberation Army (SPLA), which was at war with them in the southern part of the Sudan. It is important to recognize that the Sudanese involvement in the war brought about a lot more pain, suffering, destruction, and loss of life on the people of Acoliland since they armed the LRA with land mines that the rebels often planted on much-used roads and in fields they cultivated. The Sudanese government had hoped that by militarily supporting the LRA, they would be able to capture large parts of northern Uganda that could act as a buffer zone between the Ugandan government in Kampala and the Sudanese government in Khartoum. In spite of the strong desire by the Islamist government that the LRA capture and control territory in northern Uganda, the LRA was not able to fulfill this dream.

Instead, it resorted to the brutal indiscriminate targeting of civilians and population centers. This reign of terror aimed at defenseless people was intended to force the deployment of government soldiers to protect the population centers and roads within northern Uganda and hence make it impossible for additional Ugandan troops to be deployed in South Sudan. This brutal tactic was successful on the part of the LRA because whenever they attacked or killed people, Ugandans in the affected areas complained against the government for not doing its job. To maintain travel in the war zones meant that the government of Uganda had to deploy hundreds of soldiers along the roads and paths that civilians used.

There will always be several things confounding about the LRA because there are many aspects of the lives and activities of its members that do not make sense. Most people do not understand their need to continue fighting, abducting children, raiding villages, killing innocent civilians, and performing body mutilations like cutting off lips, since the LRA claims that it wants the country to be ruled by the Ten Commandments, which forbid murder. This is one of the frustrations that I have experienced when asked about this subject. I do not fully understand why the LRA has been fighting for all these years and why they target the local population.

However, in the Juba Peace Process conducted between 2006 and 2008, the LRA came out with a set of political and economic demands asking the Ugandan government to address the marginalization of the north and northeastern parts of Uganda. To most of the people in the war-affected areas, it was the first time they were introduced to the LRA's political thinking or heard them present an economic and political agenda.

From my close interactions and experiences with the LRA in my work in Pajule parish, I have come to the conclusion that even if it has been difficult to discern the motives of the LRA, I believe those at the top of the LRA have always had real and clear political motives for the war. The means they are using to achieve their goals may be crude and barbaric, but like all rebel forces, they want power.

First, this is because the LRA has consistently rejected any agreement that would make them surrender their weapons. The government of Uganda has been very successful in negotiating with many rebel groups and incorporated some of them into the army, and it has provided others with resettlement packages. But the LRA has not accepted such arrangements and has furiously turned down such offers, arguing that they are not fighting the government of Uganda because they are economically in need. Second, there have been numerous occasions when the government of Uganda and the LRA have come close to a resolution and the process has been held up by the LRA under the pretext that the "spirits" have spoken to its leader, Joseph Kony, demanding that the peace talks be suspended indefinitely.

In my opinion this has been a convenient way for the LRA to give itself a break in the war and then put the peace talks on hold if it sees that the terms and resolutions are not favoring it. And during this time it has bought itself more time to plan, regroup, replenish its stockpile of arms, and recruit new members—and above all, to introduce a dynamic to the talks that often cannot be addressed or questioned since these encounters with the "spirits" as claimed are secret knowledge no one can argue with or question. To be fair, I would like to point out here that it is not only the LRA that has placed obstacles in the way of dialogue; the Ugandan government has also done the same in her own ways, as we shall see in the coming chapters.

The Return of the LRA

The LRA rebels returned from the South Sudan in March of 2002, after they had been away from the country for almost fifteen months. I remember that my pastor and I had gone to Gulu, and on our way back to Pajule parish on Gulu-Atanga Road, we were halted and told that LRA rebels had laid an ambush ahead before the Aswa Bridge. So we returned to Gulu and traveled via Lira Road the following day.

Then in April, a truck traveling from Mbale was ambushed in the area of Pajule at a place called Alim village, which is about fifteen minutes away from Pajule. Those who were on board were going to buy farm products in Kitgum. At around six a.m. that fateful morning we heard the sounds of gunshots and explosions along the road; this continued for about five to seven minutes. After one hour, we learned that the military had taken control at the scene of the attack; they had rescued two people who were seriously hurt and were arranging for the injured to be brought to Pajule for medical attention. One person had been killed.

On that same day, we also came to learn that the commander of the unit of government soldiers was nearly killed in the rescue operation. When he heard that the rebels were shooting at a passenger vehicle, he literally ran on foot to the scene of the ambush, leaving behind the foot soldiers he commanded, and came face to face with the rebels, who were looting the truck and attempting to set it on fire. To save his life, he ran into the nearby bushes and only escaped death at the hands of the rebels pursuing him when the soldiers he commanded arrived.

The weeks following this ambush were marked by a heightened level of insecurity in the whole of the Pader District. On almost a daily basis there were ambushes by LRA rebels on the major highways like Kitgum-Lira Road and Kitgum-Gulu Road, and within a short period of time, many innocent lives were lost. As the attacks continued on the villages and travelers, I began to witness the loss of control of the situation by the political and military authorities, and the gradual loss of a feeling of normalcy. Whenever these attacks took place, the political and military leaders were not able to reassure the people that they would soon be in control of the situation or that they would hold accountable those who had committed the crimes—or that they even understood what was going on. There was no authority structure to depend on for safety or even for psychological comfort.

At the beginning, the attacks by the LRA rebels appeared to be isolated incidents, but at a certain point, they became a routine activity, and brought almost everything to a standstill in Pader District by July of 2002. For almost three months, the only news that we heard was negative, always about something violent or atrocious such as an ambush, a murder, or an abduction. The endless and indiscriminate violence forced many people to run away from their homes and villages and settle in camps. In Pajule, there two big camps; one of the camps was located in Lapul sub-county on the land of Pajule parish with close to eighteen thousand people, and another camp was located in Pajule sub-county with a similar number.

During this time, I also came to appreciate and learn something about human contact and communication: what a community talks about or discusses is enriched by what the community sees, reads, and comes into physical contact with; and it is very bad for any group of people to be isolated from the rest of society. In Pajule for most of March through December of 2002, we were cut off from the rest of the district of Pader and the Acoli region as a whole. If we traveled it meant that we were taking the risk of being ambushed. Because of this insecurity, close to thirty-six thousand people lived within a radius of three miles and rarely left it. The residents of Pajule seldom exchanged ideas or communicated with people from the other sections of the district. At that time there was also no cell phone coverage in the area, which meant that it was not possible to call someone outside Pajule or to receive a call from outside Pajule. The little external connection that we had in Pajule with the outside world was through transistor radios on which we could listen to the Voice of America, the British Broadcasting Corporation, Radio Uganda and the local FM stations. In the town there was one place where a few people could watch digital satellite television when electric power was available. There were no Internet or e-mail connections available. The result of this cutoff impacted our conversations and dialogue because there were few subjects we could discuss apart from the war and the violence. There were no new and refreshing ideas in our conversations; whenever we gathered together to talk, it was always about something going on in the war, and when we were finished, we would go our separate ways more afraid than before.

Another thing that I came to discover at this time when almost everything had come to a standstill was that it was really hard to know what day of the week it was. Generally, most people are constantly reminded of this by the schedule they follow during the course of the week. In a war situation, there is no schedule since everything is up in the air. The only constant is the unpredictability. Most of the day is spent by the veranda, under a tree, or in small groups talking about an attack that has taken place, or the latest rumor. I remember that after one full week of intense rebel threats on the town, I went to bed Saturday evening and forgot that the following day was a Sunday, and so I did not prepare for the two Masses that I had to lead. Most of the activities that marked a normal Saturday, such as confession, adoration, and the rosary, had not taken place because no one came for them.

When Sunday morning came, I heard young boys running in the compound, and I asked myself: "What are these boys doing around the rectory so early?" I looked out through my window only to see my altar boys dressed up and ready for the Sunday Mass. This made me almost have a heart attack, for I had not prepared my Sunday message, and yet the Mass was to start in less than seven minutes. Fortunately, all went well.

If one wanted to get some sleep the best time was during the day since most attacks took place in the night but this was not also a guarantee since a gunfight could start at anytime. One afternoon as I had a siesta, I fell deeply asleep and there was an exchange of gunfire as I continued to sleep. While Simba was lying down by the window outside my bedroom, he realized I was not awake when he did not hear me turn in my bed. Simba stood up on his hind legs and began banging on my window violently until I woke up. When he heard me turn in bed, a sign that I was awake, he ran and hid.

Chapter Five

The Attack on Patongo

At the end of June 2002, when there were about two weeks of quiet in Pajule and no rebel activity reported, my parish priest brought me a letter inviting me to go and say Mass in Patongo parish. The acting pastor was going to Tanzania since his brother was making his final vows as a member of a religious order. He needed someone to fill in for him. I accepted the invitation because it gave me the chance to go pray with the members of the parish as a newly ordained priest. The acting pastor was a Sudanese by nationality and belonged to one of the religious orders serving in the archdiocese of Gulu.

Patongo parish was about one hour's drive from Pajule parish and on the way I had to pass through Pader District Headquarters. I planned to leave on Saturday at eleven a.m. But that morning was very colorless, dull, and had a feeling of uncertainty in the air. There were a lot of rumors circulating in Pajule that the LRA rebels were waiting to strike along the route that I had to travel. Because of fear and doubt about my own safety, I delayed leaving so that I could monitor the road situation.

In the course of the day, several people who wanted to go to Pader District headquarters canceled their plans. Among them was a music instructor, Mr. Philip, who came to the parish and informed us that he had to cut short his trip since some motorcyclists riding ahead of him saw suspected rebels crisscross the road at a village called Paiula.

This Saturday was an agonizing one for me. I could not decide whether to take the risk and leave for Patongo or cancel my journey. I was deeply perturbed by the fact that if I failed to go to the parish on Sunday morning, there would be no priest to lead the Mass when the parishioners came to worship. I remember very vividly that most of the Pader District leaders who were originally from the Pajule area and now lived in the district had gone home, the main reason being that they were afraid that the district headquarters would be attacked by the rebels at any moment.

Toward evening, as I continued to share with the district leaders that I needed to go to Patongo parish and it was beginning to get late, one of them told me very authoritatively: "Father, you have to cancel your journey because it is a question of life and death." When I heard this, I reflected on it and took his advice very seriously. After I had made up my mind not to travel to Patongo parish, someone arrived in Pajule at four p.m. bringing very disturbing news that two days ago the neighboring parish of Namukora had been looted by LRA rebels. One of the associate pastors was beaten up, tortured, and his back hit several times with the flat end of an axe. When I learned of this attack on a Catholic parish and on my fellow priest, I was too alarmed to consider taking any risks. I went back to the parish with a clear conscience that as far as humanly possible I had done all I could to reach Patongo.

At about eight p.m., I went to bed exhausted since it had been a stress-filled day. The news that Namukora parish had been attacked continued to linger in my mind and made me wonder if we would be the next Catholic parish to be attacked. Even though I was not scheduled to say Mass that Sunday, the pastor asked me to celebrate the second Mass at nine a.m. But after the service, a sudden sadness descended on me and made me feel like leaving the parish immediately and going somewhere else. Because of this, I went to my room, put on my gray clerical shirt, and told my pastor that I was going home. He was surprised and asked me if I had heard any bad news from home. I told him that there was no bad news but I just wanted to be away. He was concerned about my safety on the road to Kitgum, since the roads were insecure. Seeing that I had made up my mind to travel, he wished me well and I left for home on my motorcycle. I was lucky to travel without any incident. For the forty minutes I traveled to Kitgum, I did not meet anyone on the way. Along the roads, I saw a couple of trucks that had been blown up by the rebels and several trading centers that had been abandoned for fear of attacks.

In Kitgum, I went straight home and spent some good time with my parents. While with them, my feelings suddenly changed; I felt safe, happy, at peace, and became more upbeat, partly because the subjects of our conversations were not focused on the deteriorating security situation. In fact, that very evening, there was a World Cup Soccer Final match between Germany and Brazil that my father and I went to watch at Bomah, a social center in Kitgum. It was a great evening; I saw many friends whom I had not seen for quite some time, and this was coupled with the fact that our favorite team (Brazil) won the World Cup.

The following morning, which was a Monday, I visited the neighboring parish, called Kitgum mission, which was run by the same missionary congregation that was in charge of Patongo parish. I found the priests in the parish greatly distressed and disturbed by the message that they had received through their radio-call[1] that Patongo was under heavy military assault by rebels. They were concerned about the safety of the priest in Patongo parish, who was one of their own. Since I had planned to go there to celebrate Mass over the weekend, I was able to inform them that the priest in Patongo had gone to Tanzania, and I was to fill in for him but failed to do so because of the security situation. When they heard this, they were greatly relieved. For my part, I was shaken, and a cold sensation of dread entered my body. It felt like I was being paralyzed and I immediately sat down. I realized that God had a hand in the cancelation of my trip and that He had spoken to me through my own fears and doubts and the firm advice I had gotten from one of the district leaders not to travel there.

I had planned to stay both Saturday and Sunday night in Patongo. On Sunday evening, the night before, some rebels came into Patongo and began to take up positions. No one had any idea what was going on including the security agencies. Other rebels wanted to enter the premises of the parish claiming that they were government soldiers who intended to protect the place throughout the night. Fortunately, Kim, the seminarian at the parish, refused to let them in, telling them that whenever government soldiers came to guard the parish they stayed off the premises and beyond the parish wall. Since I had failed to show up in Patongo, he was afraid to be at the parish alone, and later in the evening he left and spent the night at one of the houses within Patongo adjacent to the military barracks. When the rebels attacked the town on Monday morning, he was among those abducted after the rebels overran the army barracks and started to break into all the nearby buildings.

The attack on Patongo was very destructive; the LRA looted the parish, stole food items, ransacked stores run by local and international organizations for humanitarian aid, and abducted close to four hundred people. They also set ablaze vehicles, motorcycles, and houses. The official death toll was seven, and many people could not be accounted for. I heard a very sad story of a man who had abandoned the LRA and returned home to Patongo to become a successful, newly married businessman. As the LRA rebels were looting each and every building, one rebel stumbled upon him, called him out, and said: "You have returned home, rehabilitated yourself, and all seems to be just fine for you. You have left us to fight the war; who do you want to continue fighting the war on

---

1 A communication device that weighs about ten pounds and has a rectangular shape, uses an antenna, and can communicate for a distance of one thousand miles.

your behalf?" Before the businessman could give him an answer, the rebel shot him in the forehead and he was killed instantly.

In the whole of Patongo, it appears the only place that the rebels did not loot was the convent. At the rectory where I would have stayed, they smashed open all the doors and used an axe to break into the most secure room. I believe that it was God's hand that steered both myself and the acting pastor from Patongo parish that weekend.

However, if the rebels had gotten me, I believe they would have asked me many questions that I would have been unable to respond to adequately. The LRA were known for being aggressive inquisitors and they were both very intimidating and vile and if they had made any specific demands I am certain that I was not going to meet them. If they had asked me for money, I would not have had any to give them. If I had to explain to them that I was a visiting priest in Patongo and I did not know where the parish money was kept most likely they would not have accepted my explanation. Above all, I do not know how I would have reacted to the extreme turbulence that engulfed the place.

I believe that the acting pastor, a Sudanese by nationality, was the luckier one. The LRA had a deep-seated hatred for the tribes of the South Sudan, especially the Dinkas, who made up the bulk of the SPLA, which had on several occasions attacked the LRA in South Sudan. In fact, a few months later, because of this the LRA attacked a Sudanese refugee camp in an area called Acol-Pii; several refugees lost their lives and the camp had to be disbanded.

All in all, I believe that God spared us from the violence: the sounds of bomb blasts, exchanges of gunfire, the feelings of fear and trepidation, helplessness and anxiety, the sounds of doors being broken open with axes, the destruction of property and life, and the possibility that one of us might not have made it through alive.

Chapter Six

The Attack on the Army Commander

At the beginning of the month of July 2002, army Major Itta had just been recently appointed to Pajule barracks. He did not speak the English language fluently, or the local Acoli language, but spoke Lunyoro, a Bantu language that was his native tongue. He visited me at the parish when the place was just beginning to get insecure. He needed some gas for his official military vehicle since the following Saturday he was to travel to Gulu for a meeting with his superiors. In Pajule there were no gas stations. Small-scale traders sold gas in small amounts, mostly in five-liter containers. However, they were not willing to provide it to the army officer and his escorts since they wanted to be paid immediately and not wait till the end of the month like the army preferred. However, in the parish we had bought our gas days before in the neighboring town of Lira and stored it in twenty-liter containers. So, we gave him one of the twenty-liter containers of gas.

Between late May and the beginning of July 2002, traveling very early in the morning was terribly risky since one could end up entering a rebel ambush at any moment. Most travel started at eleven a.m. and ended by four p.m. Most people believed that if there was an ambush along the road, it would have been discovered by eleven and any possible travelers alerted. It was also presumed that by this time government soldiers would be patrolling the major routes and would have spaced themselves along the areas where the rebels usually laid ambushes. The truth was that there was no guarantee of safety for travelers.

Later, through our encounters with former abductees, we would learn that the safest time to travel was actually between eleven a.m. and twelve p.m. since most of the LRA rebels were away from the roadside cooking some food for themselves. They cooked at this time because the tropical sun was very hot and they needed to rest. This was coupled with the fact that often the wind was not blowing very hard so the smoke from the fire would not go up high enough for the government soldiers to see from a distance.

Major Itta needed to be in Gulu on Saturday at ten a.m. It meant that he had to travel earlier than usual. However, before he left, there were several indicators that the roads were insecure from Pajule to Gulu. In the town, whenever there were rebel movements in the vicinity, there were always rumors of their presence, as they did not move quietly. They would often attack vehicles or villages and loot food and supplies, and some of those who had escaped would alert the community. Because Pajule was a tightly knit community and the relationship between the army and the population was always very good, the people kept the army informed of any rebel infiltration or movements. At times the town dwellers would hitch a ride on the army transport since very few had their own.

On Friday evening at around eight p.m., the rebels attacked a village called Oralabolo on Kitgum-Lira road, about a ten-minute drive from Pajule. Literally, the name means "the swamp of bananas." The villagers were put to flight, but three of them were detained and forced to lead some of their attackers to the roadside to lay an ambush on the first vehicle that passed the following day. When these three men were released by the rebels, they ran on foot to Pajule and reported to the government soldiers that there was an ambush laid by the roadside. Strangely, earlier on between four to six p.m., I had passed through the same road and village since once a month I would go to collect dry wood along this road for cooking purposes. I must have just missed them.

When the major and his escorts prepared to travel in the morning, the message that the rebels were along the roads was well known to them, the soldiers in the barracks, and some of the civilians in the town. But this did not deter him from choosing to travel. When he went to pick up the local chief from his home for them to travel together, the local chief declined telling him that he had heard that there were rebels on the way and so the major left the town with about ten personal bodyguards in his truck.

That Saturday morning I celebrated Mass at seven a.m. as usual, and at eight thirty a.m., after my breakfast, I was taking a walk in the parish compound when I heard a loud explosion along Pajule-Kitgum Road. I saw a dark cloud of smoke going up into the sky and heard a few gunshots, but they quickly fell silent. I immediately knew that something terrible had happened. I rode my motorcycle to the center of town and learned that the army commander had just left town and there was a real possibility that his truck had been attacked.

Most of the people in the town were in a state of shock. Those whom I thought would have some information were tight-lipped, since no one wanted to speculate that the worst might have happened. For almost two hours, we were in a state of suspense and felt things were falling apart. Rumors began to fly about LRA infiltrations and attacks.

By twelve thirty p.m. we learned that the army commander had been killed. This sad news brought a sense of fear, self-doubt, uncertainty, and gloom all over town. Many people were stranded in Pajule and could not travel. I spent most of the morning hours and part of the afternoon with the people in the town and only returned to the parish when I learned that the government soldiers had secured the scene of the ambush.

From several eyewitnesses we came to learn that after the army commander had traveled for about five minutes, he was stopped by villagers at a place called Lapul and advised not to continue with the journey till he was certain that there were no rebels on the way. They had laid logs across the road to prevent any vehicle from entering a rebel ambush. At that moment, the major could have canceled his journey. I believe that if he had communicated to his superiors the reason why he could not come to the meeting in Gulu, they would have understood. Further, he could also have delayed his journey and instructed his foot soldiers to go ahead and make sure that there were no rebels along the roadside. However, he ignored all the advice and signs of danger and continued his journey. This decision was incomprehensible to us, because this man was someone experienced in war. He had fought in the guerilla war that had brought the current regime to power, and since he was assigned to work in a war zone, I am convinced that his appointing authority trusted in his capacity to discern danger and to make appropriate judgments.

On the other hand, I also think that we were in the initial stages of the return of the insecurity, and he might have underestimated the threats posed by the rebels to his life—or he did not understand what he was getting himself into. Of course, no one will ever know what was going on in his mind at the time. After he had ignored the advice of the villagers, he traveled for about ten minutes and reached the area where the rebels were thought to be. He then instructed his escorts to jump off the vehicle to walk on foot, and he stepped out of the vehicle as well.

We will never know whether he was giving these instructions in panic or as a precautionary measure. It was at this very moment that a rebel soldier shot him in the chest with a single bullet, and he was killed instantly. Two of his bodyguards were shot dead at the same spot, while two others were killed in the bushes, as they could not escape the rebels who had surrounded them.

However, six of the escorts managed to escape through the bushes back to Pajule. They were brought to the local clinic of Lucy and Simon. It was sad to see these men. They had escaped from the jaws of death and were covered with blood. The army uniforms they wore looked like rags since they had run through the shrubs and thorns, which had torn them to pieces. The condition of their feet was terrible, too. To run fast enough, they had to get rid of their shoes, and this exposed their feet to all kinds of sharp objects. This was coupled with the fact that some of them were bleeding from gunshot wounds and had their noses torn by shrubs.

This incident confirmed some of my beliefs about life. When it is one's day to die, it is impossible to stop it. In the case of the major, there were several warning signs—writing on the wall, if you will—and had he heeded just one of them, it would have saved his life. I also came to learn that each and every person in a warzone is his brother's keeper. Any information about the security situation needs to be shared because this may make the difference between life and death. And making the right judgment is very important in a war zone. One mistake alone can prove to be very costly because there may not be a second chance. This attack was a turning point because it brought the insecurity into our midst in Pajule, and for the next two years we would live in the constant fear and danger of death.

The Aftermath of the Attack

I returned to the parish to have a late lunch. I was very hungry, but I could not eat. I had too much on my mind, so I just went to bed. It was now nearing two p.m. I hoped that after sleeping I would wake up feeling less depressed and would have some appetite. However, I tossed and turned in my bed, gripped by a sense of insecurity, uncertainty, and fear. After approximately one hour, I got out of bed, warmed my food, tried to force myself to eat a little something, and eventually did so.

Then I sat outside on the veranda reflecting on the morning and what the night might bring since that was when most rebel attacks took place. At this moment a young man called Omaya came by; I knew him well since he was the local army informant. He would gather information about the rebel movements from the local population and report to his superiors. When I saw him, I expected him to update me about the security situation since he had more knowledge about it than we did. Surprisingly he did not mention anything connected to the worsening security situation but instead asked me for a cup of cold water to drink and left without saying anything. His silence left me perturbed. I could not understand why he had to walk on foot for almost one mile from the military barracks to the parish just to get a glass of water, since there were many homes and places along the way where he could have stopped and gotten what he wanted.

This was a very common experience for me because a number of people in the community would come to the parish with an administrative issue, but if they did not find the pastor, they would not present the matter to me. I believe that often they failed to make a distinction between the office of the pastor and his person. It was as if when the pastor was not physically present in the parish, he traveled with his office and everything else came to a standstill, which was not true since we consulted a lot and worked together. However, there were also some in the community who felt that I was too young to handle the serious issues going on at the time.

I learned later that as he was returning to the barracks, Omaya met the head catechist,[2] Mr. Joe and told him that he had gone to the parish to warn the pastor that there might be an LRA attack on the town that night. Unfortunately, he was not around but instead found his associate at the parish and did not divulge the security threat to him.

Mr. Joe insisted that Omaya return to explain the situation to me since he was very certain that the pastor was going to be away for a couple of days. Then Omaya told him that the government soldiers were on the alert, scared and afraid that this night there might be a rebel attack on the town, as there were rebel groups in three separate villages neighboring the town: Koyo Lalogi, Lapul, and Palenga. These villages were ten to fifteen minutes away from Pajule with the exception of Koyo Lalogi, which was forty-five minutes. And what was most frightening was that the group that had killed the army major that morning could not be traced. Because it was getting late, Mr. Joe took it upon himself to warn me about the possibility of an attack and said the army was recommending that we hide all our valuables.

---

2 A catechist is a pastoral agent who is in charge of a section of the parish community, leads Sunday services, and provides instruction on Catholic doctrine.

When the head catechist left, I almost froze. The thought of an attack on the town drained away all my energy. I felt powerless, helpless, and confused. I could not move myself from my chair. I felt like my legs were numb and getting cold. I asked myself, "What can I do at this moment?" And yet, it was evening and I was alone in the parish. I was very certain that if the rebels attacked the town, they would target the parish and come by the hundreds to loot the place and steal the radio-call and any household items and food supplies they could get their hands on.

Since it was late in the evening, I could not do anything; coupled with that I did not even have the physical strength to move or transfer anything within the house. Even if it were possible, there was no safe place that I could transfer everything to. I was particularly worried about the parish vehicle and my personal motorcycle, which were the only means that we had for getting out of the place. There was no way of hiding them, and whenever the LRA rebels attacked a parish, they would often set them ablaze. Since I was so mixed up and confused, I went back to bed at six p.m. with the hope that by the time I awakened, I would have calmed down and be able to think clearly.

After my sleep, I felt better, and it was now seven thirty p.m. I went to inform the nuns of the possibility that the town and parish might be attacked. Their convent was across from the rectory. At the time three nuns lived in this community, but in the evenings, many people from the town and the surrounding areas came and spent their nights at the convent and the tailoring school attached. As I walked to the convent, I did not know what to say. I felt that if I were to tell them about the precarious security situation in its entirety, I would alarm them and create another problem. Instead, I talked about the implications of what had happened that day in very broad and general terms, emphasizing the need for the nuns to cut down on traveling since the roads had become very insecure, and for precautions to be taken in the evenings like going to bed early and keeping things of value in a safe place. What I said to the nuns was also conveyed to all the people who came to spend their nights in the convent and school.

As I was leaving the convent and going back to the rectory, I met someone who was coming from Pajule, and I asked him to give me the latest news from town. I soon regretted that I asked this question. He told me: "Father, do not hope for the government soldiers to protect us tonight. They are equally scared like the rest of us. The second-in-command who was to take charge of the situation has left the town, disguised like a civilian in one of the passenger vehicles. So we are on our own."

This information shattered any sense of self-confidence that I was beginning to build. The evening suddenly turned into a source of terror for me. I went to bed around nine p.m. and was tense throughout the night, expecting a rebel attack to begin at any moment. Since I could not sleep, I turned on my radio at various moments throughout the night. After all the Ugandan FM stations closed, I began to listen to international radio stations like the BBC and Voice of America. Throughout the night, I kept the volume of the radio very low and kept it inside my blanket such that the sound could not be heard even by a person who was standing outside leaning on the window of my bedroom. At seven a.m., I felt a great relief that no attack had taken place, and yet at the same time, I had not slept for a single moment. This was the first sleepless night in my life.

This new day being a Sunday morning, I had two Masses to lead in the parish. I was greatly surprised that I was able to stand and lead the community in them. During the second Mass, there were twenty children who were baptized. From the celebration of the Mass, I could gauge how bad the security situation was. The people in the parish were usually upbeat and joyful in their liturgical celebration, but this Sunday they appeared cold, somber, and distracted. They were not fully engaged and appeared like their life spirit had been sucked out of them.

The readings were very appropriate for this Sunday since the gospel was from Matthew 5:14–19. It was about Christ inviting his followers to bring their burdens to Him. I urged the worshipers to bring all their burdens to Christ, particularly the immediate one of the deteriorating security situation. I believe that my homily perfectly fitted the context of the congregation and was directly relevant to them. But in my judgment, it did not enliven the spirit of the congregation in any way.

Chapter Seven

Crisis of Confidence

After the death of Major Itta, there was a terrible crisis of confidence in Pajule as a whole that made me appreciate and understand the true meaning of insecurity. From my own experience, insecurity means the lack of certainty and the loss of faith in the institutions that guarantee safety and provide stability in people's lives. For those of us who lived in Pajule, it was as if everything were up in the air. We could not count on anything. There were government soldiers to protect the town and local population, but there was no trust and confidence in them because they were equally afraid of what the future would bring.

Evenings were very tense since there was nowhere in the whole town to go to bed and sleep peacefully. Most people felt their own houses were not safe to spend the night in. Some would ride their bicycles far away from the town and furtively enter the bushes to spend the night there. The majority of the people came to spend their night in the parish school or the tailoring school, while others slept on the rooftops of their houses. These "safe places" were determined by survival instincts and not because of any real security guarantees.

There were occasions in which whole families deliberately left their house only to accidentally enter a place in the bushes where the government soldiers lay while protecting the town. The soldiers would lead them back to their houses, reassuring them that they were safe and begging them to stay inside their house. But these families just went to sleep in another part of the bush.

I distinctly remember a criminal police investigative police officer, Mr. Okidi, someone very outgoing and well-informed about what was going on in the community due to the nature of his work, coming to me and asking for a place to spend the night in the rectory. He told me: "Father, I have not had a sound sleep for almost a full week now since I am just too terrified at night. But my instincts tell me that if you give me any spot to sleep in your rectory, even on a mat on the floor, I will be able to have a good sleep." In fact, I prepared a room and a bed for the officer, and the following morning he told me that the previous night was one of the most peaceful and sleep-filled nights he had had in several months.

During this time traveling was the most risky thing. On each and every journey out of Pajule, one had the potential of being shot dead. It was like traveling with death as company since any journey beyond a radius of three miles of the township could lead one into an ambush.

Because Pajule was on the highway, vehicles that supplied Kitgum, a city with a population of close to one hundred thousand people, passed through it. We would see a vehicle full of people pass through, often with some of the travelers well known to us, and within one or two hours, we would get a terrible report that the vehicle had been ambushed by rebels, looted, and several people in it had been seriously injured or killed. Because of the attacks on vehicles, many resorted to using motorcycles to travel. However, there were many occasions when two people would leave town on a motorcycle, and within minutes, we would get a report that one of them had been shot dead.

There was a lot of fear in the air. At times, I would get information that individuals were fleeing town for fear of the rebels. I would immediately ride my motorcycle into town to find out what was happening. Often, when I asked about the cause of the commotion, the people I talked to had nothing to tell me except that they saw a neighbor running and so they also ran. Most of these incidents would start with the wind blowing hard and making a door bang loudly. Then, since the populace was apprehensive and tense most of the time, they would conclude that the rebels were in town and begin to flee for their lives. In such situations, when people saw me, the priest, not running, they would stop and come to be with me.

This crisis of confidence taught me something valuable about war. That war is not lost or won on the battlefield, but in our minds. The people did not trust that the military could protect them, nor did some of these government soldiers believe in themselves; there were occasions in which their commanders privately complained that they had a shortage of manpower because some of their soldiers abandoned their guns at their posts and ran away to save their lives.

Chapter Eight

A Sign of Hope

Pajule parish was established in 1948 by a native black African clergy. It was a parish with a unique history because most of the other parishes in the archdiocese of Gulu were started by Italian missionaries. However in 1966, it was handed over to the missionaries as well. When the parish was turned over to us, the local diocesan clergy, on September 2, 2001, the missionaries had run it for almost forty years.

The priests at the parish since the beginning of the war in 1986 were a visible sign of solidarity, hope, and perseverance to the community of Pajule and the neighboring parishes that had been deserted. Unlike many parishes in the archdiocese that were closed for long periods because of the deteriorating security situation, Pajule was closed for three months only when the lives of the priests were in actual danger.

In the late 1980s at the peak of the war, Christians from Kalongo parish, which was about forty miles away and had been left empty by their priests because of the insecurity, came to collect consecrated hosts from Pajule parish. They traveled through the bush for fear of meeting government soldiers or rebels along the way.

Once in a while the priests in Pajule parish would take the risk of making pastoral visits to the other neighboring parishes: Namukora, Patongo, Puranga, and Atanga. They would celebrate Mass with the people who were displaced, administer the sacraments, and ensure that these parishes had enough consecrated hosts on hand till they returned.

Because Pajule parish was a sign of perseverance during this civil conflict, she also had many scars of war on her face. In this parish in the early nineties, several catechists were massacred by the rebels when they had come for their monthly meeting. Even today, there is a piece of wood in the parish on which the rebels ordered the catechists to lay their heads as they chopped their necks. In 1990, an Italian missionary priest, Father Egidio Biscaro, who was the associate pastor of Pajule parish, was shot dead at a place called Porogali by the rebels as he was traveling to Kitgum town. The most recent tragedy was the death of Father Raffaele Di Bari on October 1, 2000, a few kilometers from Pajule on Pajule-Kitgum Road, as he was going to Acolibur chapel to conduct Mass and perform baptisms on a Sunday morning.

The presence of the priests in these hardships and their willingness to make personal sacrifices made Pajule parish not only a sign of God's presence to the local people, but it also made the Catholic Church a highly trusted and credible institution to all sides in the conflict. On a couple of occasions, the clergy from the parish and the local cultural leaders acted as emissaries between the government of Uganda and the rebels. Through such face-to-face encounters, they were able to emphasize to both sides in the conflict the desire of the local population for them to settle their differences through dialogue. These were risky moments for the cultural and religious leaders. The practice was for the clergy and cultural leaders to get the consent of the army before meeting the rebel commanders, but sometimes the army would send troops to follow them and then attack those at the meeting. We found this behavior mind-boggling, as at times the religious and cultural leaders came close to being killed by the army as well.

Psychosocial Support Center

Pajule parish was also a psychosocial support center. This started in November of 2001 when seventeen rebels were brought in a truck to surrender at the parish. These LRA fighters were led by a major named Philip Onekomon Kikoko. His name literally means "the one who makes women scream." This group of rebels told us that the main reason for their surrender was that they were tired of fighting and wanted to return home to take advantage of an amnesty law that was in place for any rebel fighter who gave up fighting. The law stated that any rebel soldier who surrendered would be pardoned of all past criminal activities against the state of Uganda.

The surrender of these rebels at Pajule parish happened when I was beginning my second month of priestly ministry. It was the first time I came face to face with armed ex-rebels. They looked tired, exhausted, malnourished, hungry, and their hair was unkempt. They had walked thousands of miles from the South Sudan to return to Uganda. They were fearful of surrendering to any political, military, or civilian leadership and had even exchanged fire with some of the government units along the way. They only felt safe if they surrendered to the Catholic Church, cultural and political leaders in the area of Pajule.

One thing that was very pronounced was that they were very afraid and suspicious of everyone around them. I could see that they were really fearful that they would be killed when they were asked to hand over their weapons to the government soldiers at the parish. But they felt reassured by the warm welcome of the dignitaries and the community members who came to receive them.

In fact, a cultural chief who was in the delegation that went to receive these LRA fighters in the bushes said that before they boarded the truck to come to the parish, one of them had not made up his mind to surrender and was afraid that if he did so, he would be mistreated or even killed by the government soldiers. While the rest of the rebels wanted to leave the bush, they could not board the truck and leave him behind for fear that in frustration he would begin to shoot at all of them aboard the truck, since he was still armed. However, when they assured him that he would indeed be safe, he came along.

A few of them had dreadlocks that made them look dark and dirty and covered their faces as well. Most of what they were wearing was torn; military uniforms, shirts, trousers, boots, sandals, etc. Some of the military uniforms they wore were so dirty that one could hardly tell the color. With the exception of their commander, most of them had been members of the LRA for less than five years. In fact, when the army major called Segatta in charge of the Pajule military barracks came in the evening to meet them, on seeing their condition, he sent one of his military aids to buy shoes for them.

Again when it was time for us to dine, the rebels were very suspicious and thought that poison had been put in the food to kill them. They would only eat the food on a plate that they served themselves. For them to feel secure, all the food had to be put in a common dish or dishes from which everyone served himself like a buffet. During the first meal we had with these ex-LRA fighters, their fears and mistrust were only allayed by an ex-LRA rebel called Waliki, who had surrendered earlier and now joined the government soldiers.

These seventeen ex-rebels were attended to by two social workers from the psychosocial department of the Catholic Charities of the Archdiocese of Gulu (CARITAS), and one social worker from the organization of the Acholi Religious Leaders Peace Initiative,[3] who also documented the daily activities. The three months that the first group of rebels spent in the parish were a great learning experience for all of us. We were introduced to the mindset of LRA rebels and their view of life.

In fact, we experienced how much the LRA looked down on all other people. Even if the LRA fighters lived their lives in the bushes, with no education, little or no access to phones or newspapers, and barely able to read and write in the local language, they considered themselves to be more

---

3 An umbrella organization that brought together all the faith groups and cultural institutions in the peace process.

knowledgeable and informed than many of the people in society. Most of the time they claimed they had some secret knowledge of the evil intentions of the Ugandan, Sudanese, and American governments against the people of northern Uganda; and yet, according to them the people of northern Uganda were ignorant of these evil plans.

Further, the LRA rebels looked at Catholic priests as brainwashed by Western society and at Catholicism and the Christian faith with suspicion and disdain. I remember a comment made by one of the LRA ex-combatants as we celebrated the Feast of the Immaculate Conception of Mary, on December 8, 2001. This was our parish day, since Pajule parish had as her patroness the Blessed Virgin Mary. As we were coming to the end of Mass, the statue of Mary was carried in procession, people were clapping and singing, and the congregation was in a jovial mood. Then, I heard one ex-rebel comment loudly, "See how stupid these Catholics are, for they take a statue of Mary as God." I was very perplexed to hear this inconsiderate statement. Even if this LRA ex-combatant was skeptical about what we were doing at the time, he should have kept his comments to himself since it was not an appropriate time and venue; the parish and community that he considered stupid were the ones hosting him. The rebels had some faith in the institution of the Church but did not respect its beliefs.

Further, we also saw how difficult it was for some of them to adjust to civilian life because those who were in high-ranking positions could not give up the privileges, control, and command they had over those in the lower ranks. In fact, it was difficult for them to accept the fact that with their surrender, there were no differentiations of rank or privilege among them, and all were now equal and free. A couple of them who were in leadership positions continued to issue orders to the rest to cook, buy cigarettes, and warm and take water to the bathroom for them, as if the LRA structure of command were still in operation. The ones who were formerly in the lower ranks or had no rank at all would complain to the social workers, sometimes in tears, that they were still being commanded to do things they did not want to do as if they had not yet regained their freedom. If they disobeyed they were threatened with physical violence. In fact, for most of these ex-captives, it was more of an inner struggle for them to reclaim their own authority as free people since there was no likelihood that any of them was going to be mistreated by any of their former commanders. But what was frightening to most of them was that none of them could ever remember an instance in which a subordinate had defied an instruction from a commander because to do so would have resulted in severe punishment and even death. Whenever their former officers asked them to do something, they could not say no.

It is also important to note that many among the ex-combatants who surrendered had unrealistic expectations about their future. Most of them expected to live a life of luxury and comfort in which everything would be provided for them. These sentiments were expressed very strongly by their commanders. They wanted to have the same privileges they enjoyed in the jungle replicated in their new life. There was a very strong sense of entitlement among them. At the psycho-social support center, an LRA commander had two mistresses, but in the local culture they were referred to as his wives. This was not unusual in the LRA since there were many polygamists among them. But what was strange and ridiculous was that these women were related to one another by blood. Culturally, this is unacceptable. One of the women, because she was now free, wanted to abandon the relationship to start a new life. But this ex-LRA officer would not allow her to go free. Several meetings had to be held to persuade him to allow this woman to leave. This ex-LRA rebel commander could not understand that this kind of behavior is shameful and unacceptable both in the culture and in a free and civilized society. In fact, his mentality and behavior indicated that he thought the rules and norms of society did not apply to him. He was well aware that no one in society lived and conducted himself like this, but he was unwilling to adjust. The social workers at the psychosocial support center spent several days pleading with him to change his mindset, but they could not make any progress. What they opted to do was very surprising: they resolved that this LRA officer needed prayer and not more counseling or persuasion, since they concluded that there was a "spirit" clogging his thinking. They left the LRA officer by himself and knelt down to pray for the bad spirit to leave him; when they returned to continue the discussion, the ex-LRA commander told them that he'd had second thoughts and it was fine for the lady who was fed up with the relationship to go free. This sudden reversal in thinking and behavior astounded the social workers, and many of them attributed the success of their effort to divine intervention.

For me the most moving experience in these three months was seeing the large number of people who came for daily Mass at seven a.m. to pray with the rebels and to meet them as well. In all previous occasions, whenever they heard of rebel soldiers coming in their direction, they ran for their lives; yet in their encounters with these rebels now, they were very gracious, thanking them for abandoning armed conflict and welcoming them home.

The faith the rebels had in the Church made the community see the Catholic Church as their voice for peace and protector of all in the conflict. After three months, the seventeen ex-rebel fighters were discharged from the psychosocial support center, and activities at the center were scaled down. But CARITAS retained two full-time staff members at the center.

Another Place for Rebels to Surrender

Pajule was also a place at which rebels surrendered. Whenever a group of rebels wanted to surrender, their leader would often send a lower-ranking officer or a peace-contact person to notify the army leadership or the cultural leaders about their intention, and this information would be passed on to all the leaders in the community. And in their communication often they would specify the date, time, and the route they were going to pass through to lay down their arms. They would march into town in the early morning on the stipulated routes eventually leading to the army barracks.

These moments tended to be our happiest moments during the time of the conflict. I could not believe the joy I saw in the faces and eyes of the ordinary people. Whenever they found out that LRA rebels were coming to lay down their weapons, they would welcome them with ululations all over town. The whole community including hundreds of children would line up along the roads to receive them in excitement.

This very warm welcome was often envied and resented by the LRA rebel commanders who were still bent on continuing with the war. The community's willingness to forgive unconditionally undercut their central argument for continuing the war, which was that if they abandoned armed conflict and surrendered, they would be killed by the civilian population and the government soldiers. In fact, we learned that some of these rebel commanders wanted to send some units of rebel fighters to dupe the populace by pretending to surrender, and when the people came up to receive them, then they would shoot and kill them in return. Fortunately, this evil plan did not materialize at any moment.

It is important to note that the surrender of the rebels was only made possible because there was an amnesty law in place passed by the parliament of Uganda, which embodied the cultural sentiments of the people on forgiveness. This law was passed because of the insistence of the people of Acoliland and the northern region through their religious, cultural, civil, and political leaders who wanted to put an end to the endless cycle of violence

Some of the rebels who were surrendering were well-known individuals in the community, and in some cases criminal cases could have been brought against them while others could have been held accountable for actions that led to the wiping out of whole families or villages. However, what surprised me most was that when these rebels surrendered, almost nobody talked about the past. The words I heard from most of the people assembled were "Thank you for returning home; you are safe and nobody will harm you." In the conversation of the local people, once in a while names of those who surrendered would be mentioned, but there was hardly any bitterness or anger against the ex-rebels since they had turned away from the path of violence and were now giving peace a chance.

Most of the time when the rebels were being received by the government soldiers at the military barracks, I made sure that I was physically present to witness the short ceremony of welcome. I could also see the joy and excitement in the government soldiers, who were often cold and stressed out because of the pressures of their work environment. Their spontaneous words were always something similar to "You are welcome home; you are in safe hands. Let us join hands to serve and develop our country, Uganda." And the rebels would politely reply, "Thank you."

Government soldiers were most of the time culturally diverse since to a large extent they reflected the ethnic makeup of Uganda, while the rebels tended to be more monolithic since they tended to be primarily of the Acoli and northern tribes. So, when the rebels and government soldiers came together, there were obvious differences. Most of the rebels spoke the Luo language, and yet the government soldiers mainly spoke Kiswahili, the official language of the army, and other Bantu languages. At times, they needed interpreters to communicate with one another, but this was not a hindrance to the instant trust that developed. And yet for many years, the two sides had used the same word when referring to the other: "enemy." That is, one who is dangerous and must be eliminated.

Sometimes, these occasions of surrender were separated by just by a couple of weeks or even days after a deadly clash. But on the day the rebels surrendered, there were beaming faces on both sides. What astonished me most was that when the two sides came together, the resentments and the distrust that each group had been nurturing and harboring toward each other for years disappeared like dew before the hot sun. The government soldiers and the rebels were instantly at ease with one another. And there was no instance of doubt or mistrust about the genuineness of their acceptance; they treated the ex-rebels like their very own brothers and sisters and would try to make sure that they were well taken care of before transferring them to the army headquarters in Gulu, where they would be debriefed. Those who wanted to enlist in the army were always absorbed, and those who wished to return to civilian life were always assisted.

When they reentered society, most of the former rebel fighters lived normal lives and had no psychological issues. I believe this is because of the spiritual, psychological, emotional, and spiritual support of the community and their full acceptance as members once again. Their terrible experiences were hardly a hindrance. The challenge that they often faced was that of getting a job, since jobs were scarce and most of the rebels lacked the necessary training and education to be competitive in the job market.

Personally, witnessing the act of forgiveness among the people with whom I served and worked filled me with a sense of profound admiration and wonder. Whenever I witnessed the people welcome the ex-LRA, it was like the story of the prodigal son and the forgiving father in the Christian scriptures[4] unfolding in the community inspired by the timeless traditional, cultural and social values of the people. In a war zone, most of the stories that are covered concern the cruelty of human beings to each other; hardly any mention love and compassion. I have grappled with this profound sense of forgiveness that the community has, in particular the willingness to forgive without exception. To me, this forgiveness is in the DNA of the people. In fact, I have seen the teachings of Jesus Christ to forgive and to forget lived and practiced very literally. The Christian teaching and emphasis on forgiveness contributes to and reaffirms the distinctive cultural values and beliefs of the Acoli people. For the one century that Christianity has been preached in the Acoli and northern regions, there is hardly any gospel precept and principle that there is unanimous agreement on in its application like this. And because of this I believe that forgiveness must be enshrined and considered as one of the fundamental rights of my people whenever they want to exercise it as a means to peace.

---

4 Luke 15: 11–32.

Chapter Nine

The Collapse of Social and Administrative Structures

Pader District was one of the newly created districts in Uganda. It was created in the year 2000 by an act of parliament of the Republic of Uganda. Pajule was among the towns in this new district. At the beginning of March 2002, when hundreds of rebels crossed back from South Sudan into Uganda and began attacking and destroying vehicles along the roads, the whole of Pader District became very unsafe within weeks. Within four months, almost all administrative structures in the district had collapsed. We in Pajule were equally affected. Most of the civil servants—the police, medical personnel, teachers, and social workers—deserted the place because they could not bear the insecurity anymore.

Most of the district civil and political leaders took refuge in Lira District, in which the dominant ethnic group is the Lango tribe, and would occasionally travel back to Pader District headquarters under very heavy military escort. Around this time Pader District did not yet have any cell phone connections, so it meant that when they were away, they could not keep in touch with the district. For these leaders, the neighboring town of Lira became the place from which they conducted most administrative matters relating to Pader District, in particular meeting organizations that were willing to take the risk to send humanitarian assistance to those in the war zone. Lira also became the place that many of them would go to if they wanted to have some rest and a sound sleep.

The return of the rebels and the resulting insecurity also affected Pajule very much. As it was a small town, I knew most of the residents personally and by name. And many of those who left would often come and tell me: "Father, I have a family and dependents to look after. I can only fulfill my responsibility if I remain alive. I have to leave now, I cannot bear it anymore." I heard similar statements hundreds of times.

It was painful to see them leave because I had built close friendships with many of them, and they played important roles in the community. The hardest part was that with each and every group of people that fled, it affected our morale and spirit of perseverance and the hope that the situation would ever get better. When those who opted to flee from the place came to me to say farewell before departing, I would always say a prayer and bless them. And I would particularly pray that they had a safe trip out of Pajule and Pader District since this was the riskiest part of their journey.

By July 2002, the only non-military institution that was operating on the ground in much of Pader District was the Catholic Church based in Pajule. Pajule parish was adjacent to the town, and the government military installation was about one mile away and was able to provide it with security. As a result it became a convenient place for many to assemble. Even though the Anglican Church had a presence on the ground in Pajule, it was to a large extent ineffective since it had very limited manpower and financial resources and its headquarters and church premises were located in an area that had no military protection. Its premises could only be used during the day; at night it had to be deserted for fear of an attack by the rebels.

The intensification of the insecurity made our work as priests very difficult. We could not keep regular contact with all twenty-five chapels or units that we led since most of the members were being displaced, and this made it hard for us to keep track of where they were living. The fact that most administrative structures had collapsed in the district brought a new dynamic to our pastoral duties. For the time that we had been active in the parish, we had focused primarily on spiritual things: we preached the gospel, catechized, and administered the sacraments of the Church. But since the rebels were roaming all over the district and committing innumerable atrocities we gained other responsibilities. Most of the former abductees came to Pajule parish for humanitarian aid. This was primarily motivated by the belief that the Church would always help. The needs of these abductees put a lot of pressure on us. It meant that we could not confine our ministry anymore to spiritual things since their needs were material: food, clothing, and medicine. It was a must, then, that we find a way of providing humanitarian assistance as well.

As we were agonizing over what to do about the need for social services, CARITAS provided a contingent of social workers to help provide food, medical assistance, and counseling services to the returnees upon seeing the enormous challenges that the parish faced. Indeed, this move by the archdiocesan authorities helped to ease our stress. The decision to send additional social workers to Pajule led to the expansion of the existing psychosocial support center that was in place, and gave birth to the Pajule Reception Center.

The Composition and the Role of Pajule Reception Center

Most of the people who were received at the reception center were young men, women, and children who were victims of the LRA war. Because the jungles in which the rebels operated were nearby, at a certain point the rebels released close to four hundred people, mainly women and children, who were received and taken care of by the reception center for close to four months. The majority of the returnees generally were young boys who had been abducted to be child-soldiers and had spent weeks or months, even years in captivity. Child-mothers also made up a large part of the group. These were young girls who were abducted by the rebels and forced to bear children for them. Most of these child-mothers were voluntarily released by the rebels for a variety of reasons.

First, the rebels wanted to minimize their own risks and pressures when they were being pursued by the government foot soldiers, and having mothers with children with them often slowed them down. Second, the LRA was often pursued by military helicopters that would drop bombs on them, and they felt it was inappropriate to put the lives of their children and mistresses in danger from aerial attacks. Third, even if most of the LRA rebels were polygamists, they also had strong superstitious beliefs. They believed that any woman who became a widow because her husband had been killed in combat had to be set free because they believed that anyone within the LRA who tried to inherit her would also die. Fourth, the rebels also claimed that releasing these women was a sign of goodwill on their part to show that they were serious about the peace talks and ongoing negotiations with the government of Uganda. Fifth, the rebels released child-mothers because it was difficult for them to walk for hundreds of miles in a day. They found it difficult to treat their very own like captives, whom they could leave behind or eliminate when they were tired, and so they would release them for this reason as well.

The reception center provided psychosocial support and counseling services to the returnees. It had close to thirty full-time staff members. Most of these social workers were young men and women from the districts of the Acoli region who had just finished college; for most of them this was their first job after completing school. At a human level, the staff of the reception center was a blessing to us, the priests. The large number of staff provided us with company that we badly needed since many of the people we knew had left Pajule. This helped keep our morale up. In fact, because of the strong working relationships we built with them, we could talk about our fears, concerns, hopes, and expectations. Some of these discussions were very therapeutic. Through them, we managed to encourage and be of support to one another. And this bond was further strengthened by the fact that I later became their chaplain and provided spiritual guidance to them and to the returnees.

The social workers' accomplishments were remarkable. Almost on a daily basis they witnessed and treated terrible wounds and injuries that the returnees had incurred at the hands of their captors. They would also listen to the horrible stories these returnees shared about what had been done to them or what had happened to fellow captives. Several times I got the chance to personally listen to the stories, and most of them were horrific. For example, young girls between the ages of fourteen and fifteen narrated how, after their abduction and arrival at the rebel bases, they were given out immediately as mistresses to rebel commanders, who were older men. Some of these girls were abducted while on their way to or returning from school. Many shared stories of the constant rapes that they had to endure. Young boys told stories about their initiation into the rebel ranks: they were ordered to kill prisoners of war, and those who hesitated were shot or cut to pieces with machetes while the rest of the abductees observed what was taking place. This was done to make them feel at ease with murder and expunge any sense of guilt from their conscience.

However, what I found bizarre about listening to these child-soldiers/returnees was the absence of remorse, the lightheartedness even, with which they talked about the gruesome details of the things they witnessed or took part in. Surprisingly, some of them boasted about the number of people they had killed in a single day, while others took pride in killing close to three hundred people during the time they were in captivity. I attribute this strange behavior to the trauma that each one of them had gone through during their captivity.

I witnessed some other strange behavior in the returnees as a consequence of their abduction. Some could not fall asleep at night because they had nightmares constantly. One boy who was about thirteen years old talked about being unable to get any rest because whenever he tried to fall asleep, he would see visions of those he'd slaughtered lying on the ground and looking into his face. His nights were like watching an endless bad movie since it brought back all the things that happened in captivity. This boy tried everything including seeking psychosocial help and counseling, spiritual guidance, and traditional African spiritual cleansing, but none of them made him feel any better.

Some returnees had been abducted while they were sleeping in a room, and because they were captured in an enclosed space were not willing to sleep in a house. They preferred to spend their nights in an open compound, and if they were persuaded to sleep in the house, the door had to be open all night. This was a shocking experience to us, the residents of Pajule, since we believed security required tightly locking our doors.

There were also returnees who attempted to escape but were caught and sentenced to death, and then beaten on their heads with clubs and left to die. They were later rescued by government soldiers who were pursuing the rebels.

Some returnees talked about seeing their colleagues drown in the rivers. Since not all the abductees knew how to swim, one rebel soldier would lead the way with a rope in his hand, and all the captives were expected to cling to the rope as they crossed a body of water. There were many occasions in which abductees that were weak and could not cling to the rope drowned, while others who were not tall enough or entered some deeper spots would go under water and drown, with no attempt being made to save them. Others shared stories about how prisoners of war who could not walk anymore were often bludgeoned to death instead of being carried or set free. Some of the captives were ordered to participate in these executions.

These were the kind of stories that the social workers listened to all the time. Most of them had a background in the social sciences, although none of them had a specialization in counseling or psychology. They did what they could.

In fact, hosting the reception center at the parish and attending to the returnees was one of the most stressful environments I have ever been in. In the first place, we constantly listened to the violent and troubling stories that the returnees shared; and second, we lived under the constant threat that the reception center would itself be attacked one day by the LRA because it was a place they resented as it accepted ex-combatants that had escaped from them.

A result of this stress-filled work environment was a high level of irritability among the staff. For example, quarrels, conflicts, and disagreements were common; and when they arose, if they were not immediately handled, they got out of hand. At the beginning of the reception center in July 2002, there was so much disagreement among the staff members and their manager that it was closed until a new group of social workers could be assigned. It was much later that we came to understand the real problem was that they were stressed out. They were neither resting nor sleeping enough and lived constantly under the threats caused by insecurity. This was later addressed: once in a while all of them went on vacation for two weeks in a place that was safe and where they could have a sound sleep.

On my part, I was equally stressed like anyone else. Once in a while, I would tell myself: "I wish I could have the same attention and care as the returnees at the reception center get." I believe that my level of trauma, fatigue, and stress was just as high as that of anyone else, and yet I had to attend to the returnees, the staff, and the wider community and could hardly go away from the parish for any vacation. Whenever I heard loud sounds, I would go into a panic attack, and when I felt criticized I became overly defensive and rigid in my positions.

Camp Life and Its Impact

The relocation of people into the camps was an immediate consequence of the collapse of the administrative structures in Pader District in July 2002. People settled in the camps empty-handed, making grass thatched huts for temporary shelter. Each hut was less than five meters apart, and if one of them caught fire, a line of them would burn down. These huts did not even have doors. People would look for large thin metal plates, straighten up a couple of them, and bind them together to make a door. Families of as many as ten lived in these huts, and since there were no partitions inside most of them, there was no privacy available for husbands and wives.

There was always a lack of basic necessities, and as a consequence the people scrambled for whatever they could find. Food was usually provided by the United Nations once every two months, but it was only enough for a family of eight people to survive on for two weeks.

Camp life had a profoundly negative impact on the elderly and the children because the principle of camp life was survival of the fittest. I remember old men and women carrying babies on their backs coming to my office in the mornings to ask for anything that I could give them to eat. An old man once said to me: "Father, I have not had anything like hard food to eat for the last week, I have been drinking vegetable soup only, and now I need something solid that can sit in my stomach. I have very little energy left in me at the moment." Statements of this kind were common in the parish. Hearing about the dire condition that some of the people were in made me depressed since I could not do much for them. I had just barely enough to take care of myself.

There was also an extreme shortage of medical supplies in the camps. The government hospital in the town had a medical staff, but there were no drugs that they could prescribe to patients. Instead, they referred them to the private clinics in the town. People often fell sick from malaria and did not have the money to pay for any medicine and had to endure the attack and recover without any treatment. In the local language, the people termed this as the "elephant treatment" because it is understood that if an elephant gets sick or hurt in the bushes, it does not go to a hospital for treatment but gets healed due to its inner strength and natural ability. The condition of some who had other chronic illnesses worsened, and many of the children with low immunity died.

Camp life also had an adverse effect on the character of the people. Many in the camp behaved like animals because they lived in perpetual want and need. Whenever they came across something, the tendency was to grab it for themselves and cling to it. I remember particularly on December, 28, 2003, which was my birthday, I wished to surprise the children in the camp. Their numbers were in the hundreds, and often they had very little to eat, much less any clothes to put on. So, I bought several sweets in packets to give out to each one of them. While in the camp, I picked out five ladies who were in their early twenties to assist me in giving out the sweets. The number of children who turned up was close to six hundred, and we asked them to line up. When they had all lined up, the five ladies whom I was counting on to assist me ran away with the sweets. It was a great shock to me because I had taken it for granted that adults always cared for the little ones and put their interests ahead of their own. What followed was a lot of commotion in the camp as hundreds of children began running after the women, trying to grab onto the packets they were running away with. The scene resembled a swarm of bees pursuing their target. Some were tearing apart the packets, and others were scrambling for any sweets that fell to the ground, actually fighting over them. This made me regret my idea because there was a real possibility that one of these children could have been hurt or even killed in the commotion. Some of the children remained and stood around me since I still had some sweets. However, they were not willing to follow my instructions to line up. Instead, each of them wanted to grab all the sweets in my hand for himself or herself. None of them had enough trust in me to form a line. I had no way of giving the sweets to the children and became afraid of violence from them. So, I asked one of the children to call about five adults to come to assist me. When two adults arrived, I told the children around me that we would distribute the sweets another day, and asked the adults to escort me out of the camp. I had to leave with all the remaining sweets in my hand since I did not want to cause any incident.

Finally, there was a general degeneration of morals in the camp because there was a breakdown in the chain of authority in families and society. Because of this sexual promiscuity became very high and led to many being infected with the HIV virus and other venereal diseases.

Chapter Ten

A True Heart of Compassion

While most of the experiences in a war zone show human pain and suffering, I believe that it also brought out the best of hearts in our community. I remember a man called Simon and his wife, Lucy, and how much they sacrificed on a daily basis for the people of Pajule. This couple owned and operated a small clinic. It had financial capital of not more than two thousand dollars. Lucy was a trained nurse, and her husband was a mechanic who also worked a number of trades to support his family.

This couple had several children of their own, orphans and dependents to look after. However, since there were no reliable medical services provided by the government hospital or humanitarian organizations, their clinic was one where many of the residents and camp dwellers went to get treatment. Almost half of the people had no money. A number of camp dwellers only went to the clinic after they had tried to bear an illness for several days or even weeks. Lucy treated them without asking for any payment; she told them to pay whenever they could, and if they could not it was fine. Some of her former patients much later would bring her a hen as a sign of appreciation. Often victims of ambushes who had lost everything in the attacks would be brought to their clinic for first aid and medical treatment. She treated them without expecting any compensation.

While Lucy did so much for people, it is important to note that she had serious health issues. She was diabetic and had high blood pressure as well. Sometimes she would become critically ill. There was a time when she almost died. In fact, I once received information that she had passed away; fortunately, it was not true.

During the time when she was critically ill, I remember praying to God as follows: "*God, Lucy is doing so much good in this place. She is the cornerstone of free health services and access to medical treatment for many in this town. If You intend to take her into eternal life to be with You, it is fine, but I ask that before You do so, make sure that You get someone to replace her and do her job. Otherwise, so many more people in the camps will die because of her absence.*" After one month in the hospital, Lucy returned home, and though physically weak was able to recover with the support of her mother and go back to her job. I do not have any doubts that God listened to my prayers and those of the many people who were praying for her.

I am also convinced that God has enabled this couple to pull through the many health challenges that they faced and to see their children grow up, as well as to take care of the orphans and dependents they supported. They did not have a lot of resources of their own, and yet many times they gave up what little they had to save lives. It did not matter whether they knew the people or not. It was the need that was most important to them. They taught me human virtue and true values, that however little money one may have or however much one may be in need of it, saving lives comes first.

Chapter Eleven

My First Priestly Anniversary

The first anniversary of my priesthood was on Sunday, August 18, 2002. It was an excellent coincidence, since I could pray with the whole Christian community of Pajule parish to ask for God's blessings on my priestly ministry. But on Saturday evening, I got very disturbing information through the local cultural chief. He was respected, informed, and constantly updated by the people about the security situation. He advised me to communicate to everyone in the area to go to bed early that evening since there might be a rebel attack after dark.

Whenever I got any information that was related to the safety and security of the people, my practice was to pass it to all those who came to spend their night in the parish compound. Then, instead of having dinner at eight p.m., which was my usual time, I would have dinner by six p.m., followed by my evening prayers. And I would put off all the lights in the rectory, and get into a corner of the house that I considered safe for the night.

It was important for the community to retire early whenever there were rumors of an imminent attack because this allowed the government soldiers to patrol and track any strange or suspicious activities taking place inside and outside of town. And in case a gunfight was to break out, it minimized the risk of civilians being caught up in the crossfire.

In spite of going to bed very early that evening, I failed to sleep because I was expecting shooting to start at any moment. The following morning I had two Masses to celebrate. I celebrated the first Mass at seven a.m. The parish church was about one hundred meters from the rectory. Attendance was very low since many people also had their sleep disrupted by the news of a possible attack on the town and opted to go to bed in the morning instead of coming for the first Mass. Since very few people had come to the first Mass, I had plenty of time on my hands, so I had breakfast.

The second Mass was to start at nine a.m., and I left the rectory five minutes early. The average attendance for this Mass was about four hundred people every Sunday, and my expectation was that a similar number of people would show up. But before I started the procession to the altar from the back of the church, I saw throngs of people running from the town and the camps onto the parish land toward the church, and within a few minutes close to two thousand people had converged in and around the church. The church compound was full, with only standing room available.

I could see fear in the eyes of the people all around me. They all looked at me very intently, and yet, they were not speaking to me. I had nothing to tell them. I was as equally shaken and frightened as they were, and yet, they were counting on me for their safety and leadership. To me the challenge was even greater, as I was just marking my first year as a newly ordained twenty-nine-year-old priest, and I felt too young and inexperienced to face such an enormous challenge. I opted to appear composed in their midst while deciding whether or not to celebrate the Mass. My instincts told me to proceed. The number of people inside and outside the church was so big that I could not control them, but I knew that as Mass progressed they would all calm down and be reverential and focus on it.

However, there was a greater risk as well, since it was my personal practice and conviction that whenever I started to say Mass, nothing would make me cut it short even if it meant exposing our lives to physical danger. At the beginning of every Mass, the Catholic priests in the Archdiocese of Gulu commonly say a short prayer in which we ask for divine help as follows: "Our help is in the name of the Lord." If there are altar servers, their response is: "Who created Heaven and Earth." This morning, the processional prayer to the Mass made a lot of sense, and I felt inspired by it.

I asked God in my heart what I should tell the congregation of frightened people. I realized that mentally I had no cogent thoughts to express. At times, I experienced my mind going blank and shutting down. And the worst part of it was that as I approached the altar, I had forgotten not only the opening remarks of my homily but the whole homily as well.

Whenever the entrance song was sung in this parish, it was accompanied by traditional instruments and drums, which always gave a flavor to the worship and enlivened the liturgical celebration. However, this morning the drumbeats that I usually enjoyed very much sounded different in my ears, like live bullets being fired. When I reached the altar, I could not start the Mass right away. Most people in the congregation were too distracted, afraid and looking outside the church. I felt that we could neither concentrate nor say any meaningful prayer under the circumstances. So I surprised the congregation by asking them to take their seats. This was abnormal. The usual practice was always to begin the celebration of the Mass with the sign of the cross while the congregation remained standing.

I welcomed those who were inside and outside the church and told them that, like most of them, I had spent a sleepless night. I needed to communicate to my congregation that I fully felt their fears and pains and understood what they were going through. Using a local cultural expression well known to them, I said that there were "strong winds blowing and winding round the place," meaning that the rebels were moving around and were nearby. I could not mention the word "rebel" or the LRA for fear of retaliation, and at the same time I was uncertain that in the large multitude of people assembled there were no actual LRA spies. I felt that I had to acknowledge the precariousness of the situation, and I wanted the congregation to know that they had made an important choice in coming to the church. And I went on to say that they had many options for refuge, but most of them came to the parish because of their faith in God and the fact that it is a sacred and holy ground.

I informed them that as a minister of God, I did not have any extraordinary means to protect them, nor did I have any guns. However, I assured them that since they had come to the parish, God Himself was now responsible for their security and destiny. If anything were to happen to them while they were in the parish, then God Himself had allowed it to happen.

Next, I told my congregation that we have always preached to them that God is everywhere, but one place that I am certain of the presence of God was in the tabernacle. Luckily enough, the tabernacle of Pajule parish church was in front of us, located between the sanctuary and pews of the congregation on the right-hand side of the church. Pointing at the tabernacle, I said: "As Christians, we believe that God is everywhere, but I am 100 percent certain that Christ is in this tabernacle and by implication is in this church, and is right here now in our midst." I felt that it was important for me to draw something from the faith and spiritual resources of my congregation because what we all needed at that moment was inner strength, resolve, courage, peace, calm, and reassurance.

I believe that this was the most challenging question I have ever asked in my priestly ministry of any group of people assembled: "If we believe that God is in this church, and if something were to begin to happen inside or outside the church and we made up our minds to flee for our lives, to whom would we be running?"

I could see that this question surprised the congregation. It was a difficult question, and there was total silence in the church. The congregation appeared tongue-tied, breathless and confused. At this moment I asked them to rise and participate in the Mass as a people who have faith. Instantly there was a remarkable change. The church was calm, and no one tried to look outside.

I believe that the people assembled were able to draw strength from my words because they shared the belief that cutting short the celebration of the Mass or abandoning it because of fear of danger to our lives was like an attempt to run away from Jesus rather than to take refuge in Him. Because of this belief, many in the parish were willing to take a stand as well. Just like all Catholics, my parishioners believed that at the celebration of Mass, Jesus is truly present among them. That is why they were once in a while willing to risk their lives as a testament of their faith in Christ as their ultimate protector.

Further, the celebration of the Mass for my parishioners had become their sole source of strength and renewal. It was also in the Mass that they tried to make meaning of what was happening in their own lives and environment. In fact, it is right for me to say that to most of them, the Mass was the most precious thing in their life.

We had started the Mass in a somber mood, but as we went on, by the time we had reached the Gospel procession, I could see that the congregation was brightening up and becoming warmhearted. By the time the Mass came to a conclusion, peace and calm had returned to the people. The atmosphere and camaraderie in church was like that of any other Sunday with the exception that this Sunday there were a lot more people.

After the Mass we got out of church only to find that the rebels who were nearby had gone away. Hundreds of them had spent the night about two miles away from the parish without attacking the town or harming anyone. I later heard elderly women in the parish saying, "This priest knows how to strengthen us even if he is young." I wish they knew how I felt at the time. I believe that the reason we did not have any violent incident was because God had performed a miracle to protect the town and the parish.

In the evening there was a spontaneous celebration for my first anniversary. It was a joyful evening because for a long time we had been living under a lot of tension, stress, and fear. But this time, for a couple of hours we put all that aside to socialize and celebrate. I was joined by the religious sisters, the teachers of Pajule primary school, the social workers of CARITAS, and the Christians of my parish.

In a characteristically African style, I received many gifts. I was presented with several live chickens, ducks, and other gifts from my parishioners. In fact, this anniversary celebration has left a lasting impression on me.

I remember that in the speech I gave at my priestly anniversary celebration, I said things similar to what I had said in the homily during the morning Mass about the need for peace in my ministry, and this evening in particular I said: "If there is insecurity among the people of God, that is the very reason that a priest ought to be among them and not desert them." These words of mine did not take long to be put to the test.

Chapter Twelve
Finding God in Unlikely Places

For close to five months of intense insecurity in Pajule parish, our strength as a community was centered on the Prayer of Adoration and the sacred sacrifice of the Mass. Every Saturday at six p.m. we had the Blessed Sacrament exposed for the community to worship. The time for adoration was a time for us to talk to Jesus heart to heart, to thank God for keeping us alive, and to ask for His protection in the coming week. The Adoration normally lasted for one hour.

Further, Mass was celebrated in the parish every day at seven a.m. The Little Sisters of Mary Immaculate of Gulu and many students of the parish tailoring school and Pajule technical school would participate. But most of the community came for Mass on Sundays only.

However, one segment of the population that moved me most by its devotion and faith was the military. Since the end of the month of January 1986, when the current regime came to power in Uganda, it has always claimed that religion is divisive and argued that soldiers who are interested in worship should go and look for a place to pray outside the army barracks. This stance by the political and military leadership, which is filled with disdain for organized religion, prevents most soldiers from participating in worship services since those who are deployed in the war zones are on duty for almost twenty-four hours.

It is important to note that this negative attitude toward religion and worship is because of the Marxist ideology that some of the political cadres of the regime had when they came into power and also the desire on the part of the political and military leadership to have total control over the soldiers and limit the influence of the society on the institution. A tight grip on the army is the means by which many military and political leaders have been able to hang onto power for decades. Regimes in Uganda that failed to keep a tight grip on the army only lasted for a short time.

It was under such circumstances that I was deeply touched by the faith of some of the soldiers. I remember that several of them who were on duty on Sundays would come during their break time to join the community in the celebration of Mass. They were always dressed in their uniforms because within a very short time they could be ordered to report to the battlefield. It was striking to see them in their green uniforms among the congregation, since most Ugandans have not experienced soldiers as God-fearing people who express their faith openly.

While many in the community were uncomfortable with the sight of men dressed in green uniforms at church because their presence heightened the risk of their place of worship becoming a target, they were also happy to have them around because it was their first experience to pray together. To many people, seeing the army uniform evokes mixed feelings of fear, terror, trepidation, and resentment because men in army uniforms have at different times harassed, tortured, and committed atrocities against them. In fact, the soldiers who joined us in the celebration of the Mass took a big risk on their part since they came unarmed, and if there were to be any attack on the worshipers, they would be the very first targets.

It was also common for me to meet soldiers in the town who would tell me, "Father, we wanted to come for worship today, but we were not able to because we were on duty." I assured them that it was fine, and they could still come the following Sunday.

One day in September 2002, the LRA had attacked Pajule on the previous night and looted several shops within the town, including one of a local businessman called Mr. Combon, so in the evening we were all afraid that they might return. As the sun was setting, I became restless and started worrying about what might happen. This was when I was challenged and inspired by the faith of a platoon commander. At the time the practice was to deploy close to fifty soldiers every evening around the parish to protect it.

Before I went to bed that evening, I spoke with the commander of the soldiers. Though I did not tell the army officer what I expected from him, I had hoped to hear some words of reassurance that we were going to be safe and that the Army was moving in heavy weaponry to protect the town.

So, I asked the soldier, "Because of the attack of last night and the fact that the rebels who did it could not be traced, what provisions are you making to protect the people tonight? Are you bringing in more manpower or weapons?" He gave me an answer that I never expected at all: "Father, weapons will not protect us, but God will."

This was a shock to me since I am the man of God. This statement should have come from my own lips. When I heard what the commander said, I quietly left without asking any more questions. The soldier had reminded me that as a spiritual leader, if I was going to ask people to trust and have faith in God, I had to have that same faith inside me and practice it at all times.

Chapter Thirteen
War and Alcohol

Most alcoholic drinks that the people imbibed in Pajule were locally brewed from corn flour, millet, and yeast, but bottled beers and spirits were also brought into Pajule. There were occasions when the town ran dry and new supplies could not be quickly delivered because the roads were unsafe. Whenever this happened, the lack of alcoholic drink instantly became the talk of town, an extraordinary emergency that was usually described as if it were a major security concern. Because of this, many town dwellers wondered when the next truck would bring beer into town, and those who had a few bottles left in their possession could sell them at thrice the usual price.

When there was no alcohol in town, most people would think that the situation had gone from bad to worse because they felt that everything was coming to a standstill. Others complained that if they could not find beer or spirits in town, their lives, which were already hard, suddenly became even more difficult. And when a new supply was delivered, there was a great sigh of relief and life would return to normal for a little bit.

Because the lack of alcoholic drink was considered to be a grave situation, if the military could not provide security or guarantee the safety of the roads, the townspeople would come up with creative ways to make sure that the town was kept supplied. They would hire a driver who was willing to take the risk to go to Kitgum even though he could be attacked by rebels while en route. He would affix a bad muffler or an exhaust pipe to a pickup truck, which locals called a "mamba," hoping that the loud and scary noise would sound like a military combat vehicle and keep the rebels away from the roads. The beer truck would then depart from Pajule for Kitgum at a very high speed and would not stop on the way. Because of the speed at which it traveled, it generated so much dust that it was barely visible. From afar, it could be mistaken for a convoy of trucks, as it resembled the military whenever they escorted deliveries of food supplies to the nearby camps. And we learned from former abductees that whenever lightly armed rebels saw the beer truck coming, they ran deep into the bushes. This was how Pajule continually replenished its supplies of dry spirits and beer.

However, in the month of October 2002, the driver of the beer truck, Mr. Nelson, ran out of luck and encountered an ambush at Porogali on his way back to Pajule. It was hard to tell why this evening was different. I can only speculate that the rebels abducted someone who disclosed to them that it was not a combat vehicle they were always running away from, but the town's beer truck. Or this evening, the vehicle had come across a group of well-armed rebels who were willing to put up a fight and were desperately in need of supplies. Definitely, matters were not helped by the fact that the vehicle was returning from Kitgum at five p.m., which was past the time the government soldiers provided security for travelers.

So when the rebels began to shoot at the beer truck, the driver was not aware of it. The noise from the bad muffler drowned out the sounds of gunfire and the whiz of the bullets directed at him. And because of the dust engulfing the vehicle, he had very poor visibility and could see less than fifty meters through the front screen. But as he continued driving, he began to hear sounds like a swarm of African bees buzzing about inside the truck and nearly stinging him. He immediately started to wonder how bees could have entered the front part of the truck since the windscreen was locked and there was too much dust and wind for a bee to get in. And above all, there was nothing to attract a bee into the vehicle.

As he wondered what was happening, he began to hear the supposed bees intensify and become louder; one passed above his head and made a light scratch on his hair, another passed close to his left cheek and hit the metallic part of the driver's seat, making it shake, and he heard a violent piercing sound like a nail being hammered into a wall. Then, he saw his back and front windscreen collapse and realized that it was not bees but a volley of bullets. He knew he had to act fast if he were to get out alive. Within seconds, he drove the beer truck into the bushes alongside the road, jumped out, and fled on foot for his life. That was where he spent his night before returning to Pajule the following morning, safe but exhausted.

Fortunately, government soldiers had an outpost about two kilometers away, and when they heard the sound of gunfire, they rushed to the scene and rescued the vehicle before the rebels could set it ablaze. The owner of the vehicle, a businessman of Pajule, was able to pick up his vehicle the following day, even though the soldiers had drank more than half the beer in the crates.

In a warzone, there is a very heavy consumption of alcohol for very different reasons. Many claim that there is no reason to save, invest, and plan for the future since it may never come. Some argue that without taking an alcoholic drink in the evening they will not have the inner courage to go to bed. Others say they are always stressed out and only alcohol makes them relax.

Soldiers spent most of their money on alcohol, too. For the majority of them, the future was not important since they lived each day like it was the very last. Sometimes, their lifestyle made me wonder how they were meeting their financial responsibilities since a number of them had families that depended on them.

Because a substantial amount of the money in a warzone was spent on alcoholic beverages, companies that manufactured beers and spirits also targeted the area. They designed brands of spirits for the convenience of the people and the soldiers in the warzone. The spirits were packaged in sachets like sweets or candies, since most of the local people could not come and sit and drink in a bar because it was unsafe, and most evenings it was dark because the lights had to be turned off or there was a power outage. With spirits put in sachets, town dwellers could buy several, pocket them, and sip them wherever they spent the night, either at home or in the bushes.

Packaging spirits in sachets was also very convenient for the government soldiers. They could buy large amounts and put several sachets in the many pouches of their army uniforms. It was impossible for them to go to a bar or a beer garden to sit and drink because if they tried to do so, they would be picked up by the military police, since they were supposed to be sober most of the time as they were presumed to be on duty. By pocketing the sachets, most soldiers had spirits with them wherever they went and could keep on sipping them day and night while deployed in the bushes around the town. In fact, government soldiers were much of the time tipsy or drunk, and many times this brought trouble, for whenever they heard noises or footsteps from wild animals or pigs they would panic, thinking that it was the rebels advancing, and start shooting into the air. The rest of the soldiers guarding the town would do the same, till they had confirmed that there was no real attack. Meanwhile the whole town would be tense for several minutes till the gunshots died down.

However, in the camps of Pajule, the high alcoholic consumption was mainly motivated by frustration. Most people felt worthless since they could not be responsible and productive parents. They wanted to cultivate their fields, grow some crops, and sustain their families, but they could not because it was too unsafe. Some who insisted were either abducted or killed by the rebels in their gardens. It was common to find camp dwellers drinking locally made hard liquor at seven thirty a.m. instead of having a normal breakfast. The popular hard liquor tasted like vodka. After a couple of drinks, they began to sing and dance. It knocked some down while sending others to sleep. By around nine a.m., most of the men in the camp were either very tipsy or totally drunk. Because there was a lot of heavy drinking of alcohol at irregular hours, pastoral visits were almost impossible. One day when I went to the camp, a woman who was totally drunk trailed me uninvited from one house to another, noisily introducing me to whomever we met. I could see people in the camp look at me with astonishment at the kind of company I was keeping that day. When I felt that it had become too much, I cut short my visit and returned to the parish.

I also discovered that animals enjoy alcohol as well. In the parish, I had pigs that I fed with the residue of a local brew called *kwete*, which was made out of corn flour, yeast, and water. After a few days of fermentation, it would be filtered and the corn residue remained. The pigs loved it more than anything else since it was alcoholic. They only ate the sunflower cakes that they were normally fed on after they had consumed it all.

The pigs could smell the alcoholic residue from a distance of 150 meters, and there would be a lot of excitement and anticipation in the pigsty. They would run around, scream, and some would even try to jump over their enclosures and go to where the *kwete* residue was. A single line of hair from the backs of their necks to their tails would be standing up. The person serving the residue had to keep out of the way of the pigs; otherwise, they would trample him. As soon as the residue was placed in the feeding troughs each pig devoured it as if it was meant for it alone. And in the process, I could hear their groaning, grunting, and squealing intensify as the older and larger ones tried to consume everything, while the smaller and little ones passed below their legs to get a share as well.

After this, I saw the pigs enter the water trough, which was like a wide-open bathtub or spa, and lie down, chewing what was left in their mouths. It looked like they were doing some contemplation about how good their meal was. I also guess that they were feeling comfortable and tipsy. And afterward, I would see them turn their bellies facing the hot African sun. At first I did not make sense of what was happening; it was much later that I discovered they were actually sunbathing.

Chapter Fourteen

My Journey to Rome

One evening in the middle of October 2002, I returned to the parish at eight p.m., a time that was relatively late because of the unrest. In the evenings large numbers of people usually spent the night in the parish and any buildings that could be used. But this evening there was dead silence. I did not know what to make of this. I went to bed puzzled and disturbed, wondering what was going on.

The following morning, I asked one of the local elders in the parish what exactly had happened to the many people who always came to spend their nights in the parish. He told me the parish had been cursed. In the area of Acoliland where Pajule parish is located, there is a superstitious belief called "*Kore*" that some individuals have satanic or demonic powers and can curse others and cause harm to come to them. It is believed that the intentions of those who do the cursing are often revealed in a dream; that is, their neighbors or people who live with them hear them speak aloud of their wishes and intentions as they sleep, wishing or praying harm to someone. If the object of the dream is a human being, it is believed that the person will die. And if any person has contact with a thing or a place that has been cursed, they will also die. For example, if bean seeds or meat that has been cursed is sold in the market, it is believed that individuals who purchase and consume the items will perish. Since the parish was reported to have been cursed, according to this belief system it meant that those who would spend their nights in it were all destined to die.

This reminded me of something that had happened prior to my appointment. A similar incident had taken place during the music festival that had been staged three years ago; there were rumors that it was cursed. This competition that brought together all the primary/elementary schools in the district of Pader almost collapsed because the contestants were afraid that if they took part in it they would all mysteriously die. For this reason, a woman and her daughter were almost lynched by a rowdy mob that blamed them for "cursing" the competition. The police had to intervene to save their lives.

When I reported to Pajule parish, I heard other stories about *kore* from some of the parishioners who said that they needed to protect themselves from the "curses" whenever they passed through Pader District headquarters, even if they were being driven in a truck.

The rumor that the parish had been cursed spread like a wildfire and generated a lot of uneasiness, as many of my parishioners speculated that those who came to spend their nights in the parish compound would be massacred by LRA rebels if the place were to be attacked. Because many of my parishioners are superstitious and have at one time or another participated in traditional African pagan rituals and practices, they were shaken to the core of their very being. A majority was not willing to take the risk of spending a single night in the parish compound.

After two quiet evenings and nights, and still no people coming to sleep in the parish, a man and his wife who were very concerned about me came to visit and warn me about the danger I was exposing myself to by continuing to live and sleep in the parish. There was a common tendency among the local population to look at Catholic priests as having a childlike innocence about dangers from satanic or demonic powers. Like the LRA, they view priests as either ignorant or in some instances brainwashed or Westernized by their priestly training. So when this couple explained the dangers to which I was exposing myself and what might happen to me, I told them how much I appreciated their concern and reminded them that I was an ordained person doing God's work in their midst. I was with them as a servant of God and I worked in His name. I also stated that if there were any spiritual dangers to me that I was not aware of, God would protect me from them. And, by virtue of my ordination as a priest, I had spiritual powers that God had given me. On hearing my position, the couple told me: "We are happy that you know the risk you are taking, and we hope the God you believe in will take care of you." And they left.

Personally, I believe in the existence of Satan and his powers, but I am firmly convinced that God will always protect those who believe in Him as their choice in life. I had to rely on my faith in God on many occasions in Pajule parish, but this was among the most significant challenges to the faith of the people. I am convinced that this superstitious belief in *kore* challenged the very foundations of our faith as a Christian community. My leaving the rectory to spend the night elsewhere would have validated the superstitious beliefs of the community, and in this action I would have destroyed the foundations of the Christian faith that the Catholic Church had been laying down for the last fifty years.

The encounter with *kore* pointed out to me a weakness of the Christian catechesis in the archdiocese of Gulu and Africa in general. The white missionaries and the African clergy have worked hard to spread the Christian faith, but their attitude has often been dismissive and condescending of the African traditional religious practices. They have too often been quick to condemn the local culture and label it as primitive, outdated, evil, and satanic. Some of their categorizations are correct, but they need to take time to study the depth and the degree to which the lives of the people and their worldviews have been defined by these beliefs, since they give the people meaning and security.

While the Christian faith showed to the African people a new path to salvation through Christ, it did not sufficiently demonstrate how the Christian teachings and its belief system would protect them from their fears of satanic or evil powers. As a result many Africans embraced the new faith without renouncing their traditional beliefs. This was because the new faith was taught to the people without an understanding of the local culture, partly because the culture was not well known to the white missionaries and, in the case of the indigenous clergy, most did not have the interest to learn the local culture. Africans were rightly being asked to abandon their cultural and traditional faith practices, but without a full recognition of how their lives were intertwined and enmeshed with these belief systems. It is because of this that many in my parish tended to be syncretistic; that is, they came to church and participated in the worship and all its rituals, but when they experienced serious spiritual threats like the challenge of the imminent death of a family member, the temptation was to fall back on their traditional, cultural, and African religious practices, including the reliance on superstition.

The Sunday before I left for Rome, I needed to confront this *kore* that had generated so much fear. When I brought up the subject in the church, I could notice that many were surprised, uneasy, and some looked afraid to hear me talk about it.

My whole view of *kore* and the story going around was that it was a challenge to the faith of the community. I chose to use the booklet for the prayer of consecration during the Eucharistic celebration, and I read directly from it, that is, word for word. I also had hosts and wine that had not been blessed or consecrated at the altar for my demonstration.

As I raised the host to the Congregation, I said the exact words of consecration:

The day before he suffered,

He took bread in his sacred hands

And, looking up to heaven

To you, his heavenly father,

He gave you thanks and praise.

He broke the bread,

Gave it to his disciples, and said:

Take this, all of you, and eat it.

This is my body which will be given up for you

Then I asked, "If Christ has given up Himself for our salvation to liberate us from sin, death, darkness and fear, why are we still afraid of *kore*? Do we really believe in Him?" Then, I raised the chalice into which I had poured some wine and recited the prayers of consecration, once again as I would normally do during the celebration of the Mass:

When supper was ended,

He took the cup.

Again he gave you thanks and praise,

Gave the cup to his disciples, and said:

Take this, all of you, and drink from it:

This is the cup of my blood,

The Blood of the New and Everlasting Covenant

It will be shed for you and for all

So that sins may be forgiven.

Do this in memory of me.

And I asked a set of questions similar to the above. These questions were difficult and uncomfortable for the congregation. There was total silence in the church; one could have heard a pin drop. I also proceeded to explain to the congregation in layman's terms the reasons why some people dream and how some dreams are very much a product of our own experiences.

I argued that we often dream about the things we see, think about, and expect. To believe in *kore* or the fear in *kore* is, in my view, the devil making fun of God since human beings are created in the image of God and have a unique status in God's creation. It is God who is our protector, and we should trust only in Him. I was very frank with my congregation about their superstitious "protection" practices of putting a tiny tangerine seed under their tongue and carrying a safety pin in their pockets at all times. I told them that it was shameful that people created in the image and likeness of God were now seeking protection from the seed of a plant or a piece of a metal.

I concluded my homily by drawing a spiritual message out of this fear in superstition. I told my congregation that God must have allowed this malicious and destructive rumor to spread with a purpose. Because during several months of very intense unrest so many people in the community came to spend their nights in the parish, pray daily, and claim that their only hope and trust was now in God alone, God wanted to find out if the claims of trust in Him were true. Indeed, He had found out in the previous weeks that they were false. Hearing these words made many in the church embarrassed, and I saw them look down. They were elders in the faith community and had been children at the time the church came here fifty years ago. They were now at the point in their lives to pass the faith on to a new generation of believers, and yet they had almost no real faith to pass on.

After this Sunday, life went back to normal. Those who wanted to come to spend their nights in the parish did, and others went wherever they wanted.

The Beatification of the Catechists

After addressing the issue of *kore* in the Mass, I was now ready to leave the parish that afternoon and begin my journey to Rome. All the pilgrims and I were expected to assemble in Gulu on Tuesday, October 15th, 2002, and then we would leave for Kampala. On Wednesday we were to fly to Rome for two weeks for the ceremonies of the beatification of two of our catechists, Jildo Irwa and Daudi Okello. These catechists were martyred in a place called Paimol in the archdiocese of Gulu because they defied the orders of some of the local leaders and continued to preach the Christian faith. The beatification ceremony we were going to in Rome was the first significant step in the formal process of the Catholic Church making them saints.

When I had lunch and was ready to begin my journey, a certain chill went through my body and made me begin to doubt if traveling that afternoon was the right thing for me to do. This was a very common occurrence in Pajule. Even if we had planned to travel, often our bodies would tell us to continue or not; if we felt nervous before beginning a journey, we would cancel it. In the end I traveled the next day.

I proceeded to Gulu through the Atanga route, which was considered the shorter way and yet more dangerous compared to Lira-Gulu route. But my instincts told me that even if this road was riskier, I would arrive safely. I rode my motorcycle for close to two hours going to Gulu from Pajule and did not meet anyone on the roads. At five different spots, I saw passenger vehicles that had been blown up. The sight of these vehicles horrified me. At times, the only recognizable part of the vehicle remaining was the steering wheel lying in the middle of the road. Most of them looked like "vehicle skeletons" since it was only the metallic body frame left standing. And the most troubling and frightful part for me was when I thought of what might have happened to those who were in the vehicle at the time of impact between the rocket and the vehicle.

I stopped at Atanga parish, which was along the way, and met with the parish priest Father Afrank, who was the only priest assigned there. I had not seen him for a long time, and he was very happy to receive me since people rarely visited him. In talking to him, I found that the security situation weighed heavily on his mind as well. First, the rectory in which he lived had no protection at all, and rebels could just walk in and do as they pleased. Second, there were many ambushes along the road very near to his rectory, and the constant presence of the rebels in the area and their attacks on passenger vehicles put him under a great deal of stress. Third, he was elderly, crippled, and unable to move fast enough to get to a place of safety in the event of a rebel assault. After I had rested and relaxed for about forty-five minutes, I continued with my journey.

As I was approaching Gulu, I reached a place called Cwero and saw some things lying by the roadside like huge logs. At first I could not comprehend what they were. I was shocked to realize that they were seven decomposing corpses. Seeing the dead bodies, I was instantly filled with fear. "Whose corpses are these?" I asked myself, then thinking immediately: "What if the rebels were still in the area?"

Traveling a mile ahead, I saw a military truck with a soldier leaning on it. This came as a great relief to me for I was certain that he was a government soldier. We did not talk, but he made gestures to me indicating that it was safe to continue. When I arrived in Gulu, I learned that the dead bodies I'd seen were LRA fighters; a violent clash had taken place at the location a few days ago.

On Tuesday, we traveled to Kampala on a bus and flew to Rome on Ethiopian Airlines the following day. The morning of our flight was truly exciting for many of us, since most of the pilgrims were making their first trip on a big plane and their first journey out of the continent of Africa. In fact, we took many pictures with the plane as a background.

While in Rome, the climax of the beatification was the Mass led by Pope John Paul II. At this time he was ill and weak, and many times he had to be supported while he stood and walked, but what surprised me most was the power in his voice as he led the congregation in worship. It was as if whenever he began to pray, some power and strength entered him. The most moving moment was the unveiling of the portrait of the two blessed martyrs on the wall of Saint Peter's Basilica. It was a great feeling seeing our own people given official recognition by the Catholic Church

The two weeks in Rome were a prayerful time for me. The atmosphere alone was very conducive. I had no worries about my safety. And yet, I did not stop thinking about the safety of the people I had left behind in Pajule. I continued to pray for God to protect them and us, the two priests in the parish, as we worked among them.

I felt that this pilgrimage gave me an opportune moment to offer my petitions to God, since there were so many saints who had lived and died in the city of Rome, including Saint Peter himself, who had also worked in environments in which their physical safety and security were always at risk. It was a very powerful feeling for me to pray in Rome while at the same time looking at the remains of Saint Peter in the Basilica. It was as if, seeing his remains before me, I talked directly to him and to those in heaven.

Of the different Christian sites of historical significance that I visited, the one that moved me most was the "three fonts," that is, the place where Saint Paul was beheaded. I had the chance to see the prison in which he was held in chains before meeting his death, and today this jail is inside an old church. With the rest of the pilgrims, we participated in a common practice at the shrine whereby visitors walk on foot as they trace the final journey that Saint Paul made from his jail cell to the site where he was finally beheaded and a church has been built. This journey of about four hundred meters was very moving to me, and it changed and enriched my relationship with Saint Paul, since it made his writings living words to me. All in all, the two weeks in Rome were also a time for me to once again have a sound sleep and to recharge my faith and spiritual energies.

Chapter Fifteen

The End of 2002 and the Beginning of 2003

As we entered into the final months of 2002, I was happy that the year was coming to an end. We had gone through so much violence that I was ready to put it behind me. And yet, I did not have anything on which to base my hope that 2003 would be more tranquil and less turbulent. It was just a simple desire in me that since we would be beginning a new year that something would be different.

My pastor was planning to stay in Pajule for a full month without any break, so I arranged to go to Gulu to rest for about three weeks because I was having difficulty falling asleep due to the constant sound of gunfire. I went to Gulu on November 25 and returned on December 18 to begin preparing for our Christmas celebrations.

On the day I returned, there were plenty of people waiting to welcome me. They were happy to have me back, but many complained that I had been away for too long. Their complaint was understandable because life in Pajule was always hard; it was the physical presence of one another and the spirit of community that sustained us.

I was glad to be back and found most of my parishioners to be safe and sound. But I had a feeling within myself that this was not the really the case, and it seemed that it was just a matter of time before something terrible happened to the community. For the three weeks I was away, all had been quiet and there had been no reports of any rebel attacks. And yet what puzzled me most was why I could not grasp or trace the source of my anxiety. At that time, we still had a large contingent of social workers at Pajule Reception Center and close to sixty returnees, even though some had been released to rejoin their families.

On the morning of December 24, 2002, I drove to Kitgum, for we had not heard of any rebel troop movements or incidents in the area. I wanted to do some Christmas shopping and visit my parents since I had not seen them for several months. I had to be back at the parish by three p.m. since the Christmas Vigil Mass would start at four thirty and needed to be ended by six p.m. I wanted to make sure that those who came to Mass returned home before it was dark.

While we were at Mass, some child-mothers still at the reception center saw a suspicious-looking young man about twenty years old coming from the southwestern side of the parish where a high school called Pajule College was located. At this time the school was closed and there was nobody in it. He appeared to be surveying the surrounding areas and bushes around the parish to see if the military guarded it. I believe the returnees were right to suspect that he might have been a spy because for almost eight months the rebels had been trying to attack and overrun Pajule at night. On all previous occasions they had failed to significantly penetrate the military's ring of defense around it.

When he arrived at the reception center, the child-mothers recognized him as a rebel soldier and not a returnee. This made him uneasy and fearful. He spent a very short time with them and excused himself, saying that he had something urgent to do in town. As soon as he left, these child-mothers immediately sent information to the military barracks saying that they had seen someone whom they suspected to be a rebel spy. They gave the army a physical description and some other identifiers, but the soldiers were unable to find him. It appears that as soon as he left the parish, he disappeared among the thousands of mud huts in the camps and soon went back into the bush.

After I concluded Mass, one of the social workers, Mr. Lakwo, the acting manager of the reception center, invited me to have dinner with him at his apartment within the parish. It was at this time that one of the returnees informed us that someone suspicious had been seen in the parish. In his frustration, I remember Mr. Lakwo saying: "Father, I wonder what is wrong with Pajule. It looks like we shall never have peace in this place, and I wish these rebels would for once allow us to celebrate Christmas with some peace of mind." I did not comment on what he said, but the news that a possible rebel spy had been sighted made my heart sink since it only served to confirm the fears I had felt within me since my return from Gulu. After dinner I went back to the rectory and, fortunately, the night passed without any incident. The following day we had a big celebration. Hundreds came for Mass. The congregation was larger than usual since we were joined by those who prayed and worshiped only once or twice a year. In Pajule, the festive spirit of Christmas extended till the first day of the New Year.

Following our usual practice, on the first of January 2003, we had one Mass. Hundreds of people again came to the celebration. The purpose of the Mass was to ask God to protect and bless us in the New Year. This Mass was extremely important to the residents of Pajule for obvious reasons. And since it was also the World Day for Peace, it was an opportune moment to pray for it.

My homily was centered on the first reading of the day, Numbers 6:22–27, in which Moses instructs Aaron and his sons on how to bless the people of Israel while on their way to the Promised Land: "The Lord bless and keep you, let his face shine upon you and be gracious to you." In my homily, I talked about God as the source of peace. I also urged the congregation to surrender to God all the fears and the uncertainties that would be a part of our lives in the New Year. And I stated that for some of us in the congregation, 2003 might well be the worst year of our lives, so we ought to pray that when we are faced with tough times we will have the faith to meet them. These words would turn out to be profoundly prophetic.

Around midday we received reports that LRA rebels fired at or attacked several vehicles on major routes in Pader District. When I heard this I felt cold, bewildered, and desperate. It was like what little hope that 2003 might be a better year was suddenly taken away from me. I started to ask myself, "What will happen in the remaining twelve months of the new year when the very first day alone is so bad?" It was as if the rebels wanted to make a military and political statement, reminding us of their presence and promising that the New Year would not be in any way different from the previous one. That day, vehicles leaving Pajule for Kitgum were fired at in Porogali, but luckily no one was injured; and when they returned they were provided with armed escorts.

On January 3, 2003, at around nine forty-five p.m., when the pastor and I were watching a movie, we heard a single gunshot and instantly fell flat on the floor. Then, we realized that the lights were on, so one of us turned off the light in the sitting room and the other disconnected the power cable to the television. At first we thought that the gunshot was behind the church less than fifty meters from us, but we soon realized that it was from the direction of Pajule College, which was about three hundred meters away. Soon an intense exchange of gunfire between government soldiers and the attackers began. We got up in the dark, leaning on the walls, and headed for our rooms. Even though we knocked onto chairs, tables, and doors we managed to find our way to our bedrooms, locked the doors, and lay on the floor. The night was very tense because this was the first time that the rebels had launched an attack from the side of the high school. The exchange of gunfire went on till four a.m.

Fortunately, they failed to break through the army defense lines. If they had, they would have marched into the parish, since the high school did not have anything of value except for a few chairs and tables that would be of no use to the rebels. The rebels lost one of their own, a captain suspected to have been their commander. When we got out of the house in the morning, we found hundreds of people assembled in the parish compound since they thought that the rectory and the parish had been attacked. It was common in Pajule that whenever there was an attack the previous night, the town residents would come to see what had taken place and offer their moral support and solidarity. I could see shock and concern on their faces, but they were greatly relieved to learn that we were all safe. This attack made the people begin to question the notion that the parish was safe, because till now there was the presumption that LRA rebels would respect Pajule parish since it was hosting their former wives and children.

After morning Mass at seven a.m. and breakfast, I sat down with my pastor to discuss the events of the previous night and the security situation. We were both certain that the rebels had intended to attack and loot the parish. I was of the view that the military detach that had been located behind the parish church ought to be reestablished. Troops had been stationed at the parish before because on several occasions rebels had attacked and looted it. However, my pastor was concerned about the implications of such a move on our neutrality in the conflict and the possibility that the parish might become a battleground.

In our discussion, we came to the conclusion that we did not have any good choice. Both of us were of the view that it was the responsibility of the government to protect us and that we could not hope and trust that the rebels would respect the parish since in the past they had committed atrocities in it. And if anything were to happen that we could have prevented by seeking military protection, we would look foolish and feel guilty.

Finding myself constantly in situations in which I had to act fast and be a part of decisions that could save lives or put my life and that of others in danger sometimes made me ask myself if the many years of training to be a priest had prepared me for it. I had always thought of my work as doing parish administration, dispensing the sacraments, planning the schedule for parish activities, celebrating the Mass, delivering homilies, and explaining church teachings. Even though I was well aware that as a priest of Gulu archdiocese, I would have to deal with the insecurity of the LRA war in one way or another, it never dawned on me that I would be at the epicenter of the conflict and that I would be holding not only pastoral meetings but security ones as well.

Another challenge for me was accepting the decisions made by my pastor. As the pastor, he had the final say on most aspects of life in the parish. When his decisions were about priestly ministry and parish administration, it was easy for me to go along with him. But when it involved the safety of the community and of us, I personally needed to be convinced that he was doing the right thing and his judgment was correct. Many times, I asked myself: "What would I do if I were certain that his action or inaction would put his own life, mine, and those of the community in danger?" Because of this, when it came to security issues the decisions that we made were arrived at through consensus, because each of us needed to own it since we were placing our very lives on the line.

After we both agreed that we needed a military detach set up in the parish, my pastor then went to consult other community leaders before we formally requested the army to be deployed in the parish. All the community leaders supported the idea, and I then went on his behalf to meet the military commander in the barracks. But I was told that he was away. I doubted this, since the soldiers at the entrance to the barracks had informed me that he was in. Knowing the psychology of the military, when there is plenty of insecurity, commanders are reluctant to make commitments or provide security guarantees to anyone for fear that if something goes wrong, they will be held accountable. I believe that he had instructed those at the lower ranks to tell me that he was not around. Instead, I met the army intelligence officer.

He assured me that every evening about 150 soldiers would be deployed around the parish and its surrounding area. I was skeptical of this assurance, too, for even if I did not express it to him, I knew that the total number of the soldiers in the whole town was under three hundred men. If they were to place such a large number to cover the parish area alone, it would not be possible for them to protect the entire town.

When I look back, it was as if a divine voice were speaking through us, the two priests, to the military, telling them to place a detach in the parish. If they had done so when Pajule was attacked on a massive scale by the LRA three weeks later, they would have been able to fight them on two fronts. But since they did not, they were left with only the troops in the barracks.

Chapter Sixteen

The Attack on Pajule

For a couple of days I had not felt well. Whenever I woke up in the morning, I would go to lead Mass at seven a.m., and after the Mass, my usual routine was to have breakfast and report to my office. But these days I felt sick instead and went back to bed unless someone specifically wanted to see me. I did not feel like eating, so I asked the parish cook to prepare only one meal a day, and at suppertime I took a cup of warm milk. After my evening prayers, I listened to the local FM radio station called "Radio Mega," which often played the latest music by the local artists and musicians and had several messages on peace and reconciliation.

On January 22, 2003, a visitor arrived at the parish who was a priest with a prominent role in the local Justice and Peace Commission (JPC) in the Archdiocese. He wanted to make contact with the LRA rebels to assist in resuming their dialogue with the government of Uganda. The pastor was away for a retreat in Gulu. I was also invited as well, but I declined since the idea of traveling on the roads made me feel jittery.

When he arrived at the parish, he told me that all the top rebel commanders of the LRA were not in Gulu District anymore but had moved into Pader District. This news came as a complete shock to me because we had not heard of any rebel infiltration and my fear was that whenever rebel movements could not be traced, they would often be nearby planning a surprise attack on the town. We spent the evening with the priest, though the shadow of uncertainty hung over it. I remember that as we sat outside behind the rectory he told me stories about his previous visits to Pajule in earlier times of insecurity when after dinner they would lock all the doors and stay in the house till the following morning.

At seven a.m., we said Mass together and he left to meet the government and civil leaders at Pader District headquarters and planned to return in the evening. At around ten thirty a.m., an elderly lady called Mego Jenne, who was the head of the parish pastoral council and had been a member of the parish for close to forty-five years, came to see me. I told her that I had a funny feeling like the LRA rebels might abduct me one of these days and force me to walk with them. Abduction and walking long distances were common at the time. She told me, "Please, Father, do not entertain such thoughts. To be abducted is a bad experience. God will protect his priests."

Around lunchtime, one of the peace contact persons in the area, Mr. Domenico, informed us that indeed the rebel commanders were all around: Vincent Otti, Charles Tabuley, and Nyeko Tolbert Yardin. He had met them and hand delivered the letter of the Acholi Religious Leaders Peace Initiative to them. After he left us, I spent some time with one of the social workers from CARITAS discussing the implications of the rebel presence in our vicinity. Both of us were suspicious about the intentions of the rebels. Anxious thoughts that something bad might happen before the end of the day kept going through our minds.

That day, I reluctantly had lunch. After lunch I had a siesta. I could neither relax nor sleep and kept turning over and over in my bed. Later I got out of bed and went to be together with the social workers at the reception center. While I was with them, I kept on complaining that I was bored and restless. I spent two hours with them. Then, I joined some of the returnees in playing volleyball. I used to be a good volleyball player in my seminary days, but I had not played it for almost two years since I had become a priest.

For the game, I was joined by a young army officer, Jimmy, who happened to have studied at Sir Tito Winyi High School in Hoima District, together with my sister, Palma, and we had developed a good relationship since he liked intellectual discussions. He was the army public relations officer in the area, and even if his role was to follow the official line and sometimes put the military spin on things, he always came across as credible and pro-people.

After we had played for an hour, we were joined by another soldier, who came in a vehicle. He was of medium height and a very brown man; it was very easy to tell that he was not a native of the area. This soldier had worked in the war zone for a long time, and unlike most of the government soldiers he spoke our local Acoli language quite fluently. As it approached six p.m., this soldier asked Jimmy to make the last serve in the game, and suddenly they concluded and left. I also opted to wind up and go to the rectory.

As I was taking a shower, I had my piano play some of the recorded music in it. In less than five minutes, I heard the cook panting and knocking on the door of my room, mumbling and gesturing that there were gunshots being fired at a very short range from the parish. My cook had been deaf and dumb since birth. He communicated to me through gestures since he could not pronounce any single word distinctly. To understand, he read my lips and the facial expressions and the gestures I made.

Fortunately, the visiting priest had returned by now. He ran from his room and stood in front of my door. As we were still making sense of what was happening, we heard a loud bang on one of the gates and a sound indicating that it was being opened. The visiting priest asked me if I had heard the noise and I said yes.

Then I ran to make sure that all the doors had been locked and reinforced them with heavy metals. After this the cook again wanted to run out of the house. He wanted to save his wife and children since there was gunfire coming from the direction of his house. Even though he was deaf and dumb, the bullets and bombs were so loud that he could hear them. I had to order him not to go out of the house: "Latigo, if you try to get out of the house, you will be killed." I did not want him to die in the crossfire.

Within a few minutes, I heard a whistle and knew for sure that we were in deep trouble. A whistle blast during an attack meant that the LRA rebels were advancing and acted as a signal for them to go to their different targets. I returned to my room and lay on my mattress on the floor. As we heard the crackle of gunfire coming from the direction of the town toward the parish, a young boy of about twelve years, an altar boy of mine, came to my window and began crying: "Father, Father, open the door for me to come in." This raised a big dilemma in me. I was now lying on the floor and did not want to move out of my room because the gunfire had intensified. I just wanted to tell him that I could not let him into the house, but he would not stop crying and calling for help. I felt as if the moment to do something had passed and it was safer for one to lie quietly where one was for fear that if I got up to let him in I could be hit by a bullet. At this moment I said to myself, *If I as an adult and a priest cannot take care of this little boy, then who will?* This gave me the courage to crawl on my belly to open the door for him, and we both came into my bedroom and got on the floor.

Rebels Arrive at the Parish

Less than three minutes after I had let the altar boy in, I saw through the window of my bedroom a girl and then some boys who were mostly barefooted who had been playing on the parish soccer field run into the compound of the rectory, go around the house, and jump over the wall. When I observed more people running into the parish compound and climbing and jumping over the parish wall for safety, I knew we were heading for the worst this evening. The rectory had a wall fence that was about three feet tall and four hundred meters wide all round, and at the bottom of the wall were thorny shrubs.

What was happening was that the rebels had divided themselves into three major groups. One group was exchanging fire with the government soldiers in the barracks on the eastern side of the town. There was a second group at the center of the town and camp, and a third group was to attack the parish. When the attack started in the evening, most of the people were taken by surprise. Many were in the market buying or selling goods. Some of the youth were playing games. Within minutes of the attack, people began fleeing in different directions. In fact, the rebels came face to face with people who were just running aimlessly to save their dear lives. A rebel commander was heard shouting instructing his fighters not to shoot directly at people but to fire bullets above their heads.

When the rebels began firing in town, most people fled on foot in the direction of the parish but they turned before they reached their destination since it was equally unsafe; in fact, some of the people who had tried to run and take refuge at the parish said that they found it "hotter" or more dangerous than the town because the parish had its own assigned group of rebels in addition to others who were firing heavy support weapons at the military barracks near it.

Further, the many buildings in the parish echoed the gunshots and shells that were being fired and produced very scary noises and harsh dissonant sounds. Many people who could not reach the parish took refuge in the parish cemetery. Most of them literally spent the night among the dead with the gravestones as their camouflage. This showed how desperate the people were because many people in Pajule, like the rest of Acoliland, believe that the cemetery contains the spirits of the dead and some of them are evil ones that cause harm to human beings. Under normal circumstances most people would never consider taking refuge in a cemetery.

The rebels were indiscriminately shooting at the people running into the parish compound. Fortunately, no one was killed or injured by the bullets since there were so many buildings to hide behind. The operator of the parish corn grinding mill very narrowly avoided being hit by a rebel bullet when he ran into a pit latrine but was only in it for a few seconds before he got out and climbed the wall fence to run away. A rebel soldier who saw him enter the pit latrine immediately fired at him. The bullets missed him by a hairbreadth, leaving a large hole in the wall.

After lying on the floor for only a few minutes, I heard a loud bang on the back door leading to the dining room of the rectory. Most of the doors in the parish and windows were made out of steel because of the security situation, but if the rebels could not break through them, they would break through the actual walls of the house, which were weak and had been erected at a time when there were no security concerns. Then, I heard a deep voice, cruel and fierce, like that of a wild animal: "Father, Father, Father, open the door. If you do not open the door, we shall kill you this evening." This was said about five times. As they were ordering me to open the door for them, they were also jumping and kicking on it very harshly. At this moment, the visiting priest and the young boy who were lying on the hard cement floor hid under my bed.

I knew at once that it was useless to hope that the rebels would not get in, since they had taken control of the place. I was afraid that they could begin to fire into the house. The longer I hesitated the more infuriated they would become and the more likely they were to commit havoc in the parish. It was time to act.

I called to the visiting priest, who had been a priest for sixteen years and had personally met the rebels on many occasions. After all, his primary reason for coming to Pajule parish was to re-establish contact with them. But when I bent down under the bed, he appeared cold and pale. He was in a terrible state of shock. On several past occasions he had been betrayed by the military authorities who allowed him to meet with the LRA and then sent soldiers to attack the rendezvous site. This attack apparently triggered memories of those past occasions.

I got up and shouted loudly from the hallway, "Do not knock down the door; I am coming to open it." In fact, many who were hiding in the parish compound heard my shouting within the house. I believe this was the moment that changed my role in the parish informally; from now on, I began to make many more decisions and to establish my own identity. I needed to warn the rebels in advance that I was coming to open the door because I was afraid that they would fire through the door and kill me instantly. When they heard my voice, which was indeed very deep and authoritative, they all stopped stomping on the metallic door. I opened it and came face to face with armed LRA rebels fresh from the bushes.

Chapter Seventeen

Encounter with Death

Seeing LRA rebels standing at the door of the dining room, all of them bare-chested with guns and fixed bayonets, I felt that I had come face to face with death and human cruelty in its worst form. Since it was getting dark, I could not distinguish their faces clearly, but I could see that they had very dark, shiny skin as if they had smeared a lot of oil on themselves. All of them appeared to be very young men in their early teens, and only one of them was near my height and most likely was about eighteen years old. The whole place smelled of smoke and gunpowder.

The rebels looked surprised to see me. They were so fearsome, and yet, I looked cool, composed, and calm. At this moment I think I made a big mistake because I kept quiet and retreated to my Catholic priest persona, allowing them to take control of the situation. Because the rebels understood the language of authority and are used to commands, I should have been more assertive and asked them questions like "What do you want? What can I do for you? Who is your commander?" This would have been risky, but it might have succeeded.

Since I stood silently before them, one of them shouted a question at me: "Who are you?" This question triggered many ideas in my mind, and I had to process very quickly the implications of any answer that I might give. In Pajule parish I was called by several titles. Many called me "Pare Matidi," which in the local language meant the young priest since I was newly ordained; I appeared very small in their eyes and I was the associate pastor as well. A few in the parish called me by my first name, Father Robert, and while at school I was called by my middle name, Nyeko. But I decided to tell them my last name, which hardly anyone used. So I told them that I was Father Obol. I could see that they looked surprised; it was a name that they could not connect to any that they had heard before. I was afraid that the priests in the parish might have been accused of being critical of them in our homilies and that when they came into contact with any of us, they would cause us bodily harm.

Then the tallest among them ordered me, "Sit down." I sat on the floor without any argument or resistance. They were afraid to have me stand because I was larger and appeared stronger than most of them. They might have also been concerned that I would knock one of them down, fight, or even grab a gun. I sat on the floor at the entrance of the door to the dining room, and within a second I was surrounded by eight rebels. They all had guns with knives fixed at the top, pointing at my head, holding the triggers like they were about to fire. Suddenly I could not believe the position I was in. The sight was like a crown of bayonets, and making the situation worse was that two days ago, I had gotten a haircut and shaved my head completely bald.

One of the rebels asked me in a very cruel and rude voice if we had a radio-call. I admitted that we did have one since I did not want to risk my life for a piece of property. Another one shouted at me, "Get up and take us to the radio-call." While trembling, I got up to lead them to our rectory sitting room. The radio-call was the only means of contact between our headquarters and other parishes of the archdiocese of Gulu. The rebels always targeted the radio-call since they could alter the frequencies to their own in order to communicate with other rebel units and in particular with their bases in South Sudan.

Indeed, I was lucky that the radio-call was in the parish at the time. If it had been broken and I had taken it in for repair, they would not have believed me and would have tortured me to produce it. As I led the rebels to the sitting room, I could not believe how the environment in the parish had changed. There were gunshots being fired all over the place. Even though I grew up in an environment with so much insecurity, it had never happened before in all my life that I intentionally got up to walk in the midst of so much gunfire that I could have been hit by a flying bullet. I was physically shaking so much that I could not walk straight. I knocked myself against the dining table and later again against another chair, and in the process one of rebels tried to kick me down but missed my legs.

When we reached the room where the radio-call was, the rebels immediately ordered me to sit down again. They were very afraid that I could fight back, and so they did not want to take any chances. In fact, it was a real fear on the part of the rebels since many people in northern Uganda have had the chance to work in the armed forces and have had military training.

In the sitting room, the rebels asked me for the location of the radio-call. I showed them where it was, and they immediately grabbed it and started disconnecting it from its antenna. As I sat down on the floor, I watched how my things and those of the parish were being looted; but above all, I marveled at the speed with which the house was being emptied of any property. There were rebels instructing some of the women prisoners what they were and were not to loot. Others were commanding those in the lower ranks to make sure that they had checked under each and every bed and made sure there was no one hiding underneath. This was something revealing for me because it showed to me that the LRA understood the psychology of most of the people in the society. From this moment I promised myself that I would never go under the bed whatever the circumstance. While I could not see any of their faces in the darkness, I kept hearing stern orders and warnings. The rebels could see much better in the room since they were the ones with torches.

Even though they were in control, I could feel that they were under much pressure and wanted to conclude their mission as soon as possible. They were taking anything they could find so long as it was portable, including things that I believed they did not need, like my motorcycle headgear. I knew quite well that they did not have motorcycles or ride them in the jungles. All the tablecloths and curtains in the house were being pulled down, torn to pieces, and converted into bags. In fact, the rebels in the house looked more like very experienced thieves than people who had differences with the government of Uganda. Within five minutes the sitting room was empty.

In the parish, we did have a very big and heavy video screen that we would often lend to the reception center for recreational activities for the returnees. I saw one of the rebels try to pick up the screen from the house, but it was too heavy for him. However, he succeeded with the help of another rebel.

Then the rebel soldiers remaining with me in the sitting room ordered me to take them to the location of the parish food store. At the time we had very little in our own store. But CARITAS had plenty of food supplies at the reception center. I did not intend to lead the rebels to them. Once again they instructed me to get up and lead them to the rectory food store, and I agreed since I knew that they would not find much there.

But as I got up, I heard a huge blast in front of the church. One of the rebels had fired a portable mortar from the direction of Pajule parish at the military barracks. The sound alone was nerve-racking, and the vibrations made everything shake. I physically trembled in the midst of the rebels and almost fell down. One of rebels, seeing me quivering, shouted at me, "Father, we do not tolerate cowards; we kill them." I kept quiet.

During the time I was with the rebels, they appeared not to be bothered by the sounds of gunfire and huge blasts. In fact, it seemed like a normal working day for them. Their only interest was in knowing the direction from which the bullets were coming. They seemed to be able to distinguish between the sounds of the gunshots being fired by them and by the government soldiers.

Then, another rebel came into the room and was assigned to make sure that I did not escape. He was about sixteen years old. I introduced myself to him and tried to make him a friend. I have always had the belief that I make a natural connection much more easily with men, however cruel they may be, than women, so I was willing to take my chance here. In the brief talk we had, I discovered that unlike the rest of the rebels he seemed kind and respectful. Seeing how tense and frightened I was, this rebel soldier assured me that they would not harm me. But he wanted me to be taken to meet their commander, Charles Tabuley, and the idea of going to meet the LRA commander really frightened me. Later, he asked me to lead him to the priests' food store, which I did. There was not much in the room to take. There were things like beans, engine oil, and one crate of beer. He only had an interest in the engine oil, since the rebels needed it for oiling their guns.

Then we went outside the house to the back of the rectory. By this time there were no more gunshots and the place had calmed down. I had calmed down as well. The rebels were now fully in control of the parish, camp, and town, and they had surrounded the government troops in Pajule military barracks. It was a sight that I could not believe, to find myself among them while they were looting and running all over. I thought, *So this is what the rebels look like!* They spoke the local language very fluently, if not even better than us.

Parked next to the kitchen was the car of the visiting priest, a Suzuki, and the model was a Samurai. The rebels begin to vandalize it; one of them broke the front windshield with the butt of his gun. Another rebel brought dry grass. Some of them began opening the fuel tank that was very tightly sealed, and others rushed to provide a box of matches to set it ablaze. When I saw this, even though I was their prisoner, something happened to me that I believe was a divine voice. I shouted at them with force and authority in my voice like I was back in control of the place. The sudden courage that I had was surprising.

"Do not burn my vehicle; you know that I am the priest here. My duty is to help people; how will I help people if I do not have a car?" To my surprise, one of the rebels told the rest to leave the vehicle alone. I wanted to take advantage of this, so I asked who their leader was, but none of them was willing to reply or talk to me. I could sense that there were several groups in the parish, each with a specific task to perform. I had hoped that by negotiating with their leader I could minimize the damage they were doing to the place.

As I stood at the veranda of the rectory, which was two steps high off the ground, a rebel soldier who was about the age of eleven flashed his torch onto my face. The time was now about six forty-five p.m. He had a stick in his hand and raised his gun and pointed it at my chest. Suddenly, I could not believe what I was seeing; it was like a scene from a movie. He had his finger on the trigger and was ready to fire at any second. He challenged me to say anything provocative to him, and then he would shoot. My reaction at seeing this was disbelief, like it was a scene from a hunting exercise except that this time the target was me. I also felt pity for this young boy; he was a victim of his circumstance. If he had not been abducted by the rebels, he would not be threatening to kill me. In the eyes of the young boy, I could see so much hate, rage, and contempt for me; and yet I could not tell its source. Since I knew the psychology of the child-soldiers, I remained silent and did not attempt to talk to him. I did not want to give him any excuse for shooting me. When he saw me quiet, he lowered his gun and told me that I had survived. He went into the house and looted some bars of soap from my bedroom. When he returned he said, "You are lucky; I wanted to make you lie down on the ground to cane you, but I am pleased that I got some good things from your room."

If I had not been silent, he would have killed me just to make a name for himself and help build a notorious reputation as the one who had killed the Catholic priest. This was one of the reasons why some children who were forcefully abducted stayed and became rebel soldiers themselves, because they felt that being in the rebel army gave to them privileges and power over adults; they could humiliate, torture, and kill them. They would never have this kind of power and control if they lived in society like any one of us. However horrible their actions were, it made these young rebel soldiers feel powerful.

I also noticed that this young boy also hated my physical appearance. He castigated me for being physically big. The rebels had always associated being overweight with a level of comfort in life. I believe this is an important distinction that has to be made. In Western society, being overweight is seen as a disease since it is an indication of poor self-care and there are many diseases connected to obesity; but in many sections of African society being overweight is a measure of comfort. In fact, people who have put on weight often times are envied. Since the conditions of living were very hard for most of the rebels in the jungles, many of them hoped that when they were in control of Uganda, they would also put on some weight. Further, the rebels looked at someone who is fat as a government agent or a person benefiting from the status quo. This was a source of resentment to them since they believed that they were suffering in the bushes. I noticed that continuing to stand in their midst drew a negative reaction from them, since they took it to be a hostile posture, and I sat down like a real prisoner.

I could also see how childlike and childish they were in their behaviors. Some would come out of the house with a lot of excitement about things they had plundered whose name or use was unknown to them. They would tell their colleagues that they had gotten something very precious, and when they could not identify it, they would run to me to assist them. It was like thieves asking the owner of the property to identify their loot and its value before they went away with it.

Then, a rebel soldier brought some luggage from the house and placed it at my feet. He intended for me to carry it when we began to leave for the jungle as abductees. But I declined to move my hands to pick it up. Within myself, I felt that if they were to abduct me, they would take me like one of their officers; that is, I would not carry any of the loot. This step made me know that the rebels were serious about their motive to take me along with them to the jungles.

Chapter Eighteen

My Narrow Escape from the Rebels

As I sat down surrounded, the rebels received the good news that plenty of food had been found on one end of the building. In fact, there were close to two hundred bags of corn that had been supplied by the organization of the World Food Program to feed the returnees in the parish. They all ran to that side of the building, and for the moment, they left me alone.

I immediately began to think of what to do. I did not want to be abducted and go with them into the jungles. The LRA walked on foot with their captives for hundreds of miles in a single day, and I knew that I would be unable to do so. I was also barefooted, since I had left my room abruptly without having had any time to put on my shoes. And even if I had, my regular shoes were not appropriate for walking in the bush; they would have caused terrible blisters on my feet.

In the month of January, as was the case in Pajule and Acoliland as a whole, people set all the dry grass on fire to clear the fields for the coming planting season. Sharp shoots were left that could pierce bare feet. Such injuries were very common on the feet of the returnees at the reception center.

Because of this, I took the risk to go back inside the house. The rebels were still looting the rectory while flashing their torches. I passed near some of them, since it was now totally dark. They could not recognize that I was not one of them, and in fact some of them mistook me to be among them. While in the rectory, I immediately made up my mind to enter the pastor's office. This was the one room that the rebels had not broken into since it had a strong door. I took its key, which hung above the door. This key was an interesting one. It was half its normal size, for it had broken several years back, but it still worked and so there was no need to have it replaced. But opening this door was a problem. Because it was dark and I was also panicking, I failed to place the key in its hole to open the door. What I did then was place the key in my pocket and return outside. I believe that this failure was in God's plan for me.

I could see that the rebels were very absorbed in looting the place and did not care about their surroundings at all. Surprisingly, some idea came to my mind that I had to leave. Otherwise, I would be abducted. In fact, the fate of some of our seminarians who were home for the holidays and had been abducted a couple of months ago at a place called Adilang came to mind very vividly. This made me act.

If I were to escape, there was only one direction that I could take—sideways from their midst, eastwards to the main gate of the rectory while leaning against the wall. When I reached the gate, it was unlocked since the rebels had broken it open. However, I could not go through it since beyond the gate the parish elementary school had its security lights on, illuminating the surroundings. The time was now about seven thirty p.m.

The parish church, which was in the same direction as the elementary school, appeared to be the only place that the rebels were not breaking into, but I could not go to enter it since its security lights were on. Even if I had wanted to take my chances, I did not have its key with me at the time, so it would have been impossible for me to get inside.

Since I could not pass through the gate, I made up my mind to go north. I ran from one building to another for a distance of about five meters and hid behind the wall of the CARITAS store, listening to see if anyone was trailing me. As I stopped, I heard one of the rebels shout, "If you run, I will shoot you." I immediately held my breath. I had to take this threat seriously. If an LRA prisoner of war tried to run away and was caught, he or she was to be executed on the spot. I was not certain if the LRA rebel soldier was warning someone else or me. After about five minutes, I realized that the threat was not against me.

During this time I again thought of what to do. I made up my mind to escape from the parish. I needed to go through the pigsty and then climb over the rectory wall. My instincts told me that there was no LRA soldier present, so I ran for about fifteen meters. I was lucky that my instincts were right because if I had made a miscalculation and there was a single armed LRA rebel lying on the grass, he could have shot me. I jumped into the pigsty. The pigs ran around making a lot of noise and squealing loudly. I wished this evening they could have observed some silence. I stopped and was quiet for a moment, listening. When the rebels heard the pigs run and squeal, I heard one of them say, "It is the stupid animals making noise; there is no trouble." Throughout this conflict, the animals that the LRA rebels resented and despised most were the pigs, although the origins of their negative image of pigs was difficult to explain.

When I realized that there was no one following me, I quietly crept through the pigsty to climb the wall. But the pigsty had a four-meter-high wall around it with barbed wire on top. There were also broken bottles cemented on top of the wall to prevent anyone from trying to climb over the fence. The height of the wall was slightly above my shoulder. I supported myself by holding onto the roof of the reception center, which was the building attached to the pigsty, and lifted my body up. As I held onto the roof of the reception center, I got another surprise. I received an electric shock that made me jump down and almost fall. What I had touched was an iron sheet that had contact with a live electric wire. This made me abandon the idea of supporting myself against the rooftop.

One thing I remember at this particular moment is that I was like a moving body without a spirit inside me. I felt like my soul had left me and I had been shaken to the core of my being. My breathing had changed; the sound was like someone else and not me. It was loud, warm, and stale. I felt like there was a red-hot flame in my chest. I felt like I never had before; I smelled death in the air. I was convinced that I was in the early stages of death and thought many people who died in the war passed through this same phase. I held on to the barbed wire with my bare hands and the tiny pillars on top of the wall. I lifted myself up with them and gently placed my bare feet on the broken bottles and jumped over the wall of the pigsty and the parish. My height was a great asset to me since I am six-foot-three. The surface of the ground on which I had set foot was hard and rough, and since it was now dark, I could not tell what I might have stepped on. I immediately touched my feet to see if I was bleeding; fortunately, I was not. I did not even have a scratch on my hands or my feet from the barbed wires, sharp edges of the broken bottles, or the rough surface.

When I was on the ground, the next problem that I had was where to go. I was out of the parish walls, but there was nowhere I felt safe to go. The rebels were almost everywhere. The place that came immediately to my mind was to run northward to my garden of sweet potatoes. There, I hoped that I could hide under the leaves. However, from that same direction I could hear the voices of many rebels shouting and calling out to the catechists and their families to open the doors for them and let them in. East was the direction in which the camp for the internally displaced persons was situated; what was happening there was more frightening than anywhere else; it was like hell had broken loose. I could again hear gunshots and gunfire in the camp and endless screams and pleas from the camp dwellers for their lives to be spared. I could hear the rebels trying to break open doors and using axes to smash some down. The southern side of the rectory was where the residence of the nuns was located. Fortunately, all the nuns were away for vacation, but some people regularly spent their nights at the convent. On the western side of the rectory were the residences of the other catechists. I could hear rebels forcing their doors open as well. So, there was no safe place for me to take refuge, and yet I had to move for if the rebels were to find me they probably would not leave me alive.

I ran for about fifty meters toward the camp, hoping that I could lie down and hide behind the wall of the nursery school, for it had some grass around it. As I was running, I was breathing very abnormally, and I felt like my lungs were bursting. It was a real long time since I had done any serious physical exercise. Then, I heard the steady voices of several men instructing me not to run, so I stopped. These were not rebels, but four men of the parish. They immediately recognized me and requested that I lie down. They were afraid that if I continued to run, I could be killed in a crossfire if the rebels and the government soldiers began exchanging fire. So I lay down next to them and these men for the moment forgot about themselves and came closer to comfort and support me. I was breathing very heavily, and I believe that any passerby could have heard me from a distance. Looking at them, I recognized two of the four men. I had hired them to build and renovate part of the wall around the pigsty that had fallen down several years ago. These men were builders in Pajule who would go to the area bars in the evenings and take some local brew. They were not regular churchgoers. They came to church only if a relative or someone important in the area died.

One of these men taught me some things about faith that I will never forget. First, that the Christian faith is a communal experience. That is, in a faith community, we feed and survive on the faith of one another. There are moments when the community relies on the priest to strengthen its faith, and there are also times when the priest needs the witness of faith in the community to keep his own faith alive.

Second, a priest will never be able to tell the impact of his work upon the people that he serves. This is what he whispered in my ears, words that I will continue to remember as long as I live: "Please, Father, be calm and do not be afraid, God will take care of us tonight; we have not committed any crime. And if anything bad is to happen tonight to any of us, it means that God has allowed it to happen." I could not believe what I heard. His words were filled with so much faith, and yet I did not want to entertain the idea that something might go wrong this evening. For over one year I had been preaching to the community to have faith and trust in God's protection, and today was my turn to get the same message through him.

Within a few minutes, we started to see the rebels lead captives from the camp in a single straight line. Most of them were men and young boys who were carrying their loot, and some captives that were walking too slowly were being beaten. There were a lot of screams and cries in the air. They came close to where we were but passed us by. This was a difficult moment for me. I knew most of the people being abducted and tortured. I felt so much pain for them, but at the same time, there were too many conflicting and confusing feelings inside me: sympathy, fear, horror, terror, pity, concern. It felt like I had lost any sense of balance and the primary instinct directing me was now my personal survival.

As I lay there, I started asking myself disturbing questions. *Why do I have to go through such a terrible experience?* I was also very frustrated with God and I asked Him, "Why do you make us very helpless and place us at the mercy of such violence and evil?" The armed rebels who were now in control of the place could kill any of us if they wished. At the same time one of the messages I'd preached months ago on the Feast of the Baptism of Our Lord came to mind. In the readings, it talks about the reason why Christ desired to be baptized: to share with humanity the joys and the pains of life. Within myself, I began to think that maybe this was also a moment for me to share in Christ's pain and that of my parish community.

Within a few minutes, we saw four men. They were bare-chested coming toward us with their shirts wrapped around their waists. They were searching the grass with their torches; they almost passed us by, but they suddenly stumbled upon us. When they saw us, they asked us a question that was very sarcastic: "What do you think that you are doing? Do you think that you are hiding?" In fact, their question was appropriate. We were, in fact, behaving like ostriches. When an ostrich is in danger after running for its life for quite a long time and cannot proceed anymore, it hides its head in the sand and presumes that it is safe and the problem is gone. This was a similar situation to us; apart from burying our faces in the ground, we had very little grass that was covering us.

We did not know how to respond to this question, afraid that any clumsy answer could be used as a pretext to harm us. One of us was really smart and creative. He dodged the question and said: "When things started, we were caught up here."

The rebels started to interrogate us and demand personal items. Personally, I had nothing since I had run out of the rectory abruptly. They asked for garden boots to protect their feet from thorns, but none of us had any. Then, they asked for watches; again none of us had one. Of the five of us, the other four were simple villagers who did not put on watches; they often told the time by looking at the sun. I started to get worried because I thought that they would harm us in frustration, since they had failed to get anything of value out of us. Fortunately, one of us had his transistor radio with him. At the time of the attack, he was at the market and had bought a saucepan and had placed the saucepan on top of the radio. It was common practice among men in Pajule to walk around in the evenings with their radios in their hands listening to the local news programs. So after a short search, the rebels got the radio, and it made them feel better that they had gotten something out of us.

All along we were lying facedown as the rebels asked us questions, but now they wanted to identify each one of us. They began to flash their torches into our faces. I had not said a word since they found us. One of us twisted and turned on the ground, since he was lying on the grass uncomfortably, and a rebel soldier took this as an excuse to cut his back with a sharp object shaped like an axe. The object was small in size and had a very sharp blade, and this gentleman started to bleed. I could tell from the faces of the rebels that they did not recognize any of the four men, nor did they have any particular interest in them apart from getting what they could from them.

Then, it came my turn; I kept on looking down till they insisted that I look at them. The rebels were not willing to leave without identifying me. One of them flashed his torch into my eyes and asked me a question that almost made me have a heart attack. "Are you the priest? Are you the priest? Are you the priest?" He asked almost seven times. I knew that my moment of death had arrived.

I believe that it was easy for the rebels to sense that I was different. As a priest, I live in a society that is very poor, but my lifestyle is that of a person who is middle class. Even if I am not paid a salary for what I do, I have more opportunities and a better support system than most people. Because of this, my physical appearance, body, complexion, dress, and feet looked different from the other men. In short, my external features made me a person of interest.

I was very frightened and did not know what to say. I paused, stammered, murmured, etc. Within myself, I believed that the answer I gave held the key to my life or death. I was not certain whether these four rebels had been assigned to look for me since I had escaped the rectory. If so, my chances of surviving were not more than two percent.

I therefore refused to disclose my identity or confirm that I was a priest. The furthest I could go was to tell them that I worked in the parish. As one of the rebels was getting very insistent on knowing my identity, another intervened by asking a question. I believe in my heart that this rebel soldier wanted to help me out and cool down the tempers of the others. This rebel changed the subject from my identity and began asking if they had taken the radio-call. I confirmed to him that the radio-call was the very first thing they took when they entered the rectory. So it was somewhere with one of them. Then this rebel soldier told the others to leave with him. This was a great surprise, because even if they did not do additional harm to any of us, they could still have forced us to go along with them to carry their loot. I attribute this to divine protection.

As they left, I wondered what would have happened if any of us had tried to run away in the heat and panic of the moment. I was certain that the person would have been stabbed or shot dead.

When the rebels had gone, I was calm and felt that I was myself again. I would estimate the time as being around nine p.m. I climbed inside the wall of the nursery school, which was the next building. The four men instinctively followed. Fortunately the man who had been cut was not bleeding profusely, and by placing his hand against the spot he was able to stop most of the bleeding.

However, one of the men was sickly and began to cough very loudly when what we needed was dead silence. Because he was coughing so hard, his colleagues ran away from him, and yet he did not want to be left alone and ran after them. At this moment, we whispered to each other that we all needed to go our separate ways rather than be killed together. I ran outside the wall of the nursery school and squatted under a mango tree at the edge of the soccer field of the elementary school. From there, though it was dark, I could see the cemetery, the teachers' quarters, and the camp since all were located across the soccer field.

I was now a distance of about four hundred meters away from the rectory. While under the mango tree, I began to see the rebels flash their torches nearby, and this almost scared me to death. I was taken up by fear and panic. Fortunately, at this time, there were no gunshots being fired. So, what I did was climb the mango tree and hide between the trunks in order not to be seen. As I was in the tree, I kept on wishing and praying that no rebel soldier should come under the tree and flash his torch upward. Within a short while, I found that the trunks of the mango tree were not comfortable and it was getting cold. Later, I realized how much danger I was exposing myself to; if there had been a resumption of gunfire I could have been hit by a bullet. I feel this was one of the stupidest decisions that I made throughout the war. One of the lessons that I learned was that in situations of intense and extreme danger, one should rely on one's intellect all the time rather than emotion. A single misstep may determine whether one stays alive or gets killed.

The top of the mango tree was also a bad place for me because from it I could hear almost everything that was happening nearby. Whenever I heard something fall or break in the rectory, I could feel a sharp and pricking pain in my heart. I heard the rebels break open the door to my pastor's office; this made me almost fall off the tree. I was becoming hysterical because I had wanted to hide in the room's ceiling. It felt like they had gotten me once again. Immediately, I knew that I had to climb down from the tree and go somewhere else. I guessed that the time was now coming to midnight. Even if I wanted to go far away, there was nowhere I could go. The moon was so bright; the only place with some vegetation was the garden below the soccer field, but there was no cover to get there.

However, I took the risk to run from one end of the soccer field to the other in the moonlight. I was lucky that I did not meet any rebel and that none of them saw me before I entered the garden, which had been harvested a few months back. It was almost half the size of the soccer field and was large enough to hold hundreds of people. My biggest concern was with being bitten by a scorpion, since they liked such places. It would not be fatal, but the pain would last for at least twelve hours. I was also afraid that there could be snakes in the garden, but I was also certain that snakes rarely attacked unprovoked, and if I did not step on one, I would be fine.

I was able to enter the garden without any incident but immediately discovered that it was very smelly and uncomfortable because it was used as a latrine by most of the people. I had to negotiate my way to find a spot that was dry. Even though it was dark, I found a very small space, but I had to lie completely still or end up soiled.

Chapter Nineteen

The Bright Moon

This was the beginning of one of the longest nights I have ever spent. Even at eight hundred meters away from the rectory, I was not yet certain if I had survived death. I could still hear the rebels shouting and ordering the people in the camp to open the doors of their houses or be killed, and there was sporadic shooting along with the cries of mothers and children pleading for their lives. About fifty meters from me, there was a gunman who fired bullets continually into the air as the rebels attacked the camp. It was difficult to tell his identity, but I could only guess that he was a rebel soldier who watched the perimeters as the rest of the rebels looted the camp. I felt powerless, wondering at the number of people I would find injured or killed the following morning if I was lucky enough to survive this horrible night.

I had heard many people tell of times when they were forced to flee their house and spend the night in the bush, but this was the first time I had done it. It made me appreciate my bed. After thirty minutes of lying on the bare, hard ground, I felt restless and exhausted, and I just wanted to get up and sit. But I could not since there were still bullets flying all around. I had basically two options: to lie on my back or to lie on my stomach. But within a very short time I became restless in either position. Lying on my stomach was very uncomfortable and irritating; it felt like I was constantly being pricked by a needle on account of the rough ground, the dry grass and roots, and the remnants of the stalks of the cereal crop planted in the garden. A better position for me was on my back, but this placed my ears close to the ground and heightened my sensitivity to my surroundings; I felt that I could hear what was occurring as far away as five miles, and this was nothing but violence. I had enough fear inside me already without being able to hear more.

Further, the moonlight created another situation for me. It was so bright that the garden became very illuminated. The stalks of millet stood about five feet tall, but most of them had been trampled when the people ran through, and some had been eaten up by termites, so very few were left standing to provide any meaningful camouflage.

Intermittently, as the gunshots and explosions subsided in the night, I kept on asking myself a number of questions: *God, why are you doing this to me? Why do I have to go through such a terrible experience? Why do I have to be killed after working only for one year and a few months as a priest?* As I continued to reflect on the above questions, I heard a baby who might have been about five months old cough and begin to cry, and I realized that the mother was lying on the ground about ten feet away from me. The baby was coughing and crying because it was getting too cold, and yet, there was hardly anything that the mother could do to keep it warm. In fact, this woman had run from her house in the camp with only her baby and dear life. If the situation were a little bit better, I could have shown her some sympathy or said something to encourage her, but I did not want to frighten her or draw the attention of the gunman firing close by. I dared not speak to her.

As I continued to think about my agony, I tried to make some sense of it, since it seemed that it would be impossible for me to continue to live my life without being resentful and bitter toward the rebels and the parish for having exposed me to so much danger. Searching within myself for a spiritual message out of this ordeal, I came to the conclusion that God had allowed me to spend the night in this garden with a purpose, however horrible the experience may have been. He wanted me to share in the suffering and pain of my people so as to be able to empathize with them. From now on, when anyone told me their own stories of being attacked or abducted or spending the night in the bush, I would fully understand what they were talking about.

At around two a.m., as the rebels started to withdraw; they began to set the houses ablaze. The skies were filled with tongues of fire, and the people who were still in the camp appeared like they were inside a big bowl of fire. At that very moment, I saw hundreds of children between the ages ten to fifteen run to the garden where I was and lie down. What surprised me most was that I began hearing the rebels sing the songs that we normally heard on the FM radio stations. This was an indication that they listened to and monitored whatever took place in society through the radios they stole.

As the rebels retreated, the government soldiers who had been surrounded in the barracks began to engage them in a gunfight. I could hear each side hurling abuse and curses at the other. The government soldiers were shouting at the rebels and calling them thieves while the rebels were responding and calling them cowards, as if the two sides had so much hate for one another that gunshots were not enough to do the job unless they were accompanied by words of contempt. It was also a very tense and frightening time because if the rebels had come through the garden, most likely they would have found us.

When it was approximately six a.m., I made the sign of the cross and thanked the Lord for keeping me and everyone else who had survived safe through the night. I asked God to give me the strength and courage to face the challenges that I would now find. As I got up to go to the parish, there was a little sunlight. A small girl of about eight years old who had been lying down close by got up to follow me. When I saw her, I asked her to remain where she was until we were certain there were no more gunshots. I was confident that she was safe where she was and could return home to the camp or come to the parish later, but my concern now was for her safety.

What Happened That Night in the Parish?

As I was walking back to the parish, I was still afraid, but I had some confidence that the rebels might have left by now. The place was relatively silent, and dawn was breaking so there was enough light to see where I was going. Upon reaching the parish, I found parishioners and townspeople assembling behind the rectory where most of the destruction had occurred. I saw a lot of worry in their eyes because rumors were flying around that I had been abducted and my fate was uncertain. So when they saw me unharmed, they were so overcome with emotion and relief that they ran to me and hugged me, and many broke down in tears. This touched me very deeply. I reassured them that I was fine and began to inquire about the visiting priest that I had left behind. He suddenly appeared and found us wondering about him. I hugged him and thanked God for keeping him alive. He was safe and looked tired like all of us, as he had not slept at all. Seeing him alive was a great source of joy for me. We had parted almost twelve hours ago.

I surveyed the compound of the parish and saw destruction everywhere. Most of the doors were smashed to pieces with axes; parts of the rectory's roof had been scorched by the flames from a passenger vehicle parked adjacent to the garage set ablaze by the rebels. There were a few valuables strewn all over the compound including some souvenirs from my priestly ordination. These had fallen to the ground from the hands of the rebels as they looted the rectory in haste. The destruction in the parish and the rectory looked like it bore the footprints of the worst characters from hell.

However, at this very moment the immediate need was to attend to the psychological impact on the people in the parish, especially the social workers, who had taken refuge in the convent and were violently dragged from the house by the rebels who screamed at them as they barged into their rooms. They were visibly shaken by this experience, and I could see that they were near the point of a mental and nervous breakdown. Because of this, I immediately asked that some people attend to them. When I was still coming to terms with what had happened in the rectory, I was abruptly informed that the LRA rebels had killed two people: a woman who was in her twenties and a little boy who was about five years old. They had no blood relationship except that both of them had been released one week ago from rebel captivity.

In fact, what had happened was that three groups of rebels came to loot the parish at different times. The first group came at six p.m. and was the one that I had escaped from, the second group came at around ten p.m., and the last group came at two a.m. The last group to arrive at the parish had first looted the town, and when they came to the parish they turned on all the lights in the rectory. People hiding nearby could hear them wonder among themselves about the whereabouts of the priests. In the rooms, they began to take the mattresses off the beds to see what was under them. LRA rebels rarely stole mattresses for fear they could not keep them dry during the heavy rains. They found the visiting priest, who had been hiding under my bed lying sideways facing the wall, and ordered him to come out from underneath. By this time he had been under my bed for close to eight hours. The earlier group of rebels failed to see him, but they did find the altar boy lying next to him and took him. I feel they failed to identify the visiting priest the first time because the wall was painted white, and so when the rebels looked his way he appeared to blend into it, as he was a white man. This time when the rebels saw the priest, they ordered him to come out and stand in their midst, and began questioning him. Fortunately, he was an expatriate missionary who had worked among the people for a number of years and knew the local dialect quite well and was able to answer some of their questions. Strangely, some of the rebels were of the idea that he should be killed, and yet he had not violated any of their rules by fighting back, provoking them, or trying to run. But as they continued to interrogate the priest about his role in the archdiocese of Gulu, they recognized his name, which was familiar to them since their commanders had on previous occasions talked of meeting him on the peace delegation teams. After the rebels were satisfied that this was indeed the same person, they spared his life. Instead, they asked him to give them some money. So, he led them back to the room where he was to stay during his visit and gave them his pocket money, which was about one hundred dollars. This was the room where I kept my laptop. When the rebels looked at it, they were interested in it but they did not know what it was. Some of them wanted to take it because they thought it was a camera and wanted it to take pictures. But the priest told them it was a computer used for writing letters and needed electric power all the time. Because they rarely wrote letters and did not have electric power in the jungles, they decided not to take the computer. In the whole rectory there were only two valuables that the rebels left untouched because they considered them to be useless: the laptop and the piano in my room.

However, the most difficult part of the morning was dealing with the deaths at the reception center and the burial rituals that had to be performed. Personally, I felt overwhelmed by what I had gone through during the night, and yet I had to plan for the burial of the two and organize a service as well. I felt tired and unsure what to do or say.

The killings had occurred at six p.m. when the rebels entered the reception center. As they were breaking into the rooms, they found some of the doors were very firm and locked from the inside. So they began shouting to the occupants to open the door or they would begin to shoot. The woman who was killed had run into the inner room, but after concluding that it was useless to continue lying under her bed she got up to let them in. At that very moment one of the rebels fired a shot through the door, and it hit her in the face and killed her instantly. A girl who was fifteen years old narrowly survived death when that same bullet missed her head by inches but left a scratch on the left side of her ear. The most traumatic death was that of the five-year-old boy, a death about which we will never know the whole story. This child was found dead at the reception center. The marks on his corpse showed footprints all over the body, indicating that a rebel soldier stepped or stomped on him. The cruelty with which this child was killed was the first of its kind for me to witness and the most despicable thing that I have ever encountered. It is unimaginable to me that an adult could be so callous as to kill a defenseless child. Even today after several years have passed, many of us who were in Pajule at the time become emotional when we talk about this sad event. The exact circumstances of the death were never clear, but many recalled that at the beginning of the attack, as people were running for their lives and there was a lot of confusion, a child was heard persistently crying for its mother followed by sudden silence. This could have been the moment when the child met its death. This child was among the recent arrivals at the reception center, and most people suspected that his biological father might have had differences with the LRA rebel who killed him or that his mother had refused to be the mistress of the killer.

While assessing the damage that had been done in the parish, we learned there were not as many fatalities in town as I had feared despite the violence because the rebels minimized shooting directly at people. Two people had also died in town, a woman and her child. In the course of the exchange of gunfire, a shell landed on the roof of their house and killed both of them. I also realized that God played a big part in sparing the parish building from being totally destroyed in the attack, and my own life as well.

Between twenty and thirty vehicles were parked at the parish compound every night. On several occasions when the rebels raided the town, they would set fire to the vehicles that were parked in front of the shops and private residences. Because of this most of the town dwellers and businesspeople in Pajule left their vehicles in the parish compound every evening, as there was a wall around it. However, this was not the major reason they came. When I asked some why they continued to park at the parish when they were aware that rebels had vandalized and torched its property in the past, one of them told me: "Father, if my vehicle is set ablaze, it is an indication that I have tried my best to protect it and it is God who has allowed it to happen. The parish is God's home for me and a holy place, and if my vehicle can be burned in such a place it is a sign that I have reached my limits." This reply was a great surprise to me, and a learning experience as well; I came to realize that people were bringing their vehicles to the parish not because of any security guarantees but as an act of faith. Only one vehicle had been incinerated, and since it was close to the garage, the flames had ignited part of the garage and part of the Rectory roof. If it were not because of God's intervention, I believe the rectory would have caught fire and been reduced to ashes.

What was most surprising was that the fire had scorched the external parts of the rectory roof and could have completely incinerated the house but did not. As I was contemplating my escape from the rebels the previous night, I'd wanted to climb onto the rooftop, but if I had I cannot tell how I would have reacted to the fear that the house was burning down. I also wondered what would have happened to me if I'd had to jump down from the roof with the house on fire and the rebels were on the ground looting. It would have been like falling from the frying pan into the fire.

The LRA generally set adults free because they rarely adjust to or accept their lifestyle; from their past experiences, most adults worked to escape rather than to become incorporated. But hundreds of boys and girls between the ages of eleven to seventeen were not released. This was very difficult on the parents as the news and information began to sink in on them that their son or daughter was among the abducted and was not coming home soon. None of the parents considered the idea of following the rebels to demand their children because they could not locate where the rebels were, and further the rebels could have harmed them if they did come into contact with them. Many of them informed me of the abduction of their children and asked me to pray for their safe return. From them, I heard a lot of statements of faith like; "We place everything in God's hands"; "God will take care of them." I did not meet a parent who was resigned to the loss, but instead they were filled with hope that all would end well even if there was not any good news to give them some comfort.

I remember Jenne, the chairperson of the parish pastoral council whom I had met on the morning of the attack, told me that her ten-year-old granddaughter had been abducted, but she was too young and weak to bear the strain of captivity. So Jenne said she was going to pray for her in the church and then wait at home. In fact, after two days the rebels did release her, and as soon as she arrived home, Jenne brought her to me in the parish and we went into the church to offer a thanksgiving prayer to God. What surprised me was her faith and confidence that God was going to answer her prayer.

At around ten a.m. the same morning, the rebels started to release those who were older, since they had only needed them to carry the loot. Most of the people released were not mistreated but were very exhausted by the long distance they walked and the weight of the loot that they carried. It was a difficult day for us, but community solidarity helped a lot. We did have a satellite phone in the town that we were able to use to inform our superiors about the attack and the need for them to keep us in their prayers.

Around noon of the same day, we buried the woman and the child who were killed. There were no facilities to preserve their bodies for a single day or until their relatives came to claim the bodies. Before lunchtime, the government soldiers came to the parish and made a report of what had been taken. Their interest was in knowing what the rebels could utilize in their war effort, like the radio-call and the solar panels. Around this time the visiting priest also prepared to leave. I wanted him to stay with me for one more day for some moral and emotional support, but he was very honest with me and told me that he was too scared to spend another night in the place. He drove very slowly out of Pajule to Lira, hoping that if he met any rebel soldiers along the way, they would stop him rather than shoot at him since he was moving slowly. Fortunately he arrived safely in Gulu.

When he left I was alone in the parish, it was quieter than usual, and people who normally came to spend their night were nowhere to be seen. I was certain that the rebels would not come back soon, but in the evening I became very distraught and lonely. Within myself I wished that someone in the community had volunteered to come to stay with me in the parish, but it never entered anyone's mind that I was equally shaken by what had happened, and that I also needed mental and spiritual support.

Chapter Twenty

Faith Amidst Extreme Fear in the Community

The aftermath of this attack was terrible because of the heightened fear. Since the beginning of the war, the parish compound was the only place that most people felt safe. Suddenly, this symbol of security and protection had been taken away from them in one single evening. I could see how restless the community was becoming.

A few people who had nowhere to go, mostly mothers with very young children, spent their nights at the convent. Before bedtime, I would go to recite the rosary with them. After prayer, I would wish them a good night and reassure them that they were safe. This was the most unusual experience that I have ever had. As I bid the people assembled a good night, they looked at my eyes very intently. It seemed I appeared to them like a superhuman. They would cling to each and every word of reassurance from me. Even if I was the man of God in their midst, deep down inside I was as worried and scared as all of them.

During this time, we also experienced a lot of concern and solidarity from the authorities of Gulu archdiocese. They were really concerned about my own security and my mental state. But since the rebels had taken the radio-call, our one reliable means of communication with those outside Pajule, I had to go to a place called Oguta to speak with them live. It was the only spot that had some limited cell phone network coverage, which was indicated by a single bar on the cell phone. It was on the road to Kitgum about five miles away from the parish and was a dangerous spot since LRA rebels passed through it on a regular basis.

To some in the diocesan administration, the experience I had gone through was too much for someone who had been a priest for just one year and a few months. This came out clearly in my discussions with the deputy of the bishop, who wanted me to leave the parish immediately and go to Gulu, but I was opposed to the idea. The deputy of the bishop reminded me politely: "Father, it is a matter of obedience for you to heed this directive to come to Gulu; it would be good for you to get out of the place to recover from what you have gone through." On my part, I told him: "I appreciate your prayers and concern for me, but as a matter of conscience; I cannot leave or abandon the parish since I believe that it would be the wrong thing for me to do."

The stand that I took to defy the directive of the deputy of the bishop was unusual, but I felt that I had good reasons for it since I was the only one who knew the actual situation on the ground and the needs of the people. The diocesan authorities, however great their concerns, were primarily focused on me as an individual and not on the people who looked at me as their shepherd. I was convinced that if I had left the place at this particular moment, the morale of the people would have totally collapsed since they had already lost their symbol of security, the parish. It would be too much for them to learn that the priest, now their only hope, had also abandoned them.

I firmly believed that I could still continue to be their voice and would have the capacity to use my influence and status to talk to nongovernmental organizations that needed someone credible on the ground to communicate with in order to channel aid to the people. Further, the Church was the only visible and viable structure on the ground. There were hardly any functioning institutions remaining. There were no journalists or local reporters who could make the rest of the country or the world informed about what was happening. As a religious leader, I believed I could use my influence to speak about the plight of anyone who was in need to the political and military authorities in the district, and if I left, the people would lose this important voice. And further I believed that my presence would check military abuses on the population, though they were rare at the time. My presence would mean that any abuses that took place would become known outside Pajule, since I could report this to the Church hierarchy for steps to be taken. In short, I did not want the only center of authority in the community that was different and independent from the military to be silenced.

I later heard that some of my fellow clergy joked about my decision not to leave the parish and imputed hidden motives for the choice that I had taken, that I wanted to die a martyr. This was totally untrue; martyrdom was very far away from my mind. It was the impact on others of leaving the place that was my primary concern.

Since I would not leave the parish, the diocesan authorities had to make some accommodations for me. The deputy of the bishop and my pastor planned to go to Lira, an hour's drive from Gulu, and find a driver who would take the risk to come to Pajule to bring me some money and a few clothes. I badly needed money. The rebels had left the house and my food store empty. The clothes that I had on were the ones that I was putting on at the time of the attack, a pair of trousers and a shirt. I later learned that as the deputy of the bishop and my pastor left Gulu for Lira, they reflected on the attack I had endured and my subsequent refusal to leave the parish and one of the questions that came into their mind was this: "If a young man who has been a priest for one and half years is taking the risk to be there with the people because of his faith in Christ and his desire to serve Him, what about us, who were both ordained priests almost sixteen years ago? How can we not take the same risk and go to Pajule?" This question that they asked of themselves as they traveled to Lira town made them come to Pajule. When they reached Lira, they found that the only vehicle that traveled to Pajule on a frequent basis had already left. And so they took the risk. It was a journey dependent upon faith for both of them. There was only one driver on the road called Hajji. Because he was the only one willing to take huge risks, he could charge four to five times the normal rate of transport on the route from Pajule to Lira, which was a drive of about one hour. His motto when traveling was not to stop anywhere along the road. Even if he met rebel soldiers along the road or an ambush on the way, he drove through. There were many occasions when the rebels heard him coming but by the time they reached the roadside to lay an ambush they had missed him by seconds.

When the deputy of the bishop and my pastor came to a township where we had one of our chapels located they stopped and prayed with the people, who would in turn bless them and reassure them that our Mother, Mary would keep them safe from harm. They reached Pajule on Saturday at around four p.m. We were surprised and happy to receive them since we were not expecting them. They were astonished to find us in the state we were in, since we looked better than they expected. They found us calm and preparing for Sunday Mass, though they could see that a lot of damage had been done.

The following day, we had Mass, and hundreds of people attended. Most of the town and camp dwellers came irrespective of their different faith traditions to listen to the message of the deputy of the bishop. When we were in the middle of the celebration, the director of CARITAS also arrived. The community of Pajule as a whole appreciated the solidarity of the leadership of the Catholic Church, and the risk that these two officials took to come meant a lot to us. I heard positive comments from inactive churchgoers like: "You see the Catholic Church; when they are faced with a problem they support one another." I was happy that the people could experience this because that was what our real ministry had become. Even if we could not solve most of the security problems they were faced with, we could offer them our solidarity and presence.

Before the end of the Mass, the deputy of the bishop blessed every place in the parish with holy water asking for divine protection: our living rooms, the rectory, the convent, and the reception center where the two killings had taken place. After the Mass I could see the community breathe a sigh of relief since it felt like God was once again in charge. Then, that same day, they all returned to the headquarters of the Diocese in Gulu. My pastor could not stay since his journey to Pajule with the Deputy of the

Bishop was unplanned and he needed to pick up his personal belongings in Gulu and report the urgent needs of the parish to the bishop.

A week later when our lives were settling down, some hunters found a decomposing body of a man. He had been hit by a stray bullet as he ran for his life on the night of the attack. He had died lying behind an anthill, and yet many thought that he had been abducted.

I still recall one of the many inspiring letters I received around this time from a fellow priest, Father Matthew Lagoro, the pastor of my home parish, expressing concern for what had happened in Pajule parish. I recall these very few words: "Father Robert, it is unfortunate that you went through this, but by your insistence to continue serving the people of God in Pajule, you teach us faith."

My Vacation in Kampala

The rebel attack combined with the constant sense of insecurity at the parish for close to one year had left me traumatized. Whenever I heard gunshots or huge explosions, I did not physically tremble as most people did. Instead, I felt pricking and sharp pains in my heart and the lower parts of my ribs. These pains were also triggered by news of ambushes, attacks, and killings. Even the mere hint of an attack on the town by the rebels caused it. It was much later that I discovered the severe pains were an indication of the high level of stress I was experiencing.

This attack on the parish had made it worse for me, in particular the fact that the rebels kicked at the metallic door to the dining room so violently while demanding that I open it for them. Any bangs from anything metallic, in particular the doors during the windy season or the screeching noises that the doors and windows in the parish made while being opened or closed, brought back fresh memories of the attack of January 23. Even when I was alone, I would hear voices in my head like the rebels had returned.

After two weeks, my pastor had returned, and it was a good time to take a vacation. On a Sunday during Mass before leaving, I told the Christian community that it was time for me to take a break. I needed to go to a place where I could have a good rest and buy some personal items and clothing. My usual practice whenever I was planning to leave the parish for a while was to inform the Christian community during the Sunday Mass so that anyone who wanted to see me during the course of the week knew I would be away. However I did not reveal the date or the exact time because of concerns that someone would use this information to plan an ambush on the road to attack me.

When the day came for me to go on my vacation, I left for Gulu, where I met my sister Flora, who like all my family members was gravely concerned about my psychological and physical state. I could see she was really happy I had survived the ordeal. On my part, I was filled with joy to see her, for in her, I saw all my family members once again. This encounter reminded me of our times growing up as little children and the genuine love and sincerest concerns of my own family members. Above all, it made me develop my own concept of the meaning of a near-death experience—that it is almost being taken away from those who value you the most.

In Gulu, I met with many friends who worked for CARITAS; most of them had spent some time in Pajule parish during the insecurity. It was a happy reunion for me. What surprised me most was that within hours of people learning that I was out of Pajule and could be reached on my cell phone, I got calls from almost all over the diocese and the country wishing me well and thanking God for protecting me. The support and encouragement I received meant so much to me. I could have stayed in Gulu since the situation was not as bad as Pajule. Gulu was much safer than Pajule; unfortunately, the rebels continued to attack the outskirts of the town every night, and so every morning there was some bad news. And yet, I just wanted to go to a place where I would have some peace of mind.

After a week in Gulu, I traveled to Kampala and spent seven weeks with the family of a friend who was like a parent to me. I had met him many years back at Christ the King Teachers College in Gulu on the Feast of Christ the King in November 1994. Apart from welcoming me into his home, he counseled me. The seven weeks that I lived with him were a great time of recuperation for me. He took me out several times to relax, visit his friends, and share my stories and experiences with a wider audience. This was a healing experience for me, and in the process I tried to make sense of what I had gone through. Many people were interested in learning about my experiences and stories, and even more so about the insights I had gained.

During the first weeks, sharing my stories about the events of January 23 in Pajule brought back painful memories and left me in almost a state of shock and disbelief that I had gone through such a traumatic experience. However, as time went on, I was able to talk about my experiences without the strong emotions. At his home, I was able to have the first sound sleep since my last visit to Rome. It was a nice feeling to go to bed without thinking that I might have to wake up or be woken up, leave my bed, and sleep on the floor or run out of the house in the course of the night.

My time in Kampala was not only a time for me to heal psychologically and get back my equilibrium; it was also a great moment of introspection. I reflected on the meaning and value of life. I appreciated the fact that God had kept me alive. It was a time in which I experienced and lived my own preaching and that of others. On several occasions, I preached on the text of Ecclesiastes 1:1–18, that is, on the vanity of vanities, meaning that human possessions are worthless and human life and our relationship with God are the most valuable things that we have. I recognized how precious my life was since I still had it after losing almost all my material possessions.

It was also a time for me to reflect on the love that I experienced from unexpected quarters since I had real needs and nowhere to turn to meet them. Since I was a public figure, there were many people who knew me and yet I did not know them. Their concern toward me was so moving. I remember one of them called Billy came to me and said, "Father, I am sorry for what happened to you; I have heard of what you went through. I would like to take you to a tailor to take your measurements; I want to get you a shirt and a pair of trousers." Such kindness from people who were not directly responsible for my needs was very uplifting.

Ultimately, this time was a great moment for me to reflect on the meaning of my vocation as a priest and how to live it in concrete terms. Some tend to think that being a priest is about power, prestige, respect, and comfort—but on the contrary it is about people and serving them and their needs. I was also able to recognize my motivation for continuing to work in this life and death situation. I understood that I was taking the risk because of my love for the people, and even with my limitations I wanted to keep Christ and the Church alive as a sign of hope in their midst.

A cross section of the social workers. It is amazing how these young men and women kept Pajule Reception Center running against all the odds.

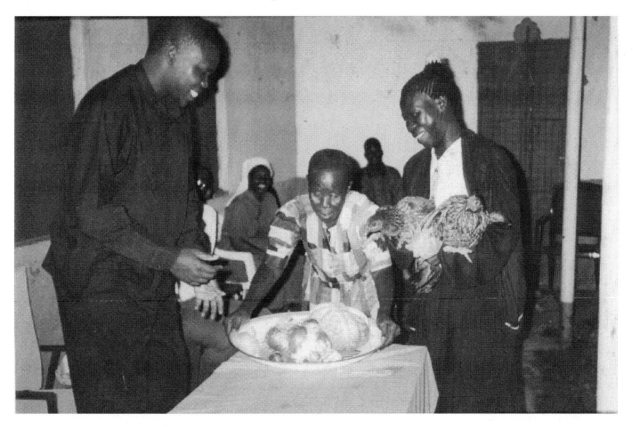

This was the evening of my first anniversary after a very tense morning at Mass. I received gifts including live hens and ducks

As one of the pilgrims from the Archdiocese of Gulu in October 2002, I visited the Three Fountains in Rome. This was the most moving of all the places I visited.

Within minutes after I returned from my first night ever in the bush in January 2003. Most of the people assembled at the parish were in a state of shock and wondering what might have happened to me.

One of the footprints of the LRA. I am standing next to the vehicle of a local businessman that they set ablaze at the parish. I was convinced that one day I would tell the story no matter how long it would take.

Relaxed behind the rectory reading a newspaper and sipping a cold cup of water. Even in a warzone there are surprisingly quiet days. Whenever possible I always tried to leave whatever I heard or saw outside the walls of the rectory.

The members of the lay apostolate and Oliver Stoltz, (kneeling at the center) and his team. They came on a different mission but turned out to be a great blessing for the parish.

As the chaplain of Pajule Reception Center I attend to one of the former child soldiers. However difficult their ordeal, it did not prevent most from making a successful transition to a new life.

The inside view of Pajule parish church and the congregation. In a warzone the only place where most people heard a refreshing idea, and felt some peace and joy was at the celebration of the Mass.

At the Mass for the children. They seem to be having the best time of their lives.

Chapter Twenty-One

My Return to Pajule

After spending seven weeks in Kampala, I returned to Pajule to continue with my work. I felt well rested, and the level of trauma was substantially reduced in me since I could go to bed and sleep soundly once again. On a Sunday afternoon, I boarded a bus and traveled to Gulu, where I spent a couple of days planning to return to my station of duty. At that time, it was hard to get a vehicle traveling from Gulu to Pajule via Lira or Acolibur since both routes were risky. But frequently the CARITAS trucks traveled with a white flag mounted, indicating that they were vehicles belonging to a humanitarian organization. The hope was that the two sides in the conflict would easily identify and respect it. Most of the trucks were "double cabins" and were painted white.

On March 25, 2003, I boarded a CARITAS vehicle that was traveling from Gulu to Pajule taking supplies to the reception center. At the beginning of our journey, as was the common practice, we prayed for a safe travel to Pajule and went via the Lira route, which was the longer route and commonly thought to be less risky. The journey to Pajule normally took about two hours. The shorter route would have been for us to travel to Pajule via Atanga, which would have taken about forty-five minutes.

To reach Pajule on our way from Lira, we would travel for forty-five minutes on roads that were still relatively safe, but the farther we moved into Pader District the more insecure the roads would become. After passing Puranga, we would start traveling in very deadly and dangerous territory. This journey would take twenty-five to thirty minutes, but each and every minute of it would be very tense since we expected an ambush at any moment. So rather than worry about an attack, we recited the rosary.

Within one hour we were in Lira; we rested, had lunch, and planned to leave for Pajule. As we drove out of Lira, we reached a spot at a place called Ngetta where the tarmac road ends and the dirt road begins. At that time a National Teachers Training College was in the area. Then, we saw a double cabin painted red moving very fast, and those inside gestured at us to stop. In the vehicle we found the program coordinator of the Acholi Religious Leaders Peace Initiative and other executives of the organization. They had spent the night in Pajule and made contact with a group of LRA rebels, who expressed their desire to declare a ceasefire and give dialogue a chance. After their meeting they had driven to Acol-Pii, which was the army headquarters in the district of Pader, to inform the army commander of the intention of the rebels.

There was a lot of elation within the delegation of the Acholi Religious Leaders Peace Initiative. First, at encountering us because we knew each other quite well, and second, because their work was beginning to bear some fruit since the rebels had started to show an interest in dialogue. Third, they had driven safely out of Pader District. Whenever one entered Pader District for any reason at the time, it was difficult to tell if they would leave alive because LRA ambushes were very common. Reaching this spot that marked the end of the dirt road and the beginning of the tarmac road was a source of relief and a reassurance that they would get another chance to see their families.

At this spot in Ngetta, we asked the team of the Acholi Religious Leaders Peace Initiative how safe the road was; they told us it was fine. Their answer was based on the fact they had traveled without any incident. After twenty minutes we parted, continued for one hour and we reached Alim inside the danger zone. This area is under Pajule parish and has a chapel built by the roadside. There we found that government soldiers had set up a roadblock. This was unusual unless something significant had occurred. The soldiers stopped us and told us that we could not proceed with our journey to Pajule till the road ahead of us had been secured. A red painted civilian truck with close to thirty passengers had passed them about five minutes ago going to Pajule and they suspected it had been ambushed by the LRA. They told us they heard gunfire and had sent some of their units to rescue the passengers who had been ambushed.

What struck me most was the way one of the soldiers talked about the incident, as if it were a joking matter: "I could not believe the barrage of gunfire and the volley of bullets directed at the vehicle. In fact, the rebels must have done a lot of damage today." If one had not paid close attention to the soldier, one would think he was praising the attackers.

As we were standing by the roadblock, a soldier with his gun strapped across his back arrived on foot from the direction where the ambush had taken place. He was physically shaking and trembling and in a terrible state of shock; he could no longer hold his weapon and handed it over to one of the other soldiers. Then, he described how he had narrowly escaped death. He said that he was a few meters away from the spot when the vehicle was attacked. He was walking on foot, and as he looked back, he could see and hear the shots being fired at the vehicle. This soldier believed that the attackers must have seen him but decided not to kill him.

I thought that this soldier would get some sympathy from those at the roadblock since he was one of their own. But I was surprised again since they made the situation sound so frivolous. I heard them saying "You, man—today you missed being turned into human flesh, you would be a carcass by now." I may never understand the temperament and behavior of the soldiers. I guess that working in a stressful area made them downplay any bad news, and this helped them cope with the violence and death they saw or experienced on a daily basis. The distress of their colleague was very genuine. Whenever LRA rebels saw government soldiers moving alone, they would often kill them and take their guns. There were several incidents in the area in which government soldiers moving on private transport like bicycles and motorcycles were attacked on the way and had their guns stolen.

Within a few minutes, a survivor of the ambush arrived. I knew him well since he was a businessman in Pajule. He had run through the bushes for his life, and I realized that the very shirt he was wearing, now torn to pieces, was a gift from me. Since he had abandoned his shoes to run more quickly, his feet were bleeding profusely. He was greatly relieved to see us. He told us that armed men ran at the vehicle from the bushes while firing, but many of the passengers managed to jump out and flee for their lives with the exception of a few mothers with children.

For almost one hour now, the road had been quiet and we had not heard any more gunshots. Then, it started to rain heavily. The soldiers who were with us retreated to their makeshift huts called *mama ingia pole pole* which is a Swahili word meaning: "Madam, please enter carefully and cautiously." Because the government soldiers shifted their location from time to time and lived in temporary structures, they dug a rectangular hole in the ground and created a space large enough for one or two people. The hole was shaped in such a way that it prevented the rain from flowing into it, and then they would thatch some grass that would be elevated above the hole to act as a roof. Whenever a male soldier had a visitor such as a lady friend or a mistress, she had to negotiate her way carefully into this hole. Otherwise, her clothing, hair, or back would bring down the whole roof. However, the main purpose of these huts was for the defense of the soldiers. If they were attacked, their adversaries were the ones out in the open while they were several inches below ground level, minimizing their chances of being hit.

As the rain started to pour very heavily, we entered the vehicle, but not all of us could fit. The local businessman who had escaped refused to come inside, and yet he was feeling very cold. I wanted him to sit in the car, but he was not willing to because his clothes were dirty and stained with blood. Instead, he sat under the car as it rained, and I could see him getting soaked by the rain and muddy water under the vehicle. At this moment I instructed Mr. Aludi, the driver, to defy the instructions of the military and go to Pajule. We asked the businessman to sit in the back of the truck and drove off. The soldiers had all entered their temporary houses and we were certain that none of them would stop us. We were also convinced that by taking this risk we would be able to save the lives of some of those who had been ambushed.

It was common knowledge that whenever the rebels attacked a vehicle, they normally took less than twenty minutes before leaving. We drove for less than five minutes before we were at the location of the attack. It was a sad scene. There were people lying all over the road with huge cuts on their faces, legs, stomachs, etc. Most of them were helpless and exposed to the rain, and some were also lying in muddy water since it was a dirt road. It was a surprise to me that no one was screaming or crying, but I could see that there was a lot of pain all over the place. And since it was a passenger truck transporting some businesspeople from Pajule, some of the items they had bought in Lira were scattered all over the place. Above all, there was human blood flowing all over. The vehicle had overturned at the time of the attack, but fortunately, the government soldiers had raised it up and it was on the left-hand side of the road facing the bush. A few of the injured sat in the front seat in the midst of the broken glass from the windscreen. These people were waiting for any help that would come their way.

Looking around, I could see I knew almost everyone involved in the ambush. I had either prayed with them in a Sunday Mass or chatted with them in town. The soldiers had secured the scene, but none of them had any first-aid kits or training. This was a common occurrence whenever an ambush occurred; the rescue operation was basically the military securing the scene and the injured waiting until some vehicle traveling in the same direction reached the spot and took them to a hospital.

I asked some of the soldiers standing around if there were any deaths or people whom they thought should be given priority. But most of them were not willing to talk and instead appeared shocked to see us. They seemed to have other priorities, and when we asked them to help us lift the injured and place them in the truck, they refused. So the driver, some of the victims of the attack who were strong enough, and I joined to put all those who were seriously hurt into the back of the truck, even if it involved touching the blood of the injured and we could have gotten a blood infection. As we placed the injured into the vehicle, the soldiers opened boxes that had been strewn all over the place; some of the contents included salt, sugar, and cartons of cigarettes.

In fact, two people had been killed in the ambush, a police constable and a middle-aged man from Paiula along the road to Pader District headquarters. Another police officer, who was the registrar in Pajule Police Station, had knocked his head very hard against the bonnet of the vehicle and had a deep cut on his forehead. He was not dead but seemed to be paralyzed, though he could open his eyes. But the most serious injury was that of a mother who had a bullet rip through her stomach; her bowels were visible and she had lost a lot of blood. She was powerless and left with very little energy. And yet, her one-year-old baby boy clung tightly to her and continued to suckle her breast. When I came to hold her hands, she recognized me as the priest but was in a lot of pain. We were able to carry her and place her in the truck and later gave her son to her to hold. Inside the ambushed truck we found Mr. Ongaya, a medical practitioner who had a private practice in Pajule. He had a broken leg and was all wet and shivering terribly. He was in a lot of pain, but when he saw me he smiled because he was certain that we would make sure that he and all the rest reached the hospital. We placed all the injured on the truck until the vehicle was really overloaded. We could not leave anybody behind except for the dead bodies, since we were the last vehicle traveling on the road that day. Driving very slowly, within twenty-five minutes we were in Pajule and found it gripped with sadness and the residents standing on either side of the road trying to get a glimpse of the injured.

It was now coming on six p.m. and too late to drive out of Pajule. But the kinds of injuries that the people had were so serious that we had to get them to a hospital. The closest hospital in Kitgum was normally a forty-five minute drive away from Pajule, but since the vehicle was overloaded, it had to move very slowly. And the driver had to avoid hitting bumps that would cause more discomfort to the injured. I did not proceed to Kitgum but stayed in Pajule. At Pajule, I wanted to take my things out of the vehicle, but I could not since so many injured people sat on them. Fortunately, the driver traveled safely to Kitgum, and most of the victims were saved with the exception of the mother who was seriously hurt. She was able to reach the hospital but died the following day since she had lost so much blood and the gunshot had destroyed some of her vital organs.

That day, I got back everything that I had tried to get rid of during my vacation. Alone that evening after taking a bath, I continued to smell blood in the air. Even as I went to bed, the sight of the injured lying helplessly on the ground kept coming to mind. This made me sleepless. The following day, hardly anyone asked me about the seven weeks I was away; instead they asked about the ambush and the people we had rescued. After two days, my traveling bags were brought back from Kitgum town, but most of the new clothes and the books that I had bought to read, hopefully to take my mind off the insecurity, were stained with blood, and some of them had to be thrown away.

At this moment I felt like I had a theological conversion. It was not possible for me to go for another vacation, and I said to God, "I am going to stop worrying about myself anymore since this is where You have sent me." From this moment onwards I stopped dwelling on instances that could have caused me serious injury or even death as I did my work. In fact, I began to compartmentalize more, and even if I witnessed something really bad or nearly got involved in something fatal, as soon as I entered the rectory I would try to leave it by my door.

However, this ambush, unlike many others, left the community divided and suspicious of the army. Most of the attacks in the district were committed by the LRA. But this time, a number of people, including Mr. Munana, the caretaker of the vehicle, and the driver, Jakeo, pointed fingers at the government soldiers who purportedly came to rescue them. They were convinced that they were attacked by the same government soldiers who claimed that they had come to rescue them because there was no exchange of fire between them and the so-called rebels. This complaint was reported to the military and civil authorities at the time, but no follow-up was made and nothing came of it. As I look back at the incident, the discomfort of the soldiers that we met on our arrival at the scene should have raised a red flag for us at the time.

In fact, this incident pointed to one of the challenges we faced. There were no institutions we could rely on to do any independent documentation or investigation. It was enough to say that the LRA had committed an attack, and that would be the end of it. Further, there were so many acts of violence and killing that unfortunately many had come to accept them as a part of life. Most people preferred to move on and focus on what the next day would bring rather than look back. This was also the way in which I lived; I looked to the future most of the time rather than the past. I found it a big challenge to be a strong advocate for the respect of human rights in the community because personal safety was not guaranteed. If someone wanted to get rid of you, it was not difficult to do so because in the end the rebels would be blamed for it.

This incident left me reflecting on how much we lived our lives based on luck, chance, and providence in a war zone. Those who entered the ambush could have missed it if they had traveled slightly earlier or later. And on our part, we could have been the victims if we had traveled an hour earlier or had not stopped at Ngetta on the way. The executives of the Acholi Religious Leaders Peace Initiative whom we met on the way could also have been the ones to enter the trap. They survived because when they reached Acol-Pii, they did not go back to Pajule but they continued straight to Lira town and then proceeded to Gulu. I believe that this was also a manifestation of a divine hand to steer away the peace team. It would have been terrible to hear that advocates of peace were killed. But above all, it pointed to the many things that people survive in a war zone and yet are never aware how close they came to a fatal incident.

Several Months Later

After almost eight months had passed following the attack on Pajule parish, one of the rebels who had found me hiding outside the wall of the parish after I had escaped from the rectory surrendered to the government soldiers in Pajule and was brought to Pajule Reception Center. This happened when I was away from the parish for a few days. The ex-rebel revealed that he was among those who had attacked and raided Pajule town and the parish. And on the night of the attack, he found the priest, meaning me, hiding with my head buried in the grass behind the nursery wall, and he interrogated me very rudely and nearly frightened me to death. Those who were listening to him were greatly perplexed by the unremorseful way he talked about his role in the attack because in that attack lives were lost, much property destroyed, and he was now talking to the victims of their violent actions.

However, it was not uncommon for former LRA rebels to talk about their past violent activities in a joking, trivial, and casual manner. Part of this was because they had been involved in so much cruelty that violence had lost its sting. Because most of them were traumatized, it was almost impossible for them to exercise prudence in what they said. When they opened their mouths to speak about their time in the bush, they did not sort out what should be said and not said; they did not consider the audience they were addressing. When they began to talk, they talked endlessly like a tape recorder being played. It never came to their minds that some of the people they had wounded were among the ones listening to them, and that their loose talk and inappropriate disclosure might be rubbing salt into the injury. Fortunately, the society as a whole understood that they were traumatized and needed help rather than judgment. There was never an occasion that I remember when fingers of blame were pointed at ex-rebels since the community never wavered in forgiving.

It was always interesting to hear the ex-rebels describe their primary activities in the bush. For example, the rebels referred to the attacks on civilians traveling on the roads or in their homes as actions done when they were "on duty," "at work," "doing an operation," or "accomplishing a task.". I found this manner of description repugnant and ridiculous, especially when some of the local people in the community bought into it, since it only served to sugarcoat their heinous crimes.

For example, when the rebels attacked a vehicle on the road, looted a place, or even killed people, many in the local population, instead of stating specific actions like looting, killing, or destroying property, would instead use expressions like "the rebels worked in the place," "the rebels had an operation," or simply "the rebels disturbed people." I was convinced that ordinary citizens needed to call these actions what they were, condemn them, and state the barbarism in them whenever possible. Using milder or softer words gave these atrocious actions dignity.

As the discussion progressed with this ex-rebel soldier who had surrendered, those listening to him asked him what his faith tradition was. His answer was that he was baptized and raised a Catholic, but as a young adult he had drifted away from his Church and his faith. Then, someone asked him, "If you are a Catholic, why didn't you treat your priest with some respect when you found him hiding, since he is your spiritual leader and an elder in the community?" His answer was interesting: "I did not need to give the priest any special consideration because I was on duty and carrying out my job, and above all, I was executing the instructions of my commanders."

Chapter Twenty-Two

An Unexpected Meeting with the Rebels

My visit to the LRA rebels at the beginning of April 2003 was not something I had planned. While those within the hierarchy of the Catholic Church in the archdiocese of Gulu, the Anglican Church, and cultural leaders had met the LRA on many occasions, I had not made a single visit to them. First, I was of a junior rank, an associate pastor, and second, I was not connected to any of the departments of the Catholic Church. However, when the Acholi Religious Leaders Peace Initiative came to Pajule parish prior to traveling to their destination, I hosted them before and after their meetings. Personally, I had no desire to be part of any delegation to meet the rebels. While the rebels gave the impression that they trusted the Catholic Church and the institution of cultural leaders that mediated between them and the Ugandan government, they constantly attacked Church property and personnel.

So, my meeting with the LRA rebels was not something that I had wished for. I was in Gulu on parish business and needed to return to Pajule, but there was no means of transportation other than to travel with the Acholi Religious Leaders Peace Initiative. A delegation was going to a place called Koyo Lalogi to make contact with the LRA, and the driver of the vehicle was the brother of one of the rebel commanders. We left Gulu via Lira going to Pajule. Our plan was to have them drop me off in Pajule parish, and then the delegation would meet the LRA rebels without me.

By this time, the government of Uganda had designated the whole of Lapul sub-county, in which Koyo Lalogi was located, a ceasefire zone in order to give dialogue a chance. As we were approaching Pajule, I noticed that the delegation members began to panic, breathe loudly, and shift nervously, and they started pleading with me to accompany them to meet the LRA rebels. Yet on my part, I was very hesitant.

My personal rule when traveling at the time was that once I had decided on a plan, I would not change it since I believed my first choice was the safer one and God's voice. I felt that abruptly changing my travel plans could expose me to an ambush since I was being unfaithful to my inner voice. And the LRA was often suspicious and hostile to visitors they did not expect or invite. However, they insisted that I go along, so I kept my discomfort to myself and accompanied them. At that moment in the truck, I was the authority figure among them, and I immediately took on a new role in representing the Catholic Church as I was the only Catholic priest among them.

The junction to Koyo Lalogi was about one mile from the main center of Pajule, and it had the signpost of a primary school called Gore. I was greatly surprised when we entered the junction and traveled less than five hundred meters and saw two rebel soldiers very near to the main road, monitoring and watching those who might be heading in the direction of their hideouts. This came as a great shock to me because this spot was very near to town. It was now clear that the rebels constantly observed who was going in and out of the town, and if they had any ill intentions they could easily carry them out. Since these two rebel soldiers had advance information that a delegation from Gulu was coming to their base, they stopped us and assured us that it was safe for us to proceed and that we would soon meet more rebel groups ahead.

After driving for fifteen minutes into the bush, we met a large group of rebels who were really excited to see us. Their attitude was festive, like we were coming to a picnic. There was a lot of youthful excitement and happiness among them. I noticed that most of them were in their early teens. Several of the rebels boasted of having their own personal guns, and others bragged about their large numbers in the place, and that even if the government soldiers were to try to attack them they would never be dislodged. Some of them came and introduced themselves to us, but they all had funny names like the crocodile, cow, goat, rabbit, or guinea fowl. These fictitious names helped them to hide their true identity.

As we traveled deep into the jungle, we could hardly see what was ahead of us since the grass covered all the roads into Koyo Lalogi. The little we could see were marks of destruction: burned buildings, crumbling walls, and abandoned houses. The primary signs that people had once lived there were the orange and mango trees that were in the compounds. At this time of the year in early April 2003, the trees were full of mangoes and oranges that were ripening, but there were no people to pick and eat them.

The elementary school of Koyo Lalogi was the only permanent building left standing. Its renovation had not been completed before the place became insecure. When it was raining heavily, the LRA rebels used it for shelter, or for cover when there were any suspicious planes flying overhead.

This trip was remarkable for me since Koyo Lalogi had occupied a large part of our lives since the resumption of conflict in 2002 because it brought so much fear and uncertainty into our daily regimen. The LRA rebel commanders would send some of their units every day from it along different routes in Pader District to attack passenger vehicles and steal food and supplies.

Supplies for Kitgum District that had to go through Pajule could not reach their destination on many occasions because of the attacks on traders and travelers. Some of the political and civil leaders in Kitgum District accused the people of Pajule of collaboration with the rebels. To an outsider this accusation had a semblance of truth because the attacks were mostly concentrated in a particular locality. But the reality, the truth about the situation was that the jungles of Koyo Lalogi were behind Pajule, and they contained the base from which the rebels operated. If travelers were ever to move safely in Pader District while passing through the Pajule area as a whole, something had to be done by the political and military authorities to eliminate the rebel stronghold.

Something I learned from living in a war zone was that the perceptions of those who live in the situation were often very different from those who lived outside the actual situation. It was almost impossible for outsiders to know what was actually happening since most of the information they received was based on false rumors and was wildly inflated by imagination. And the government was the worst culprit in the game of disinformation since it put its own spin on everything. Personally, I also came to recognize that, over time when the security situation is not improving, people become frustrated when trying to comprehend what is happening. It is at such moments that there is the danger of making rash judgments or oversimplifying the issues. This is the exact path that the civil and political leaders in Kitgum District embarked on.

When we had reached the center of the village of Koyo Lalogi, the rebels led us to an abandoned home and we sat under a mango tree to await the two rebel commanders, Nyeko Tolbert Yardin and Raska Lukwiya. After about thirty minutes, the entourage protecting the two LRA commanders began to arrive in two lines. As soon as they came face to face with us, they spread out, lay down, and encircled us at a distance of about four hundred meters. This continued for the next ten minutes, and at the end of the two lines were the two LRA officers. The rebel soldiers on the ground were meant to provide security for their officers, but I did not feel safe at all. It seemed as if I were now in a prison cell cut off from the rest of society and had surrendered my life into their hands. I prayed that they did not have any ill intentions toward us and that there were no government soldiers in the vicinity, because if they tried to attack the place, we civilians would get caught in the crossfire.

The two officers were well dressed in full green military attire, and had their rebel military ranks on them. I was surprised by their smartness and neatness. Their uniforms were clean and ironed. This was contrary to the image I had of people who lived in the bush most of the time. But it was easy to recognize that most of the rebel soldiers who guarded them were having a rough life, as they appeared weak and emaciated. They were dressed in torn and dirty clothes, wore sandals that left most of their feet exposed to injuries from thorns and sharp objects, and had no protective boots to wear.

As we sat down, I noticed that one of the rebel commanders, Raska Lukwiya, was irritated by my presence in the delegation. He constantly looked at me in a strange and ominous way. I could feel that he did not want me around; he seemed to be thinking that I was a government agent or spy. Matters were not made any better by the fact that I had not put on my clerical shirt or my white cassock, as I had dressed very casually and looked like a businessman or government official in town. Whenever Catholic clergymen visited the rebels, they normally put on a cassock or a Roman collar. It did not help that I am light-skinned, which made me appear slightly different from the rest of the delegation, since most Northerners and in particular the Acoli people have a slightly shiny, darker skin texture. It seemed to me that Raska Lukwiya was thinking that I must have been a Westerner/Southerner who had sneaked his way onto the LRA rebel base since I had light-brown skin. Because the Westerners and Southerners were ruling and dominating the affairs of the country, one of the reasons why the LRA was at war, I was the wrong person to have come to Koyo Lalogi.

Raska Lukwiya came very near to my face and stared directly into my eyes. This really alarmed me. Let alone his physical appearance, he was close to seven feet tall, slender, and very dark skinned and with very red eyes. I felt deep in my gut that I was seeing death. But I remained composed and looked backed into his eyes as well; if he expected me to panic or blink instead I disappointed him and held my ground.

When the local chief we had traveled with noticed the extreme attention that I was getting from Raska Lukwiya, he intervened. He introduced me to him by saying I was the man of God working in Pajule parish who has been receiving their mistresses and was not someone foreign. It was at this point that Raska Lukwiya changed his attitude and became relaxed. The intervention of the chief made me breathe a deep sigh of relief. To confirm that I was not a stranger, Raska Lukwiya initiated a conversation with me in the native Acoli language; we chatted for a while, and I could notice him become at ease with me.

The forty-five minutes that our meeting with the rebels lasted was like a second captivity for me comparable to when the rebels had detained me at the parish. From the very moment we set foot in their base, my heart at each and every moment focused on the minute we were to leave. Fortunately, deep inside we all felt the same way. We made our discussions and interactions very brief and precise.

In our delegation, we had an elder who came to encourage the rebels to give the peace talks a real chance since the government had responded positively to their unilateral ceasefire. He also wanted to communicate to the rebels that it was now a common trend in the region for conflicts to be handled through dialogue. For example, the South Sudan, which had a history of armed conflict since her independence, had put an end to the war through dialogue.

In our informal discussions with the rebels, Raska Lukwiya told me something that was very revealing and yet at the time did not make any sense to me. It was a statement I kept reflecting on for several months. "Father, if things go our way, we shall also have softer bodies like yours." At this particular time, I was slightly overweight. This statement should have raised a red flag within me about the commitment of the rebels to the peace process—for when I look back at this statement after a couple of years have passed and then contrast it with the actions of the rebels at that particular time, I have come to the conclusion that Raska Lukwiya seemed to say that when the rebels captured state power, they would have the resources that they needed to live comfortable lives and grow fat like those who were in the government. This meant that the rebels had no genuine desire for peace but were only playing mind games with everyone.

I believe that it is safe to say that the unilateral ceasefire that the rebels declared was a hoax. The two rebel commanders were sent to divert attention from the offensive they wanted to carry out. They used this period of the so-called ceasefire to build up their capacity and to expand their area of operation. It was during this time that they went farthest into eastern Uganda.

This is one of the challenges that the religious and cultural leaders always faced in the conflict during the pursuit of peace. It was always difficult to tell what the truth was and who was telling it. I believe that on many occasions, both sides exploited the sincerity of the religious and cultural leaders in their quest for peace. The truth was always hard to find, and suspicion filled the air between the two opposing groups. Each side distrusted almost everything that the other had said and it was very difficult to find common ground on anything.

I also came to learn that the rules of conduct and human behavior in conflict zones are very different for those on different sides. When regular folks say something or make a commitment, most of the time they intend to keep their word. But telling a lie is an accepted part of military strategy. For example, an officer can be in favor of a meeting and be against it as well. There were occasions when religious and cultural leaders got the approval of an army commander before meeting with the LRA, and after he had given his blessing, this same officer would send soldiers to attack the venue while the meeting was going on.

The short time I was in the company of the rebels, I saw how security conscious and tense they were most of the time since they did not want to be in a particular location for long. At each and every moment, they updated other groups about the progress of our meeting through the radio-call. In fact, the radio-call they were using looked like the very one that they had looted from Pajule parish on January 23, 2003, but I did not have the courage to inquire about it or make any comments. The furthest I could go in my conversations with Nyeko Tolbert Yardin, who was their chief of staff (the third highest ranking member of the LRA), was to tell him that I was the priest present in the parish at the time they attacked it. I just wanted to hear what he would say since he was well aware that Pajule parish was at the forefront of humanitarian efforts to receive ex-LRA fighters and reintegrate them into society. Nyeko Tolbert, surprisingly, did not make any comments. Unlike Raska Lukwiya, he appeared friendlier and normal; I could not detect anything that was strange about him and his worldview. He expressed the hope that one day he would return home and live a free life like anyone else. And this is what puzzled me most about him. He made me constantly ask myself several questions: Why does a person who appears to be normal like anyone else kill other human beings? Do these rebels really value the lives of the delegation that is now visiting them? Nyeko Tolbert Yardin was among the top LRA officers who every evening instructed their units to ambush vehicles, and on some days close to ten people or more would be killed in a single incident. This is an aspect of the LRA war that I have not yet found a comprehensible answer for: I do not understand why people who appear to be normal like anyone else in the way they talk, think, and behave are not bothered by the constant shedding of the blood of the innocent.

As we interacted with the rebels, one who was about twelve years old wanted a particular book with pictures from me. I did not know what book he was talking about. Even if I had the book, I was certain that I would not be returning to visit them in the near future. So I did not want to make any commitments. From past experience, I had learned that most LRA fighters had a childlike mindset. If I gave the impression that I was willing to consider his request, he would take it to mean I made a promise to him. If I failed to deliver the book to him, this LRA soldier would think I broke my promise, and if they attacked someplace where I could be found he would look for me to account. Further, I did not want to do anything that I would later have to explain. We were not to provide the rebels with anything that would aid their war effort. I knew that a book with a couple of pictures had no military value in it, but I did not want to put myself into a situation where I might have to explain my actions to anyone.

As the time came for us to leave, we immediately boarded our truck to depart. The speed with which we left was striking. Normally before a journey we would say a prayer through the intercession of St. Christopher, the patron saint and protector of travelers, but this time we forgot. Yet there was plenty of need for us to pray since we were about to begin driving through the jungles and were uncertain of what might be waiting along the way.

As the car was leaving the place of the meeting, strangely, Nyeko Tolbert Yardin came forward and stopped the driver, asked us to get down, and asked me as God's representative to pray and bless them before we left. "Father, as a man of God, you have not blessed us; bless us before you leave." As I got out of the vehicle, I kept on wondering why prayer was important to this LRA officer; and above all, what kind of prayer was I going to lead? Did it make sense to pray that God bless the rebels in the plunder and murder they commit? What if they were not happy with my prayer and felt that I had judged or criticized them? What if they decided that I should remain at their base? I asked God to provide me with the words to say, and I believe that He did. This is what I remember loosely to have been my prayer:

"Lord God, as your minister, you know that we all love this land, I would like to thank you for the beauty of Acoliland and its people, children, soil, skies, and rivers. You have blessed this land with every good gift."

"Unfortunately, we cannot enjoy your many gifts in this land. Because of this war, we are refugees in our own land. I pray that you bless every sincere effort by the government of Uganda, the LRA rebels, the people of Uganda, and the religious and cultural leaders toward peace in Acoliland." And we concluded our prayer by reciting the "Our Father" and the "Hail Mary."

The rebel commander, Nyeko Tolbert Yardin seemed moved and pleased with my prayer and asked that on a future visit I bring them rosaries. Again, since I did not want to commit to anything, I told him that I could not make any promises since we did not have rosaries in the parish and we rarely traveled because of the security situation. This request for rosaries once again brought back bad memories of the attack on the parish, during which they took all the rosaries in the house, some of which had engraved pictures of John Paul II I had bought in Rome when I went for the beatification of two of our catechists in October 2002.

As we boarded our vehicle and left the rebel base, I asked myself many theological questions on prayer. Why did these rebels value prayer? Did they pray to the same God as we all do? What did prayers mean to them? What did reciting the rosary mean to them if in the evening they lined up along the roads to shoot and kill innocent people?

Chapter Twenty-Three

The Peace Team Survives Death

This incident took place a week after my unexpected trip to the LRA camp. After our visit, the rest of the delegation returned to Gulu the following day and reported to their main offices that we had been well received and that a priest who was initially not part of the team accompanied them. This news inspired some in the office of the Acholi Religious Leaders Peace Initiative to finally physically meet the rebels, since they had for many years confined themselves to behind the scenes activities like arranging and attending conferences, conducting seminars on peace, and lobbying for funding to enable the organization to continue its activities.

The following Saturday morning, the program coordinator of the Acholi Religious Leaders Peace Initiative arrived in Pajule parish. He was a warm and outgoing middle-aged gentleman who was very enthusiastic about whatever he did. At times he talked too much. Formerly, he had been a national youth chaplain. He was full of excitement at the prospect of meeting the LRA for the first time. I wished him well and promised that I would prepare lunch for them. They went to the jungles and returned after three hours, which was normal for most face-to-face encounters with the LRA.

When the delegation returned, it was lunchtime and we ate with them. As usual whenever a group went to visit the LRA, there was always curiosity on the part of those who remained behind. At the table I kept on peppering the delegation with questions about their visit, but no one was willing to speak. I could sense that they were not their usual selves. When I looked at their faces and into their eyes, they appeared troubled. Whenever I brought up the subject of the visit, they looked at each other and did not respond to my inquiry. For the forty-five minutes we were at the table, no one in the peace delegation talked about anything connected to the visit. My insistence was not that the delegation share with me the substance of the meeting but rather the nature of the encounter and the demeanor of the rebels that they had met. This is because the contents of discussions with the LRA rebels were kept confidential and were only to be heard by those concerned. After lunch the delegation immediately left for Gulu town with the exception of the local chief, who lived in Pajule. The fact that the delegation did not say anything at all about their visit made me wonder what might have happened, and this intensified my curiosity.

In the evening I went into town to socialize with the people, and I ran into the local chief who had been part of the entourage that went to meet the rebels. Even now he still looked uneasy and in low spirits. When I saw him, I insisted that I wanted to know what had happened, and at that moment he chose to open up. He said, "Father, you the priests have good training. You are trained to tell when one is unhappy and troubled. We were almost killed by the rebels today." I was totally shocked to hear this. The chief went on to explain: "The rebels had instructions from their superiors to kill all of us this morning. The only reason we were spared and are alive is because our driver happened to be the brother of Nyeko Tolbert Yardin, one of the two commanders that we met." I could not believe what I was hearing. The chief told me that as soon as they reached Koyo Lalogi, the rebels talked to them very callously as if they had not met them before and accused them of collaborating with the government of Uganda to have them exterminated, contending that they ought to be executed right there and then.

Further, they also came out with specific accusations that the ceasefire zones the government had designated and the areas in which the rebels could assemble like Owiny Kibul, Lapul and Lagwara had all been infiltrated by government soldiers with land mines and booby traps set to blow them up. The rebels claimed that they had found empty beef tins strewn all over the ceasefire zones as an indication that these areas were constantly being monitored and watched by the government soldiers in an effort to wipe them out.

And they also said that the "spirits" had spoken and revealed to their leader, Joseph Kony, that the government was not sincere about the dialogue but was instead planning to eliminate them. According to the LRA commanders the delegation was to be executed as a result of its deceit and untruthfulness since they were colluding with the government to annihilate them. But above all, they were certain that the "spirits" would never mislead or tell them a lie. This execution would send a clear warning that the LRA could not be duped.

Two bizarre things took place that convinced the cultural chief that the LRA was bent on killing them. First, Nyeko Yardin showed a weapon to the delegation and asked them if they could identify to whom the gun belonged. The group had no idea. He told them that the gun belonged to a former LRA fighter called Waliki whom the LRA had killed almost two months ago. Waliki had abandoned the LRA and joined the government army, and his presence on the side of the government had become very helpful in reassuring LRA fighters who wanted to abandon rebel activity that they would be safe. In fact, Waliki had been killed at a place close to Acolibur together with five other people in an ambush on a passenger vehicle on his way to Kitgum. I remember meeting him on the day rebels surrendered at the parish at the beginning of my priestly ministry.

After Nyeko Yardin had showed them Waliki's gun, he warned the delegation that if they continued to insist on peace and dialogue, they would also die like Waliki, whom he accused of thinking that he alone could bring peace by abandoning the LRA.

The next thing that the rebels did was to order all in the delegation to surrender their belongings before the planned execution. The team gave up their watches, socks, and money. When they were about to be executed, Nyeko Tolbert Yardin, whose brother was the driver of the delegation, broke down and began to weep uncontrollably, saying that he could not kill his own brother. After he regained his self-composure, he canceled the orders for the execution. He said that even if there were standing orders for him to execute them, he was not going to carry them out even though it would mean that he would be punished by his superiors. When the chief shared all this with me, I was overwhelmed but not surprised because the LRA has always been unpredictable. I am certain that the accusation that the government of Uganda was collaborating with the cultural and religious leaders was totally false. The delegation genuinely wanted peace and cared wholeheartedly for both sides in the conflict. In retrospect, more than ever I believe that from the very beginning the rebels were not sincere at all when they declared a unilateral ceasefire.

I believe that the rebels had come to a point where they were fed up with pretending that they were interested in dialogue. After this encounter, contact with the rebels broke down and the security situation deteriorated very rapidly. I am now convinced that the two commanders, Nyeko Tolbert Yardin and Raska Lukwiya were based in Lapul sub-county at the time to hoodwink the Religious, Cultural, Military and Government leaders into thinking they were interested in peace. During this period the rebels advanced as far as Kumi District in eastern Uganda, along the way abducting and forcefully recruiting many youths into their ranks. In fact, they only lost their momentum when one of their commanders, Charles Tabuley, was killed in the eastern region.

Chapter Twenty-Four

My Tense Encounter with the Mayor of Pajule

One morning at ten a.m. at the beginning of the month of May 2003, I was informed by a catechist who was also in charge of the parish cemetery that the military were burying a returnee who had died in the barracks. Ninety percent of the burials at that time took place in the parish cemetery since most people could not use their family burial grounds due to the insecurity. This returnee had been in the barracks for close to one week without receiving any medical attention and had died from the injuries sustained while in LRA captivity. He had reported to the mayor of Pajule, who took him to be debriefed at the military barracks but did not make any attempt to get medical treatment for him. It was a regular procedure for all returnees to meet the military intelligence personnel since it was thought that some of them might be able to provide useful information.

On hearing about this death, I was struck with disbelief. I felt that there was no reason that any returnee who needed medical attention could not get it at Pajule Reception Center since it provided it free of charge. The emotions in me soon turned into anger directed toward the mayor of Pajule. I felt very strongly that he should have made arrangements for the returnee to get medical treatment following his debriefing at the barracks. He knew quite well that most of them were sick, weak, and exhausted on their return.

What was most painful and frustrating to me was the thought that someone had defied the odds by surviving captivity, escaping, and returning home, yet in the end died of neglect. Since I was filled with so much anger, I sat at my desk and immediately wrote a letter to the mayor asking him to come to meet with me as soon as possible. I tried very hard to hide my anger. However, I indicated that I had something important to discuss with him about the conduct of his office. It was unusual for me as an associate pastor to invite him, but since my pastor was away, I felt I needed to make him aware of the callousness and negligence of his actions.

As soon as the mayor received my letter, he got on his bike and in less than fifteen minutes was in my office. The speed with which he responded to my invitation took me by surprise. In Pajule things normally moved slowly; an immediate response could mean attending to something within one or two hours. He found me gathering my thoughts as to what I intended to tell him. I noticed that he was extremely tense, breathing very loudly, and his hands were trembling. On seeing him in my office, I became nervous and tried to calm down. I was afraid that if I did not, I would begin to shout at him, and this would not have done either of us any good. I invited him to take a seat and began to talk about issues other than what I had originally intended to discuss. We talked about the delayed rains, the insecure roads, etc. I guess that he must have been wondering why I had called him to come to the parish with a lot of urgency, and yet, I was reluctant to get to the point.

After about fifteen minutes, when the atmosphere in the room was more relaxed, the mayor himself indirectly brought up the matter by saying, "Father, as a spiritual leader in the community, you hear many things about the elected leaders of the people, and I would ask you to please bring to my attention anything you hear about me in regard to the shortcomings of my administration—or if you have any concerns and suggestions of your own, in particular things I could do better!"

In reply, I said to him, "The way you are running your office and conducting business as the mayor is my main concern and the reason why I have invited you here. Do you understand that because of your actions we have lost a life that could have been saved? I am very disappointed with you." He listened attentively to me and went on to tell me that he personally regretted the death that had occurred. He explained that because he did not want any problems with the military, whenever any returnee reported to his office, the first thing he did was to take that person to them. And so, he was following the established procedures at his office. I understood this point.

But when I asked him why his office or the army did not take the next step to make sure that the returnee received medical attention after being debriefed, he could not give me a good explanation. He told me that since he had delivered the returnee to the army, it was now up to them to take care of him. But I reminded him that he could not have left the person with the army since the returnee was a civilian and not a military man. Because I would not accept his explanation, he said that he regretted the fact that a death had taken place and he was going to reexamine the procedures in his office. I was certain something could have been done, since if returnees were critically ill, the military intelligence personnel normally debriefed them while they were getting treatment at the reception center on the day they reported or even much later depending on their health condition.

Finally, I asked the mayor of Pajule to provide me any information on the identity of the deceased. His answer was a complete shock to me. He told me that he did not have it. I found it hard to believe that an escapee from captivity could report to the office of the mayor and there would be no documentation. My desire was to trace the family of the deceased and inform them of the death of their loved one. But I guess that the mayor was afraid that if he gave me these details, he would indirectly be keeping the matter alive and get some of the blame for the circumstances surrounding the death. When I tried to follow up the subject of the identity of the deceased with the military, they were equally unhelpful. They told me that they did not record the name of the deceased since they were interested only in military matters.

I felt that as community leaders we had failed in our obligation to take care of the deceased. It went against all my basic cultural and religious beliefs about the dignity of life, that when it comes to saving human life, we fight for it, whatever the cost especially if we can. Death only grabs and violently snatches someone away from us. And I also felt a lot of pain for the many families who had lost loved ones in the war who would never have closure since they would never know what happened to their son or daughter.

I came to understand much later that World Vision, a Protestant-leaning nongovernmental organization (NGO) was at the center of this. This NGO at the height of the conflict in 2002 had tried to open a reception center for returnees in Pader town but could not sustain it. Pader District was too insecure for their social workers to live in. They were open to working in the district, but they did not want to take daily risks of being shot at or killed. And they did not have a supportive structure like CARITAS which had the Catholic Church. In fact, many NGOs at the time had explicit instructions from their headquarters not to travel to Pader because of the insecurity.

Most NGOs get funding from donors if they can show that they are providing services to the people on the ground. The immediate need at the time in Pader District was the provision of services to returnees since most humanitarian activities had come to a halt. World Vision could easily raise money from their donors for this, but they had to demonstrate that they were actually doing the work. The problem at hand for them was how to get returnees, the majority of whom surrendered in the area of Pajule, which was the most insecure part of the district and where most of the rebel activities took place. Returnees could report to several places like the office of the mayor of Pajule, the mayor of Lapul, the traditional chiefs, Pajule parish, and the army. Through their connections in Pajule, World Vision made arrangements with some of the local leaders in exchange for some "facilitation" to take the returnees to the military barracks in Pajule, from where they would transport them to the military headquarters in Acol-Pii and eventually to their facilities in Lira.

On paper, it appeared to be a good arrangement. But the problem with their plan was that there were no provisions in place. In Pajule barracks where the returnees were received, there were no first-aid kits or any medical drugs. The returnees were kept locked up in an empty room without any furniture, and sat and slept on the cement floor. And above all, there was no food, and the military trucks that were to transport them rarely came.

Even if little immediate good came out my discussion with the mayor of Pajule at this particular time, I believe that I succeeded in making him aware of my displeasure with his administration, and we committed ourselves to work together in the future to save lives. I was unable to track all the places to which returnees were sent on their arrival, but after this incident, I did not hear of the death of any returnee as a result of neglect. At a personal level, I began to develop a relationship with the mayor and could count on him in the months to come whenever I needed the participation of the local leaders. As a young priest and a leader, I learned that confronting an issue head on or talking with the person concerned face to face is worth trying rather than going around him or her, because some good may come out of it.

Chapter Twenty-Five

An Invitation I Cannot Forget

One of the most moving and trying occasions I remember was the request that came to me from a catechist who was dying at the end of the month of May 2003. This was a young man that had followed the family tradition of serving as catechists. Like his own father, he was now the catechist and head of the chapel at Alim along Kitgum-Lira Road. For close to four months, he had suffered from liver complications and his health had steadily declined.

One morning, he sent someone to inform me about his declining health condition, which I was unaware of. He needed to be anointed since the medical doctors had told him that there was not much more that they could do to keep him alive. The distance from Alim to Pajule parish was a drive of about only twenty minutes, but it was terribly risky because LRA rebels were along the roads. The messenger of the catechist was a friend of his since childhood. I was surprised to see him in my office very early that morning; he had left Alim on his bicycle at dawn coming to Pajule with no security guarantee at all. His only hope was that by riding a bicycle he could travel silently and not alert any rebel soldiers. He told me that the catechist of Alim had one request, that before he died he would like to receive the sacrament of anointing of the sick.

This request was a very big challenge to me. The road to Alim was very risky, as for close to two months LRA rebels had attacked, abducted, and killed those who traveled on it. My gut feeling was to say that I could not go to Alim since the roads were very unsafe. Within myself I debated about how much damage I would do to his faith if I were to tell him that I could not go, since he had demonstrated how selfless he was. So, I told him that I would consider all options and thanked him for bringing such an important piece of information to me. When he left my office, I continued with my internal debate.

As I agonized on what to do, what kept on coming to my mind was the nature of the request. The sacrament of anointing of the sick is at the heart of my ministry and identity as a priest. Since I was the only priest in the area at the moment, I was the only person who could do this for him. And the reason why I was taking the risk to be in the parish was because I wanted people to have access to the sacraments of the Church.

I asked myself, *If my personal safety has become my primary preoccupation, why should I keep on working in such an insecure place?* I also reflected about how much the family of the catechist had done for the Church; his own father had retired from the same job a couple of years back. I felt very strongly that if I took the risk and anointed him, it would be an act of gratitude by the Church for his service and an expression of solidarity as well.

As I considered traveling to Alim, I focused my thoughts on the priestly duty I had to perform instead of the fact that I could fall into a rebel ambush. I convinced myself that whatever happened along the way, good or bad, God would take care of it since I was not going on personal business. So after this internal debate I prepared to go to anoint the catechist. What I did first was to call the parish staff and workers who had reported for duty that morning and brief them on what I intended to do since I could not predict what was ahead. There were so many people in Pader District who left home to begin a journey and never reached their destination or returned home. I told them of the urgent request that I had received to go to anoint the catechist of Alim and my intention to travel there even if the roads were risky. Most of them looked surprised and puzzled at first, but when I told them about the health of the catechist they were understanding and supportive as well.

Instead they asked me how I felt. Since there was no way of telling how risky or safe the road was, we always relied on our instincts and feelings. I told them that I felt peaceful and calm, and that I believed that I would be able to travel to the place and return safely. If I had told them that I felt anxious or worried, they would have advised me not to travel that day and wait for another day. Then all the staff and workers said a prayer with me and blessed me individually, assuring me that I would be safe along the roads since I was going to do God's work.

After the blessing, the challenge that I had now was to select a means of transport. I could not use a bicycle since I was not physically fit and it would have taken too long. I had to choose between using a motorcycle and driving a truck. I did not want to use a truck because the roads to Alim were dirt, and moving in a vehicle would create so much dust that the rebels would see me coming from a distance and get a chance to run to the roadside and lay an ambush. And the noise of the engine would also alert them that a vehicle was on the way.

So, I rode my motorcycle since it produced less sound and would raise less dust as I traveled. I also put on my white cassock to minimize my chances of being shot at. I believed that identifying myself as a priest would make a rebel soldier think twice before firing at me. If the rebels wanted to shoot me, I intended them to know that they were killing a man of God.

I left Pajule at eleven a.m. moving very slowly to Alim, since I did not want any rebel soldier to have as an excuse for shooting me that I was riding very fast or trying to escape from them. Within my heart I felt that if the rebels were along the road it was better for them to stop me. Because Alim was not very far from Pajule, within thirty minutes I reached it. There was total silence along the roads; I could see spots where ambushes had taken place, but there were no signs of life at all. Even the birds that commonly filled the air were nowhere to be seen. My arrival was a surprise to the people at Alim since they had been cut off from Pajule, but they were also happy that I had come and brought the sacrament of anointing of the sick to the catechist.

When I reached the home of the catechist, he was overwhelmed and started to weep. This was very moving to me, since in the local culture men are not supposed to cry. The catechist cried not because of his health condition but because of the love I showed toward him and the risk I had taken for him. Since the journey had made me very tense, I focused on what took me to him, and we went to a separate room where I counseled him. When I was about to anoint him I invited everyone to join me in praying with the catechist and then I anointed him, granting him his final wish.

After the anointing, I immediately returned to Pajule parish. Fortunately, there was no incident. The catechist passed away a month later. But this is an invitation that I will never forget.

Chapter Twenty-Six

Orders to Kill the Priests

One evening in the middle of June 2003, after our night prayers and supper at eight p.m., we two priests in Pajule parish went immediately to bed. Before falling asleep, my pastor always had the practice of putting on his radio at a very low volume to listen to some world news before falling asleep. However, that evening, he listened to the BBC report that the Ugandan Army had intercepted a communication from the LRA High Command in the South Sudan instructing the LRA fighters in Uganda to kill any Catholic priest that they would come across in the archdiocese of Gulu.

Since my ordination almost two years ago, no other priest had been ordained, so we were sixty-one priests being targeted. When my pastor heard this grim news, he immediately came knocking on my door so I could come and listen. This information was also being reported by the Voice of America. What we heard made both of us very nervous. We wished one another a safe night and promised that we would discuss the news report in the morning. We were always aware that we served in a very risky place, but this rebel threat put the spotlight on us. We felt that we could not take it lightly because our parish was at the epicenter of the conflict since most of the other Catholic parishes in Pader District had closed. The two previous deaths of priests who had worked in the parish weighed heavily on our minds as well.

The following day we woke up and tried to see what our options were. We had basically two choices. The first one was to pack up our things and leave the place. The second was to continue working and make new security arrangements.

As we agonized on our next steps, my pastor was firmly of the idea that we should move out of the parish as soon as possible. He was of the view that we could return once in a while and conduct Masses and administer sacraments when we considered it safe. At the parish we had two vehicles in running condition that we could use to flee to Kampala or to Gulu. Kampala was almost three hundred miles away from the conflict area and would give us a moment to rest from all the violence. However, this option was not very practical to me since it would require money to live there. Pajule parish was a very poor parish since financial support toward the Church was less than five hundred dollars a year, and the priests of the archdiocese are not paid a salary.

The second option was to go to Gulu, where the headquarters of the archdiocese was, and stay in one of the parishes or institutions. But this did not make any sense to me since that place was not safe either. A week ago, I had been in Gulu and spent about two weeks at the archdiocesan seminary high school on a solidarity visit. The LRA rebels had recently abducted close to forty-one seminarians. Evenings in Gulu and the surrounding areas were as tense as in Pajule since the rebels roamed at night and committed atrocities. Personally, I also had real misgivings about going to Gulu, as I believed that after a few weeks we would become the target of unwanted attention and begin to appear like shepherds who had abandoned their flock. This was because those who would be hosting us were also experiencing the same level of insecurity and threat to their lives as we were, but on their part they were persevering and making sacrifices to be present at their stations of duty.

However, as we thought of what to do, a factor that complicated our deliberations was the community of the religious sisters. At the parish we had four nuns who ran the school. If we, the two priests, were to flee from the place, we could not leave them behind, so whatever decisions we were to arrive at had to factor them in. As we discussed what to do, we made sure that the head of the nuns came to our meetings. These nuns were a very important pillar to the community; they were teachers who ran one of the two remaining elementary schools still operating in town serving close to 1,500 children; if they were to move out, there was a real possibility that everything would come to a halt.

What to do became a big bone of contention between us. We wanted to continue serving the people, but at the same time, we needed to avoid taking stupid risks while working in Pajule. Throughout the insecure period in Pajule, the principle that guided me all along was that I would only leave the place if the rebels were looking for me personally to eliminate. If my hardships were basically a sharing in the hardships of the community as a whole, that was not a sufficient reason. This threat on our lives met my criterion, but I was not for the idea of leaving the parish. I believed that we did not have any good options even if our lives were directly threatened. I was opposed to the suggestion that we periodically travel back to the parish to lead Masses and administer sacraments because this would keep us constantly traveling on the roads and make us more vulnerable to LRA attacks. I was also convinced that if we were to leave the parish, there was no guarantee that there would ever be a time when we could say that the place was secure enough for us to return. To me the insecurity and constant threats that the people and the priests lived in was now second nature, and there was no prospect that it would come to an end soon.

Further I considered the impact of the priests and the nuns leaving Pajule parish as being devastating to the community. For almost eighteen months the strength of the community had been based on the Church and the fact that one of the two priests was always present in their midst. It was also my firm conviction that God was the only one who always protected us from the dangers of working in Pajule since the army had failed several times. However, since the attack of January 23, 2003, they had also learned their lessons and become more vigilant and deployed around Pajule on a twenty-four-hour basis. I believed we were safe within the town. Personally, I also felt spiritually and theologically challenged by the situation we were in, and I continued to ask myself if I ran away from the parish, how could I ever ask my congregation to have faith and trust in God for their security? What kind of credibility would I ever have as a shepherd among them?

This was something that created some friction between us, the two priests. We could not agree on what to do to take care of the people and our own lives. My pastor was firmly for the idea of periodically returning to the parish while on my part I was of the idea that we should stay in the parish but that security be beefed up by having more soldiers assigned specifically to protect the place, and this view was supported by the head of the nuns. Because we could not arrive at an agreement, we consulted the diocesan authorities in order to give us some ideas about what to do.

When we called the deputy of the bishop, he told us they did not have any directives for individual parishes and it was up to the priests and their communities to take the necessary precautions. We did not get any clear guidance on what to do. So we resolved to write a letter to the military authorities in Pader District headquarters, requesting them to beef up security around the parish. We spelled out the threat on us and stated clearly that without a guarantee from them to provide us with additional protection, it would be a stupid choice on our part to continue working in Pajule parish.

After writing our letter, we went to Pader District headquarters to hand deliver it. The journey was very stressful because the road had been cut off for several weeks as the rebels constantly abducted travelers on the way. Because it was during a wet and rainy season, the roads had become very bushy as well. Tall grass had grown on both sides of the road, and in many places the top of the grass leaned across the road and we could hardly see more than fifteen meters ahead of us. We traveled separately, the pastor in his truck and me on my motorcycle, because we did not want both of us to be blown up or killed in the same truck. As we made our journey, I was afraid that at any moment a rebel soldier would jump out of the bush and stop us since the truck had to move very slowly because the grass was so thick. At certain spots it could have broken the windscreen, while on my part the tall grass kept piercing my body and face.

On reaching Pader town, we met the political and military leaders, who were very understanding. They immediately held a security meeting and resolved that they would now assign a specific number of soldiers to protect the rectory and parish premises in addition to the protection that the parish had as part of the town as a whole. That very evening we saw several soldiers stationed specifically to protect the parish. This was a great relief to us. The civil and political leaders in Pader did not want Pajule parish to be closed since they knew how important our presence was to the whole community.

Around this time, I also learned that hardship in wartime builds strong bonds in the community and brings the people closer together. In Pader, we had to unite to survive. Political differences and rivalries were often put aside in the interests of serving people and collective survival.

Because of this direct threat on us, we now had to reduce our travels outside Pajule to the minimum. So long as we were within Pajule, which had a radius of three miles, we felt safe. But occasionally we were to attend to the chapels outside this area. By this time the majority of the chapels had been closed, and most of the people had assembled in Pader town and Acolibur chapels. These places had close to thirty thousand people in each of them, and once in a while we had to take the risk to go to minister to them. Whenever we traveled to these chapels we put on our clerical shirts or cassocks because we thought that it might make the rebels think twice before attacking us since we were doing God's work. When we had not visited a chapel for a number of weeks or months, we would have someone come to us on foot or on a bicycle informing us that the Christian community would like to receive the sacraments. Usually, the people wished to receive the sacraments of penance/confession, the Eucharist, and baptism. If we took two to three months between visits to a chapel, we would have close to seventy to one hundred babies to baptize in a particular Mass.

This is an area I will always be proud of and grateful to the people that I worked among for their patience, understanding, and flexibility. There were numerous occasions when I prepared a program for baptisms in a chapel, and several families would prepare for it and the social celebration. However, I would then wake up in the morning planning to perform the baptism and learn that the road was insecure because rebels had been sighted in the area, or at other times I suddenly felt nervous and afraid as I was about to set off to a chapel and I canceled my trip abruptly. Because there was no way for me to inform the congregation that was expecting me, they would wait for hours, and then at a certain point the catechist at the chapel would make the judgment that I was not going to be able to come that day and he would conclude the day with a prayer service and later come to the parish for us to set a new date for the baptism. Whenever I canceled spiritual programs, the people did not complain but understood that my safety came first and that I listened to God's voice in me.

It was when we had taken steps to have the security around the rectory boosted that I received a memorable letter from my sister Silvia, the sixth born of the nine children in my family. Because I am the firstborn and began boarding school when she was three years old, I did not have as deep and as close a relationship with her as I wished. Silvia wanted to update me about what she was doing in Kitgum, as she was looking forward to starting college that coming fall semester. She also wanted to hear from me how I was taking the threat of the LRA rebels to kill the Catholic priests. This is what she wrote:

"Father Robert, we heard the news that the LRA rebels have ordered the killing of priests; hearing this made me deeply troubled and worried about you. I want to know what you have made

of this news. Remember, Father, I will always be praying for your safety and that of the other priests of the Archdiocese."

Her concern and love expressed in this letter moved me very profoundly because she was the only one who related to my anxieties, insecurities, and need for spiritual and emotional support at the time. I wrote back thanking her for her letter and her prayers. I also informed her that we were fully aware of the threats against our own lives as priests, but that God had been protecting us in our work. I promised her that I would avoid taking any unnecessary risks.

In fact, working as a priest in an area of danger put a lot of pressure on my family. Whenever they heard of an ambush along the roads, an attack on a parish, or even Pajule being raided by the rebels, they were always thinking of my safety. I remember the best advocate for me to God was my mother; she would always say one rosary daily for my safety. Even if Kitgum where my parents lived was just forty-five minutes away from Pajule parish, because of the insecurity I often spent six to nine months without visiting them.

All in all, I do not have any doubts that the army heard the rebels issue a directive to kill the priests, but we may never know the reasons for this threat. We were gravely shaken by it, and we could not take it lightly since the LRA had a record of violence against Church personnel. However, I also think that the threats against the priests could also have been a tactical move on the LRA's part to sow seeds of panic in the Church, since most people at this time depended on the Church. If they had been able to put the priests to flight, they would have won a psychological victory over everyone involved.

Chapter Twenty-Seven

Some Hope for Those in the Camp

In May of 2003, a form of dysentery and malaria started in the camps, and many young children started to die deaths that would have been preventable in peaceful times. Previously, they could have been taken to the hospital in the neighboring district of Kitgum. There was a temporary government hospital in Pajule, but it had no medicine or drugs, nor was there a laboratory to perform any medical tests. Until now, whenever I dealt with the people in the camps, my focus had been very narrow and strictly focused on spiritual and religious issues since that was my area of competence and comfort. But this was soon to change as thousands of displaced people settled on parish land, and whenever a family member passed away they buried the deceased in the parish cemetery. Around this time, the number of child deaths dramatically increased. In previous months, one or two children had died every two weeks. However, by the middle of June 2003, four or five children died in the camps on a daily basis. I remember on one day I had seven infant burials. This was one of the most depressing days of my life. Because of this I made up my mind to do something about it. Whatever hat I had to wear to make it happen, I would. I felt that it was time for me to mobilize the civil society, political and cultural leaders to address the plight of the little children.

However, I found it very frustrating when I began to talk about the high infant mortality rate to the politicians and local leaders, most of whom were unaware of the gravity of the situation and therefore did not see any urgent need for action. The first thing I had to do was to convince them that there was a real problem. I was also surprised that it was only at Pajule parish that we had a detailed report of the high infant mortality rate, since we kept records of all the child deaths and burials that took place in our cemetery.

The sad fact was that the high frequency of deaths in the camps had become routine, even normal to most people. Also, many of the community leaders lacked a clear sense of priority since there were so many needs to address. Further, one of the lessons I learned from living in a war zone was that people tended to get disoriented and expend most of their efforts on personal survival.

Even though I had a strong desire to do something for the people, one of the very first challenges I faced was getting into contact with those who were influential. I knew well that there were humanitarian organizations, both local and international, that wanted to help the people in the camps, but because of security concerns they could not come to Pajule. Further, I knew that no medical doctor would agree to work in Pajule since two of them had abandoned the place in 2002 for safer locations and better pay.

To convince humanitarian organizations that there was a need for them to intervene in the camp situation in Pajule, I needed to present to them a detailed and convincing report on the situation. Because there was no one apart from myself who had the ability to do this I had to teach myself how to write a project proposal and how to compile and design a statistical report. This was an interesting experience for me. During the many years I was in school, I did not like dealing with numbers, figures, and charts. But this time, there was no other way since it was the only means I could use to make other people understand the tragic situation.

I requested the local leaders who were in charge of the different sections of the two camps to compile additional data for me regarding the most recent deaths in their jurisdictions. Some of the leaders responded immediately and provided me with all the information I asked for; I had to work harder to hear from others. After I had all the information I felt I needed, I invited two local health officials, one being the clinical officer who worked at the government hospital that did not have drugs, since they understood the plight of the people much better and knew the kind of drugs the community needed. I also invited the mayors of Pajule sub-county and Lapul sub-county. These mayors were technically called local council III chairpersons. In early 2002, the town of Pajule had been split into Pajule and Lapul sub-counties depending on which side of Kitgum-Lira Road that one lived.

This gathering was a great learning experience for me and broadened my perspectives since it made me understand what was really happening. In fact, it marked the beginning of a constructive relationship and engagement with the local politicians, and at a personal level I experienced the strength of the civil, cultural, religious, and political leadership when it chooses to collaborate in the interests of the people. The two health officials and the mayor of Pajule sub-county turned up for the meeting at the parish, but the mayor of Lapul sub-county did not show up. With the statistical data I had compiled, in three days we were able to come up with a budget for the medical needs of the camp dwellers for a three-month period. I also drafted a cover letter. It was my hope that the two mayors and the clinical officer in charge of Pajule Dispensary would sign the letter, and if there was a need, I was willing to do the same since I believed that it would give it more credibility. When it came time for the letter to be signed, what surprised me most was that the clinical officer refused to. This was a red flag; I felt that something was happening that was not right. I wondered why this man was not willing to commit himself to this project we had worked together on for the last three days since he understood the medical needs of the place much better than any of us.

However, this little setback did not deter us. Instead, the mayor of Pajule and I signed the letter, and we made sure that the mayor of Lapul sub-county also signed it. We then distributed copies to several humanitarian organizations. Within weeks, we began to get positive responses from different quarters. Some wanted to donate medical equipment. Others wanted to send people to do needs assessments, but their headquarters and country offices would not allow them to take the risk.

It was from these responses that I received one of the greatest shocks of my life. Among the many organizations that we had appealed to was an Italian organization called AVSI (Association of Volunteers in International Service) that had worked in northern Uganda for decades. We came to learn that throughout the entire time of insecurity, it was supplying medical drugs for the people in the camps of Pajule and Pader District as a whole.

But in reality, what was happening was that the drugs were always sent to Kalongo Regional Hospital in Pader District since it had an airfield. From there they were sent to the district medical superintendent, who was resident at Pader District headquarters, and she was to see that all the different camps in the district received them. However, the district medical superintendent had a large network of "scavengers" around her, and when she received the drugs, they were diverted and sold on the black market. Her office took advantage of the insecurity, for she was well aware her activities would not be monitored by the donors because of the security situation. When she received information that there were questions being raised about the shipment of medical supplies to the camps of Pajule, she wrote to the CARITAS office, which had a station in Pajule parish, and any other organizations that were asking questions, stating that she could not send the drugs to the different health units in the district because of the security risks involved in traveling—and additionally her office did not have a truck to transport the drugs.

To address her concerns, through the director of CARITAS, we volunteered to provide a vehicle to pick up the drugs. We waited in vain for days, weeks, and months to hear from her office. Instead she went on the offensive, enlisting the collaboration of one of the local politicians to attack me and the Catholic Church, claiming that our primary reason for raising the issue of the lack of drugs was because I, the priest, had ulterior motives and wanted the Catholic Church to take over ownership of the government health unit in town. Their calculation was to change the subject by inciting religious polarization and suspicion so that the people would not talk about the drugs that were being stolen.

This diversionary tactic was a shock to me. More so, the local politician who was at the forefront of this distortion was a representative of the area in the district council, which is the US equivalent of the state senate, and half of the population that was in need of medical drugs had voted for him. Some of those who were frail and sick were his own family members! Even the religious division he was trying to sow in the place did not make sense, as he himself was a Catholic. Almost two decades ago, when he was seriously injured by a bullet that almost took his life, it was Pajule parish that cared for him. The Christian scriptures are full of stories about wickedness, but I believe that this man was truly evil.

This was a rude awakening to the world of local politics. I came to discover that the truth and good intentions were not always enough, since many politicians in the community had no heart for the people they were elected to serve but only knew how to position themselves on issues, to campaign, and to win elections.

Further, I also came to learn the reason why the mayor of Lapul sub-county often did not show up for the meetings. The two mayors were often quarreling over the market dues. When the sub-county was split, the local market was located in Pajule sub-county, which meant that Pajule sub-county continued to generate income from it. The mayor of Lapul wanted the revenues shared, but this did not happen, and it created bad blood between them. I had to learn how to delicately work with them in future joint ventures.

At the beginning of July 2003, when I was feeling really discouraged since I had prayed a lot and had drawn attention to the need for medicines in the camps and there was no concrete response, while I was contemplating how to respond to the attacks on the Church from the district medical superintendent, two German film directors came to Pajule on an exploratory visit. They were Oliver Stoltz and Ali Samadi, and they said they were interested in making a documentary film on child-soldiers. They wanted to see the area, identify a place in which they could live, and visit the reception center. These film directors were moved and touched by the hard living conditions in the camps, which had close to seven thousand babies.

These Germans asked if they could live with me at the parish on their return visit, and I told them that it would be fine with me. They were surprised by the speed with which I agreed to host them and the fact that I did not consider asking any payment. My acceptance to host them turned out to be a big blessing for the community.

On this initial visit I took them around and told them about the high death rates in the camps. The Germans were surprised to see the camp dwellers had almost no material possessions, and yet they were very happy people and wanted to share the little they had. On returning to their home country, they made appeals about the urgent need for medical services to save lives. Their request touched the hearts of the people in Germany. It was through the generous financial donations from Germany that CARITAS was able to set up a health unit in Pajule parish offering free medical services to all the people in the camps, beginning with the children, for the next three years.

This whole experience was like a miracle to the community. Within a month, we were able to end child deaths in the camp and above all relieve mothers of the worry of what they were to do if their children fell sick. This experience deepened my faith; I saw the hand of God at work. It was a long, slow, winding, and twisting road, but when one door of opportunity was closed by the district medical superintendent and the vultures around her, God created another opportunity through the film directors.

Above all, it was a learning experience for me. It strengthened my convictions on social action and collaboration with other public officials because my perception of what I could do for the people and how I could go about doing it suddenly broadened. From this experience, I came to the conclusion that however strong personal differences may be among political leaders, they must not deny the people service because that is why they are put in office. In the past I had focused primarily on spiritual issues in my work. But from now on, I became convinced that if there was a need in the community that was not being addressed, I would exert my power and influence for the good of the community.

Chapter Twenty-Eight

"Craziness in Wartime"

This incident took place at the end of July 2003. A common job for young men today in Acoliland is in the business of transportation via bicycles or motorcycles. This business is popularly known as *boda-boda*. It got its name from the means of transportation between Uganda and Kenya at the two border entry points of Malaba and Busia in eastern Uganda. For those who needed to travel from one side of the border to the other, a bicycle was a reliable means of transport. As passengers called out for the owner of a bicycle, they shouted, "Border, border," and several men riding bicycles would rush over, hoping to be the one selected to provide the ride.

At the beginning of August 2003, a young man in his midtwenties who was a *boda-boda* traveled from Kitgum via Pajule to Pader town carrying a passenger who had some business to perform at the district headquarters. Even if movement along the roads was still very risky, the transporters never stopped, since they needed to work to put food on the table. This young man had a safe journey to his destination, but on his return journey, he did not find a passenger to transport. And unfortunately, after he had left Pader and cycled for about ten minutes, he stumbled upon a large group of LRA rebels at Paiula, a place that the rebels often frequented. They stopped him, hit his head several times with the butts of their guns and metallic objects, kicked him in the stomach, and eventually stabbed him to death. This young man, innocent as he was, was killed in the most brutal and gruesome way. The rebels even set his motorcycle ablaze. As if these actions were not bad enough, they set up an ambush at the spot where they had killed him that lasted for a full week, waiting for family members or interested parties to attack and kill if they came to retrieve the corpse.

However, the government soldiers learned through an abductee who had escaped from the rebels that a man had been killed on the road and used military force to secure the area and retrieve the body. It was badly decomposed. They did not have a stretcher to carry it but improvised one constructed of thatched grass and dry wood, and requested that their headquarters in Pader provide a lorry for the body to be delivered to Pajule parish. The parish was at the forefront of humanitarian activities even if it had very limited resources, and also its relationship with the military leaders was good.

When the soldiers arrived at the parish, they found me in the middle of a meeting with my altar boys and liturgical dancers. I excused myself to attend to them. They informed me that they had been instructed by their commanders to bring a corpse to the parish so that arrangements could be made to contact his family to pick it up. I was sympathetic to their request, but unfortunately I had to tell them that we did not have any body bags or any facility in the parish where we could store a decomposing body. I advised the government soldiers to seek the help of the medical personnel at the government health unit in the town. I could see that the representative of the soldiers was not happy with my response. It seemed that he was thinking I was unwilling to help.

When the soldiers reached the temporary government health unit, they did not find anybody at work so they looked for them in the town. Unfortunately, when the health workers learned the reason why the soldiers were looking for them, they literally ran away and hid. I guess the primary reason was because they did not have any equipment to handle a decomposed body. The real government health unit was about fifteen minutes away on Pajule-Kitgum Road, but it had been abandoned several months ago because it had no military protection. One of the health workers should have explained to them what the real situation was. So the soldiers became angry and frustrated and returned to the parish, feeling that no one was willing to assist them.

What followed next I could not believe. As I continued with the meeting, a young man ran up to me and interrupted: *"Father, there is something urgent you have to attend to. I saw government soldiers lower a dead body at the entrance of the church and then leave."* I immediately stopped the meeting and ran to the church. As I approached it, I could see the army lorry covered in dust already almost a mile away. There I was face to face with the corpse, not knowing what to do or where to begin. It was swollen thrice the normal size of a human body. It had a terrible stench, and the face was unrecognizable. I could see that the body had been pierced in several areas, including the head, chest, and stomach. The fingers and legs were all swollen, but if someone had known the deceased before, it appeared there were some identifying marks.

A number of people had gathered, and I could see that a few of them were afraid of a dead body; most could not stand the sight of a badly decomposed corpse and its strong smell. Even though I wanted to take the body away from the entrance of the church, no one seemed willing to come near and give me a hand. Removing the body had now become my problem. I needed to withstand the stench and the sight alone.

Fortunately, as I was faced with this dilemma, my pastor arrived from Puranga parish and found me at the entrance of the church in need of help. We covered the corpse with a blanket and placed it in the back of his truck to take it to the abandoned hospital for the night. We were certain that we would not find any facilities at the abandoned hospital but we only needed a room to store the body. Our only concern was to prevent a wild animal from eating the dead body; however, we were confident that if we closed the doors tightly everything would be fine. At this moment a police constable and traffic officer, Mr. Onen, came and confirmed to us that he personally knew the deceased and would get his family contacts for our use.

We drove to the abandoned hospital and arrived there at six p.m. Fortunately we reached it safely. The rebels had recently broken down the doors, smashed open the windows, looted the remaining drugs, and left it in a general state of devastation. On the floor we could see broken bottles, glasses, and syringes. We were able to identify a room and carry the corpse into it while at the same time avoiding sharp objects. We placed the corpse in a room with a door that could close, even if the door handle was broken. We felt it was safe enough for the body to spend the night and left for the parish.

As we were returning to the parish, we resolved that if we could not contact the family, we would return the following day to pick up the corpse and bury it in our parish cemetery. Luckily that evening we were able to use a satellite phone and get in touch with his family. They were shocked by the news but had been expecting it, and assured us that they were resolved to pick up the corpse. I could sense their relief at the opportunity to bury him, since it gave some closure to the week of anxiety they had gone through.

After four months, I met the father of the deceased and I expressed my sympathy to him for the loss that his family had experienced. I wanted to know how he was doing. This is what he said to me: *"I am sad that I lost my son at an early age, but I am not the only person going through such a loss in this troubled land of ours. I would like his death to be an offering for peace in this land."* What struck me most was the total lack of anger and vengeance toward those who killed his son. This was a common attitude in families who lost loved ones during the war.

Chapter Twenty-Nine

My Appointment as Pastor of Pajule Parish

On August 4, 2003, I was appointed pastor of Pajule parish. My appointment was not something that either I or the members of the parish expected. According to long-standing tradition in the archdiocese of Gulu most of the priests who were elevated to the pastorate had to be ordained for five or more years and were much older in age. I received the news of my appointment when I had two weeks left before the celebration of my second anniversary of priestly ordination. It came at a time when the security situation was still bad and it was particularly unsafe to travel, and yet we two priests continued to also serve Puranga parish, which my pastor had been in charge of prior to being transferred to Pajule parish.

That day around noon my pastor returned from Gulu and told me that he had big news: *"Father, I have good news for you in particular; the archbishop has appointed both of us parish priests. You are to be in charge of Pajule parish and I will be in charge of Puranga parish once again."* I could see that my pastor was really excited for me to be given this opportunity. I just felt overwhelmed by the news. Seeing my troubled face, he encouraged me to take up the appointment since he thought that I would make a fine pastor, for I had run the place ably in his absence.

My appointment came as a great surprise. I had not thought of ever becoming pastor of Pajule since my bishop had explained to me the day before my ordination that he intended my appointment in Pajule to be for a short while. So, I expected to work in the place for a few years and then be sent to do further academic studies and finally be assigned to teach in a Catholic diocesan institution, where he felt my services and talents would be of greater use.

After about two hours, during which I had time to digest the news, my pastor told me that the bishop needed to hear from me to get my consent before the end of the day because without it the appointment would not take effect. By now I was leaning toward accepting the appointment. The tricky part was how we were to get back to the bishop, since we did not have any reliable means of communication. The radio-call had not been replaced, nor were we intending to replace it since that would only entice the rebels to attack the parish again. Both of us had cell phones, but there was still no cell network coverage in the town, so we had to drive to the town's "calling place" at Oguta. I believe this spot was accidentally discovered by a traveler who had tried to use his cell phone in the course of his trip. To communicate from this spot one had to go to a shrub, stand very close to it, and lean one's head against one of its branches. If one was too tall or too short, one would miss the exact spot where the network signal was. If the wind was blowing too hard and the leaves and the branches of the shrub were unstable, identifying the exact spot of the network signal became impossible. For the two of us it was not a problem since we had communicated from it on previous occasions.

When we reached the spot, it was quiet and there was no one around. My pastor called the bishop, who had just completed his siesta, and told him that I was ready to talk to him. Then my pastor passed his cell phone to me. The bishop asked me how I was doing and indirectly brought up the subject of my appointment. I was expecting him to ask me a direct question like "Father, I want you to be the parish priest of Pajule parish; do you accept the appointment?" But I was very surprised by the way that he brought up the subject to me. He said: "Father, the primary reason for me wanting to talk to you is: I am putting you in charge so that you will report directly to me." And that was all.

Since my pastor had already briefed me that the bishop wanted my consent, I accepted and told him that I was willing to take up the responsibility as pastor, and that I was confident that with God's help, his own, and that of the out-going pastor, I would be able to do my best. With his proclamation that I was now the parish priest of Pajule, I felt something like a crushing weight on me. The sensation was as if my pastor had taken the heavy load he was carrying on his head and placed it on mine. At the same time, I felt like it was not real; it was like I had been made a pastor too soon in my priestly career. I also wondered why the bishop communicated his intentions toward me so obliquely. If I did not already know what he wanted from me, I would not have been absolutely sure what he was talking about. Since this was my first experience at being given some real responsibility, I convinced myself this was the way people in authority communicated.

After we returned to the parish, we wanted to inform some of the people that I had been made the new pastor. We debated it among ourselves but settled on not informing anyone until we had a written document. I would have loved to spend more time with my pastor, but he had to leave that very evening to prepare for the Sunday celebration and take up his new assignment. Since we did not have any Internet connection or mail service in the area, I had to wait until the letter of appointment was hand delivered to me by someone who picked it up in Gulu.

My hope and plan was to announce my appointment on the Feast of the Assumption of the Blessed Virgin Mary on August 15, 2003, since on that day we would celebrate only one Mass with hundreds of people. As this feast approached, I got very nervous because I had not yet received the appointment letter. Two days prior to the feast, I finally received a letter from the bishop's delegate in charge of Kitgum Vicariate, Monsignor Mateo Ojara, who wrote about recent appointments including changes in Pajule parish.

On the Feast of the Assumption of the Blessed Virgin Mary, as expected, many people turned up for Mass. We started at nine a.m., and it lasted for three hours. At the end of Mass, I told the congregation that there was a special announcement for them before the final blessing, and I asked a member of the parish pastoral council to read it. First, he read of the transfer of the pastor of Pajule to Puranga parish. As this was being read, many in the congregation looked surprised, since my pastor had been in charge of the parish before. Then the announcer proceeded to read to the congregation that Father Robert would now be the new pastor of Pajule parish. When my name was mentioned, there was dead silence. Many thought that they had misheard. This information had to be read again. When they were certain that I was the one who had been appointed pastor, I saw an overflow of emotion in the congregation. Some of them began to sing; others danced, jumped up in joy, ululated, and thanked God aloud. I was touched and moved by this response, and I became teary-eyed.

This news was a great surprise to most of the parishioners assembled since they had not seen a thirty-two-year-old priest appointed pastor before. Their experiences with pastors in the recent past were of priests in their fifties and sixties. After the Mass, I noticed that there was still much excitement in the people. I could hear people say that God really loved them and the parish. It had never before dawned on me how intensely the community felt about me. I came to realize that during the two years I had been with them, they had come to see me as one of their very own. This was because throughout this time, if they were happy, I celebrated with them; if they mourned, I joined them; and when they were afraid and ran for their lives, I was also frightened like them and did the same.

When I had settled down into my new role as pastor, I paid a visit to the bishop to see what his intent was in giving me this new assignment. He told me that he was confident I could execute the responsibilities of a pastor, and that it was now time for me to put my creative ideas into practice. I thanked him for his trust and confidence in me and promised that I would not let him down.

Back in Pajule, I wrote a letter to the missionaries who had served in the parish before to introduce myself as the new pastor of the parish. I felt that my appointment was a historic event for me and for them. God had united us because of our common service to the Church in Pajule. Above all, what was more gratifying to me was that my new position gave me the platform to express it. In my letter I also thanked them for their service and told them that I was following in their footsteps and much of my work would be based on the foundation they had laid. I believe that the act of acknowledging the missionaries who had worked before me was significant since it renewed their relationship with the parish. It also made them feel recognized and appreciated since it indicated that the community had not forgotten them. My letter received a very positive response from them.

Chapter Thirty

A Narrow Escape

This was at the end of September 2003; we still continued to live in a time of uncertainty. The irony of life around this time was that at the center of town, life went on normally unless there were attacks by the rebels. Within a radius of three miles within Pajule town, there was some relative safety. But if we moved outside the town, the level of risk went up to almost 100 percent.

I had been invited to an urgent meeting at Pader District Headquarters, and there were documents I had to personally sign. By this time, most of the people who were displaced lived in three big camps: Pajule town, Acolibur, and Pader camp, and sometimes I was their spokesperson because nongovernmental organizations often wanted to hear from someone credible on the ground

The security risks in moving from one place to another were very clear, but we could not stop traveling. I had parishioners under my care that I could only reach by taking the risk to go where they were camped. There were also services not provided in Pajule town that forced us to travel. The bank and the hospital that served the people in Pajule were located in Kitgum. And if I was invited to a clergy meeting at the archdiocesan headquarters in Gulu, it meant that I had to take a risk.

Pader District headquarters was about fifteen minutes from Pajule. The roads were often quiet and lonely, and surrounded by thick bushes and trees. Most of the people who lived along the road had abandoned their homes because of the constant attacks by the rebels. Along the road to Pader, the most frightening spot was at Paiula. There were several natives of Paiula in the LRA rebel force, including a notorious captain called Guli, who knew the place quite well and often returned to his now-abandoned home village. The physical conditions of the roads were bad especially around Paiula. The roads had deep gullies created by the heavy rains, and there were huge rocks in the middle of the road because of the soil erosion. Further, road maintenance at the time was very poor, and because of this a vehicle or a motorcycle on reaching Paiula had to slow down or stop completely. It was at such spots that LRA rebels often laid their ambushes.

On the day I was to travel to Pader, I woke up as usual in the morning, said Mass, had breakfast, and got ready to leave. The previous evening as I received my invitation I had learned that in the morning hours, LRA rebels had been along the road at Paiula, abducting travelers until they were driven away by the government soldiers. But as I left Pajule parish for Pader, I was really nervous, and that was not a good sign. I met some people in Pajule town and told them that I needed their prayers since I had something to do at Pader District headquarters that I could not postpone, and yet I felt tense and my heart was beating very hard that morning. I traveled very slowly, hoping I would be able to stop and ask other travelers how safe the road ahead of me was.

Unfortunately, there was hardly anyone on the road. As I traveled, I passed through one of our chapels called Ogan, which is about a five minute ride away from Pajule town on the road to Pader. It was only when I had passed the chapel at Paiula which is half way between Pajule and Pader town that I saw an army truck that looked abandoned in the middle of the road. I wondered if the rebels had attacked it at dawn, but if any attack had taken place earlier I would have learned of it, and if it had just happened I would have heard gunshots.

The stationary military lorry in the middle of the road made me stop and contemplate my next move. As I wondered about what to do next, I saw two government soldiers come out of the bush and stand by the truck. In fact, they were guarding it. This gave me some reassurance that things were okay. I later realized that below the army vehicle were two army mechanics who were hurriedly trying to repair the truck, which unfortunately had developed a mechanical fault at a very dangerous spot on the road. There were many more soldiers who had taken up positions in the tall grass and bushes around to protect the truck in case of an LRA attack. Since I was confident that they were government soldiers, I felt safe.

When I reached the soldiers, none of them appeared interested in talking to me. They looked tense, indifferent, and even hostile. A hundred meters behind the army lorry, I saw two civilians I recognized, including one that I knew well since we were students at Alokolum Seminary in the early nineties and he was now an official at Pader District headquarters in charge of Community Development. When they saw me, I could see that both of them were relieved. They were caught up in the same dilemma of not being sure of what to do next. They were traveling to Kitgum for the weekend to be with their families. They had followed the military truck on their motorcycles because it gave them some peace of mind and also provided them with company. These two men asked me if the road behind me was safe. Their greatest worry was how to reach Pajule. I told them that I did not know if the road to Pajule was safe, but I had been able to travel without any incident. This vague answer was enough for them; they convinced themselves that since I was not harmed along the way from Pajule to this point they, too, would be safe. Because the army truck had traveled from Pader District headquarters and had been followed safely by the two motorcyclists, I also convinced myself that I could travel safely. I continued to ride through Labongo Olung, Apiri and Olworongur and reached Pader District headquarters safely.

As was always the case whenever I reached Pader District headquarters, I reported to the branch office of CARITAS. I met the coordinator and informed him that I had come to have a meeting with some district officials and I expected that the meeting would conclude in an hour's time. Then I left for the meeting.

At the meeting, the district officials kept on asking me about the safety of the road from Pajule to Pader since they had all heard that there was a lot of rebel activity on the road the previous day. I told them that I was able to ride through, but I could not tell whether the road was unsafe or secure. Many at Pader District headquarters had their families in places like Kitgum, Gulu, and other places; if the roads were unsafe, it made it almost impossible for them to be reunited with them.

After the meeting had ended and I had signed the forms, I met a military officer who was from Gulu town called Colonel Ogema. I had met him before, but this was his first trip to Pader District. He told me that the previous day he had ordered soldiers to clear up the roads around Paiula, which the rebels had made impassable, and reminded me that he was going to be in Pader District till the security situation had improved. He was nice, friendly, and upbeat, but his talk did not really lower any of my anxiety since I knew that without a permanent presence of government soldiers along the roads, it was just a matter of hours before the rebels would return.

Then I returned to the CARITAS office and met the branch coordinator. He was very warm and welcoming, and if I arrived at his office around lunchtime, he would always take me out for lunch. But this afternoon when he suggested that he wanted to take me out for lunch, I told him that I did not feel like eating since I was very tense and wanted to ride back to Pajule as soon as I could. In the local culture, it is bad manners to turn down an invitation to share a meal, since sharing a meal is an expression of brotherhood. Fortunately, the branch coordinator did not insist, and I left immediately.

As I left Pader, the roads were quiet. My worry was about how I would pass through Paiula, and about two miles before I reached it, I began to see bushes and grass along the roads on fire. I continued to proceed toward the flames because I felt that it could not be LRA rebels burning the grass since they would need it for camouflage. When I reached the spot where the grass was burning, I found that it was government soldiers who were on patrol, burning potential rebel hideouts. I waved to them, but none of them bothered to wave back to me; they looked indifferent and focused on what they were doing. On my part I did not bother to stop but just continued with my journey. I was dressed casually, and I believe that they did not realize I was the priest from Pajule.

After traveling for about three more miles between Ogan and Paiula, I met two young men in their early twenties who were riding bicycles going back to Pader. They were *boda-boda* cyclists, but they had no passengers. They had just passed the chapel of Ogan, and I waved to them and they waved back to me. Seeing these two men made me feel confident that I would now reach Pajule safely since they had been able to go along the road ahead of me and the parish was not far from Ogan. In fact, within less than ten minutes, I was back at home.

But when I reached the parish, a social worker at the reception center came to me. I could see he looked surprised and puzzled, and he began asking me how I had passed through Ogan. They had gotten reports in the past hour that LRA rebels were on the road abducting people. I told him that I had not met anyone in the area with the exception of two *boda-boda* men. Since I was tired and liked to have siestas, I went to bed to have some rest.

At around four p.m., I woke up and received information that two people who were riding bicycles on the road to Pader had been killed in a very gruesome way. They had been stabbed to death and an eyewitness reported that the spot on which they had been killed was drenched with blood. On hearing this, I felt a sharp pain in my heart. This was common whenever I heard bad news.

In fact, they were the two cyclists that I had met. They had traveled for less than two miles from the spot where I met them when they were pulled down from their bicycles and met their cruel deaths. I was horrified by this incident. For weeks, I did not know what to make of it. I was not mentally at peace at all. I wondered whether the rebels either did not see me or let me pass since they knew that it was the priest who often used a motorcycle. Or were the rebels just too late in coming to the roadside to lay an ambush for me? At a certain point, I made up my mind that it was not productive for me to worry and second-guess what could have happened to me; I needed to move on. I concluded that so long as I continued to remain here, I would be taking risks all the time, and so I needed to work as if nothing had happened.

All in all, this incident left me convinced that so long as God had a mission for me in Pajule, even if I came very close to being harmed or killed, I would still be safe. Instead of focusing on my personal fears, I needed to continue focusing on my priestly duties and God's work.

Chapter Thirty-One
The Rebel Attack on October 10, 2003

The LRA attack on Pajulc that took place on October 10, 2003, a day after the National Independence celebrations of Uganda, was the worst of all the attacks. That morning alone ten civilians died in town, nine rebel soldiers were killed in the fighting, a government soldier died of shock, and close to forty people were seriously injured. This attack took place at a time of relative quiet.

On the sixth of October, I used my motorcycle to go to Acolibur chapel. As I was leaving Pajule, I met a man called Oliri. He was very concerned about my safety because I was heading out of town. I told him that to minimize the risk of an attack I was riding a motorcycle, but above all, I needed to go to Acolibur since I had not conducted any baptisms there for almost one year and close to 250 children needed to be baptized.

Oliri was a funny man; he drank a lot of alcohol, and it was rare to meet him sober. He regularly came for Sunday worship. The congregation loved him because he amused them at worship especially the way he prayed to God since the prayers of the faithful were always said aloud. The spontaneous prayers that he said at Mass were often serious, direct, and with a touch of humor to the ears of many. I still remember very vividly one of his petitions after a full week of insecurity. Throughout that week we kept getting reports that the rebels were on their way to attack the town. Because of this there was so much tension built up that people began to run in panic whenever they heard any indication that the rebels might be approaching. Most people had become tired, frustrated, and fed up with the whole situation. So the following Sunday, Mr. Oliri communicated his prayers aloud as follows: "God, see what is happening to Your people now! Every day we cannot go to cultivate our fields, work, rest, or even sleep. All the time, we are on the run like wild animals and mad people. Save us from this situation." He concluded his prayer by saying, "Lord, hear our prayer." Whenever he offered such petitions, the congregation, which had been reverent, focused, and absorbed in prayer, would often burst into laughter because his petitions best expressed their sentiments and he put them across to God in such a direct way that none of them could ever do.

I traveled to Acolibur chapel located on Lira-Kitgum Road, which is a drive of about thirty minutes from Pajule parish, without any incident. In peaceful times, I would often go to this chapel and stay about three to four days in the Christian community, praying with the members of the chapel in the mornings and evenings. During the day, I would visit the sick in their homes, and after dinner the members and I would sit around a fireplace, tell stories, and conclude our day by reciting the rosary before going to bed.

This time, because of the intense insecurity, my pastoral activities were going to be very limited in scope. I was going to spend my time mainly baptizing the children and administering the sacrament of penance. And since I had been made the new pastor of the parish on August, 4, 2003, I wanted to visit them as their new spiritual leader and encourage them to continue persevering since so many of them had abandoned the place because of the war. My visit was very successful; I did baptize about 240 children and administered the sacrament of penance to hundreds of people.

In my message to the members of Acolibur chapel, I encouraged them to continue to be hopeful that God would intervene in their situation even if at the moment Pajule parish had the largest number of armed rebels roaming and committing violence and atrocities in the area.

I spent my nights at one of the shops along Kitgum-Lira Road that passed through Acolibur since the home of the catechist and the mud huts where I had stayed on previous visits were deemed too insecure for fear of an LRA attack. Before falling asleep, I listened to my radio. Around this time, the dominant issue in world news was the recall election in the US state of California and the controversies and accusations of alleged past transgressions against the Republican candidate for governor, Arnold Schwarzenegger, who eventually won the election.

On October 8, after spending three days and three nights in Acolibur, I returned to Pajule parish since the following day was the national celebration of the independence of the country. At the parish center, we always held the customary big celebration beginning with an open-air Mass that around nine hundred people would participate in. After Mass the social celebrations would start.

After the celebration of Mass, which was joyful and well attended, I joined the community of the religious sisters for the social celebration; however, as the day was coming to an end, a businessman and one of the local leaders called Pontiano, whose name many found easier to pronounce as Aponya, invited me to his home. This businessman's residence was located behind his commercial building, and he had invited most of the leaders in town to celebrate with him. I went with one of the nuns.

The evening was very interesting and exciting as well since almost all the political, civil, and cultural leaders in Pajule were present. What was striking about this evening was the fact that most of the men had come with their wives, which was not very common in the culture since men and women in the society tend to spend their social time separately. The extent of the celebratory atmosphere this evening could be seen among the polygamists (polygamy is legal and widely accepted in the culture), who had all their wives sit and dine together at the same table. At some tables, there were two or three co-wives. This was the first time I ever saw this happen, since from common knowledge and my life experiences, polygamous relations among the women are normally full of rancor and tension. But this evening, all of them appeared to be on their best behavior.

When I look back at this evening, I believe that it was providential for each of us. It was like God wanted each one of us to wish one another well and say good-bye to the other before what would befall the town the following day. At the party I sat next to Jimmy, the army public relations officer. I had been with him playing volleyball at the parish minutes before the attack of January 23. He came from the southern part of the country; he was a Munyoro by tribe and greatly loved his work and the people. Jimmy was good at networking with the people and at gathering information and did not have an antagonistic relationship with the locals. I had developed a good relationship with him. As the party continued, I asked him a question that I had not planned: "Jimmy, if the rebels were to attack the town tonight, what would the military do?" Jimmy did not give any answer at all to my question; in fact, he behaved like he did not even hear it.

Personally, I was always security conscious around days of celebration since the rebels often took advantage of any lax behavior. An attack on such an evening or early morning was a real possibility since the rebels often took it for granted that the people and the military were partying, drinking, dancing, and not paying any attention to their movements. Because Jimmy was also very conscious of the security situation, at seven p.m. he excused himself and left for the barracks. After ten minutes, the nun and I also left the party. I drove her back to the convent and returned to the rectory, planning to go to bed early since it had been a long day.

At around eight p.m., before I had gone to bed, I heard a single gunshot. I thought that it could have been fired by a tipsy government soldier, but what followed was very surprising and ominous since all the loud music coming from the town suddenly stopped. I heard soldiers shouting and ordering people to disperse and go to bed. This should have raised a red flag in me, but because I was very tired I ignored all the warning signs of danger and got in bed. We came to learn later that this lone gunshot was fired by an LRA rebel who belonged to a group advancing from the direction of Pader town. As he was approaching Pajule, he came across some soldiers on patrol, and in panic he fired into the air and ran away.

In fact, during the day an advance team of the rebels had already infiltrated the town, yet nobody including the security personnel was aware of their presence. Some who later surrendered confessed that they were at the Independence Day Mass celebration at nine a.m. We learned that in order for the rebels to blend into the community, they tried to appear like the youth and the men in the town; they had portable radios in their hands as they walked, they had kempt hair such that they would not become persons of interest, and some put on jeans and shoes so as to look like any of the other youths in town, while others dressed up in the most current fashions. And those who had weapons hid them in their portable bags. In fact, throughout the day they had been spying on the number of government soldiers in town, their activities and locations, what the civilian population was doing, and the shops they could loot in the course of the attack.

As soon as I went to bed, I fell asleep. The whole night was quiet, but at six a.m., I heard the first shots fired at the army barracks followed by a massive and savage assault. The rectory started to shake and vibrate, and my bedroom was filled with dust from the ceiling. Anything metallic in the house made noise: the iron sheets on the roof, the door bolts, bedsprings, and wall clocks. I immediately jumped out of bed and went to confirm that the doors were locked and reinforced. My running to check on the doors was an automatic response that always occurred when I heard gunfire. As I ran I feared that I would be hit by a bullet passing through the windows of the public bathrooms. That is why at a later date I built a wall inside the house to keep any stray bullets from entering the hallway.

Fortunately, all the doors to the house were locked and had additional metal bars to reinforce them. After I did this, I was very confused and shaken; I felt like the last attack on the parish in January was being replayed. This time, I was not willing to let them get me. I immediately got two chairs, placed one on top of the other, and climbed into the ceiling. The roof of the house was high, but I was able to hold onto a piece of wood and pull myself through the small opening into the ceiling. Within less than two minutes, I realized that this was not a good idea. The vibrations from the heavy gunfire were so strong that I could not stay up there. Since I was in the ceiling of the house, I also could hear bullets pierce and tear through the iron sheets that had been used to roof the rectory. There was a real possibility that a bullet could hit me, and if a shell hit the rectory, it would be fatal. What little protection I had was a pile of about three bricks placed one on top of the other.

After about three minutes, I made up my mind that it was not rational for me to keep hiding in the ceiling. I jumped down, ran back to my bedroom, and lay on the floor. After less than one minute I heard a chorus of people shouting and knocking on the parish door: "Father, Father, Father, open the door for us." This really frightened me. At first, I thought the rebels had broken through the defense lines of the government soldiers and were now in the compound of the rectory. But the voices I heard were of women and children, and this emboldened me to leave my room, enter my office and climb on top of a table to identify the people calling me. From the ventilator, I could see that they were unarmed and helpless women and children so I climbed down and let them inside while the firing continued.

It was the wives and children of the soldiers who had run from the barracks to the rectory. When the attack started, the soldiers instructed them to run to me at the parish. The trust they put in me that their wives would be safe was fascinating because I hardly knew those who were in the lower ranks, although on many occasions I visited their commanders. One woman had been hit by a bullet as she ran out of the barracks and died a couple of meters away.

When I allowed the women and children into the rectory, I told them to take any room that they felt safe in, and I went back to my bedroom and lay on the floor. As the fighting at the barracks continued, I kept worrying about Jimmy; I constantly wondered if he would survive the morning. Inside me it felt like he was the only one in the barracks. This is because the amount of firepower that the rebels unleashed on the barracks was so heavy I could not compare it to any previous attack.

This attack had started at six a.m., and by eight thirty there were no signs it was coming to an end. I was tired of lying on the floor, and by now fear had sunk deep into me. The LRA rebels generally ended most of their attacks after less than an hour. I was getting concerned that they might overrun the barracks, and if this happened their next target would be the parish. I went to the wives and children of the soldiers and told them that I needed to get out of the rectory since I did not feel safe anymore. Surprisingly, they did not ask me any questions about where I was going or object to my leaving the house. When I left, one of the women locked the door behind me. Culturally, during times of extreme danger, people respect what one decides to do so long as one's decision is not seen as too risky or stupid because at such moments individuals rely mostly on their survival instincts.

With the keys of the side door to the church in my hand, I went out of the rectory into the compound that had a wall surrounding it, where I met several bare-chested returnees, who immediately ran over and began to question me. They asked if the rebels had overrun the barracks, and I told them that I had no idea what was happening. Most of these returnees were in their early teens and had been at the reception center for less than five days; I could see they were gripped with fear. Some of them had just escaped from the rebels, who would execute them if they were to overrun the barracks and recapture them.

Since my intention was to go into the church, I climbed over the wall fence of the rectory, and many of the returnees followed me. I stopped and told them that I did not have a place to take them where I could guarantee their safety. I did not want them to follow me into the church, since it was a confined space. When I insisted that they should not follow me, they obeyed. I did not want a situation in which all of them could be massacred if the rebels were to break into the church.

When I entered the church, I knelt at the center with my back facing the wooden door of its main entrance; if a bullet were fired through the door, it could have struck me. I said to myself I would not change positions until I had completed my prayers since I felt that this was the best place to intercede for the people. This was my prayer:

God, this morning, as I speak to You, I do it as Your only servant and priest in the community. I am the only one among them with the special function to intercede on behalf of all others. I ask You to listen and answer my prayers as You did for the prophets of old in times of crises and great difficulty. The people in Pajule town and the surrounding camps whose lives are at stake now from the huge explosions and bombs blasts are innocent; please spare them!

When I had finished my prayers, I went to the sacristy I used to vest for Mass. This small room was connected to the sanctuary. Even in the church itself, I was still fearful, so I crawled under one of the tables on which my vestments for Mass were laid out and sat down on the floor. This table stood between two huge closets used for storing liturgical vestments. After spending about ten minutes under this table, I looked out through the window of the church. There was still heavy fighting going on in the town and the camps, but there was no fighting around the church or the parish compound. While on my knees, I could see the grave of one of the priests who had been killed in 2000 in the parish, Father Raffaele Di Bari. I felt that he must be aware of what was going on in Pajule this morning, and he must be praying for us. Then, I went back and sat under the table.

After about twenty-five minutes, I began to hear a strange sound in the distance. At first, I thought it was a military truck or tank, but I came to realize that it was a helicopter. When I was certain of this, I took a deep breath and gave a sigh of relief that God had answered my prayers. I was sure that with the helicopter overhead the fighting would not last much longer. When it arrived and flew over the parish and barracks area, the momentum of the fighting immediately changed in favor of the soldiers, as the rebels who had surrounded the barracks and were on the verge of overrunning it suddenly felt in danger of being bombed. Immediately, they began to withdraw from the area around the barracks, since it was in an open field. Within minutes I began to hear the firepower of the rebels lessen. As they withdrew, they set the houses in the camps ablaze, and the smoke served as camouflage for them. Interestingly, we later learned that the helicopter did not have any bombs attached, as it had left in great haste from a town in eastern Uganda called Soroti, which was a three- to four-hour flight from Pajule.

What Really Happened?

What happened that morning was that Pajule was attacked by hundreds of LRA rebels led by three commanders, Nyeko Tolbert Yardin, Raska Lukwiya, and Vincent Otti. Most of the rebels traveled on foot from the jungles of a place called Kalongo, which is a ninety-minute drive away, through the bushes to Pajule, and that is why we did not have any advance knowledge of their presence in the vicinity days before the attack.

As the rebels attacked the town at dawn, they divided themselves into three groups. The first group was to overrun the barracks, the second to abduct people from the camps, and the third was to break into the shops and loot supplies from the town. The rebels were able to abduct close to eight hundred people in the camps, men, women, and children, including a local chief, Ywakamoi.

One of the local chiefs who escaped abduction shared his story about what he saw during the fighting. He said that he looked outside through the ventilators of his house and saw dozens of people sitting outside the compound of the police station. He kept on wondering why they were sitting in the open when there was a lot of gunfire. In fact, the people sitting outside had been abducted. But at the moment, the traditional chief could not make this connection.

Around the barracks where the heaviest fighting took place, the sight was gruesome since nine rebel fighters had been killed, most of them having their brains blown out. Two government soldiers were seriously hurt, my friend Jimmy and Omaya, the army's informant. Most of the dead rebel fighters were grown men and physically well built with the exception of one who seemed to be in his early teens. As I inspected the dead rebel bodies strewn before the defense line of the barracks that morning, I kept on asking myself how much more advanced and better off our society would be if all these able-bodied dead men had used their energy for something more productive than waging war, let alone the fact that they would still be alive and with their families.

In my opinion, the attack by the LRA rebels on the army barracks was a very reckless move, and they seemed desperate to overrun it. As they advanced, the rebels were in an open soccer field with no vegetation for cover either above or below them. And yet the soldiers were in their trenches, so in order to shoot at them the rebels had to constantly stand up to fire, which made them easy targets for the heavy weapons that the soldiers used. As the fighting intensified, the rebels constantly hid behind the cows standing in their enclosures all around the trenches of the barracks. Most of the cattle owners considered the surroundings of the barracks to be the only safe place for their cattle herds. Fortunately, no bullet hit or killed any cow in the heavy fighting around the barracks. The reckless assault on the barracks caused me to wonder about the rebels' logic and seemed to confirm the popular belief that the LRA was not always guided by reason in what it did but by the conviction that it had a spiritual mission to fulfill.

I believe that if the troops had not fought hard, the rebels would have overrun Pajule barracks and the town. One of the army commanders called Paulo, who was stationed in Pader, rushed to Pajule in his truck with his escorts when he was informed the place was under heavy attack. When he was five minutes away from Pajule town and had reached a village called Ogan, he entered an LRA ambush. The rebels had placed their big support weapons along all the major roads leading into Pajule town to repel any potential reinforcements. The rebels fired at him, but fortunately Paulo was able to jump off his truck before the shot hit it. Four of his escorts died in the truck, and some had their limbs blown off so he singlehandedly engaged the rebels. He was lucky, as he was soon rescued and backed up by soldiers in a lorry that was following his truck.

Further, the actions of Major Nyero, an energetic and youthful military officer, were also very remarkable and courageous. He was stationed at Alim, about a twenty minute drive away from Pajule. The forces under his command literally ran on foot through the bushes to save the people in Pajule, and he himself came to a place called Lanyatido that was a ten-minute drive away from the epicenter of the battle. The forces that he commanded entered the town from the eastern side, and their arrival was timely because by this time the rebels had taken up positions surrounding the buildings in the area and were using axes to break into each house and were looting and abducting the people inside. When the soldiers began to fire at them, they stopped.

I was moved by the discipline of the government soldiers and their respect for the rule of law. After the fighting had come to an end, they brought a child-rebel soldier who had been hurt in the fighting to the reception center to be treated. This young boy was among the first group of rebels to fire at the soldiers and was hit by a bullet as he tried to jump over their defense line while attempting to get behind them. If the soldiers had killed him, it would have been easy for them to cover it up by saying that he died in the actual fighting. They could also have ignored the need to bring him for immediate medical treatment, since soldiers also get angry and hurt if they lose colleagues in an attack.

The civilians who died that day numbered about ten people. Many of them died in the crossfire since the rebels and soldiers fought in densely populated areas. It is surprising that many more people who lived very close to the barracks were not harmed because for nearly three hours, they lay on the ground and did not raise their heads even once, to avoid being hit by flying bullets.

It was around midday before we were able to establish the magnitude of what had happened. Close to forty people had been seriously hurt, and most were brought to the parish for treatment, though we did not have a medical doctor to attend to them, only a nurse with limited training. Some of the injured died on the doorsteps of the rectory since their injuries were too grave for a nurse to handle. That day as I entered the rectory, I could see human blood everywhere. Those severely injured were driven to Kitgum midmorning in the CARITAS truck, even though there was no guarantee that the roads were safe. All I could do was to pray and bless the driver of the truck and the injured before they left. Fortunately, they drove safely and nobody died on the way.

By around one p.m. we began to hear horrific stories from people who had escaped or were released by the rebels. They said the rebels had killed some of the abducted who were too tired or weak to walk. One of them was Mr. Lachum, who was lame and happened to be the secretary to the mayor of Pajule. Hearing such news was unsettling because we knew that many people had been abducted, and most were not used to walking long distances or were sick. And we were also informed that the rebels were very angry since a number of them had been killed, and the government soldiers had also captured one of their portable mortars, which they used as a support weapon in the attack. Because of these losses, they wanted to return and launch a fresh attack. The prospect of the rebels returning kept us in a state of constant tension.

After a late lunch at two p.m., I felt it was time for a siesta. But after about thirty minutes, I heard a lot of commotion and footsteps. People were running from town toward the parish and the rectory, and many of them continued to run through the parish into the bushes since they deemed the church compound to be unsafe. When I heard what was happening, I jumped out of bed, ran out of the house, and met a retired military officer called Major Ocan, a former mayor of Pajule, who was running inside the parish wall; he always found some corner to hide in at the parish when there was an attack. He told me that the rebels were coming from the direction of the town; indeed, we could hear gunshots coming from that way. I did not consider the parish compound to be a safe place, so I ran, intending to hide in the bushes surrounding Pajule College, which was about four hundred meters away on the western side of the parish. As I darted away, I caught up with a large group of people, including the three nuns in the parish who were all on the run. Reaching them, I asked everybody to slow down and advised them to listen first to the direction of the gunshots because we might run very fast only to fall into another ambush. When we reached the compound of Pajule College, we stopped to review the situation. Luckily, we soon came to learn that the rebels had not returned; rather, a government soldier who had drunk a lot of alcohol accidentally fired into the air, and in response to this single gunshot all the government soldiers started to shoot into the air from their various positions around town. Since the community was already tense, people panicked and began to run for their lives.

Most of the people who were abducted by the rebels were released after three days; it was a huge crowd numbering close to seven hundred people. They were tired, hungry, and sick. When they were to be released, the rebels informed the peace-contact person in Pajule that they needed to be picked up since most of them were unable to walk anymore. Several trucks left the town to get them, and they were brought to the parish where I led a Thanksgiving Mass. They were reunited with their families and friends at the parish. It was unbelievable to see how many people the rebels abducted; they seemed to number more than the people who regularly attended my Sunday worship service.

Chapter Thirty-Two
The Death Sentence

The attack on October 2003 was the most devastating of all the attacks on Pajule so far, and in its aftermath it generated the highest level of panic in the people I ever witnessed. After the fighting stopped, I saw hundreds of families boarding trucks and leaving Pajule that same day. Some of the social workers at Pajule Reception Center also packed up and left. The vehicles that transported people out of Pajule were extremely overloaded. I could see the fleeing people squeezed together and stepping on each other because there was barely space for legroom. And since there was hardly any room for property inside, it was tied to the outside of the vehicle and left dangling, and pieces kept falling to the ground. This exodus of large numbers from Pajule continued for almost one full week.

This was a very stressful time for me. All along I had maintained a very strong will to persevere and stay in Pajule, but this time I found that my determination was diminishing since there was almost no hope that the situation would ever stabilize. We had managed to live through the insecurity because we supported one another, so seeing hundreds of people leave daily was very demoralizing. Most left empty-handed with no money or means of survival. In the one and a half years since the insecurity had started again, they had used up most of their savings or consumed all the food in their personal food stores, as most of them were small-scale farmers who survived on what they cultivated.

Those who fled were going to a place called Bweyale, which is in the southwestern part of the country, about five hours' drive away from Pajule in a district called Kiryandongo. This place was peaceful since there were no LRA activities in the area. Many people had gone there to escape the war, but this new batch of refugees did not have any support system or a means to begin a new life, nor could they count on any humanitarian organization to help them transition.

In the mornings as I drove to town to watch those who were fleeing, I saw some of the town dwellers approach my truck to peep inside and see if I was leaving. For most of them, my fleeing the place would have been a sufficient reason for them to consider leaving immediately. Around this time all the priests of the archdiocese were invited to a clergy meeting in Gulu, but I could not go for fear that my actions would be misinterpreted as an indication that I had fled from the place, and cause widespread panic.

And if the tension in Pajule was not high enough already, four days after the attack on October 15, 2003, we received a very threatening letter from the LRA. At around ten a.m., a nun came running to tell me that the rebels had written to the people of Pajule, ordering me and the local chief, Ywakamoi, to leave Pajule immediately. This letter had been dropped near the community water well at Pajule primary school and was now in the possession of military intelligence. What she told me was indeed true. In the letter the rebels also warned that they would be returning to attack the place on October 25, and the civilians who refused to leave the place would be massacred in proportion to the mass killing in Atiak. At Atiak in 1995, in a single morning LRA rebels massacred close to four hundred civilians in cold blood.

This threat from the rebels spread like wildfire in the community; those who were leaning toward leaving departed within hours, and the following week many more fled. The ones who remained numbered close to twenty thousand and had neither the means to leave nor anywhere to go. This specific and concrete threat made our lives very difficult. Each and every day we counted the number of days we had left to live. I went to sleep wondering if this was my last night alive, and many in the community felt the same way. In the whole town, we all felt like we had been communally sentenced to death and were waiting for our execution day.

I did not doubt the rebels' threat because in the past, they had done terrible things to the traditional rulers and the clergy. At the same time, I saw the threat as a calculated move, since they were certain that the strength of the community was in the Church and the institutions of traditional cultural leadership. If they had succeeded in making us leave, they would have broken the two pillars of the community and psychologically scored a major victory since many people who were supposed to feel safe and protected would flee.

For almost two weeks on a daily basis, after I had said Mass and had breakfast, I would go to town to watch those who were running away. It was during this time that I feel I prayed the most as a priest. I felt a sense of helplessness and experienced an intense battle within me over what to do. But it also made me realize that I am a problem solver because I could not accept that the situation was out of our control. I believed that more could still be done, along with praying and hoping for the best. Fortunately, Ywakamoi, the local chief, was also determined to continue to live in the place, and this was a source of hope and encouragement for me.

In my prayerful reflection throughout this time, I felt deeply that this situation needed divine intervention on a large scale similar to what God had done for the Israelites when they were in captivity in Egypt. I rarely pray for miracles, but this time I prayed for one. I always told God in my moments of prayer and meditation that in His divine store, I was certain that there were many miracles, and I wanted Him to make one available to us.

My Visit to the Army Captain

One morning after I had spent about three hours at the center of town watching people leave, I went to see the military commander at the army barracks and have a talk with him. I believe this was around October 16 or 17. I felt that what the community needed most was a word of encouragement from him and reassurance that they were in control of the security situation. I wanted to suggest that the military organize a rally and address the people. I believed this would give all of us some peace of mind.

Personally I still had some hope that the soldiers would take charge of the situation since they were able to prevent the town from falling into the hands of the rebels on October 10. The army captain I went to meet in the military barracks was the person in charge at the time of the first major attack on Pajule on January 23 when the rebels overran the town. He was blamed by the local population for failing in his responsibility and was reprimanded by his superiors for it. He was from the southwestern part of the country and belonged to the Nyoro tribe, and had been in Pajule for over one year. He was a good man but reclusive, and his social skills were very poor. He had also failed to build trust with the local people. Part of his difficulty was cultural; he could not speak the local dialect. To me he was a man of good intentions, but hardly anyone in the community was aware of this. On his part he constantly complained that some people in the community were rebel collaborators and some did not want to work with him or would not trust him because he was of a different tribe. Both of his complaints had some truth to them. There were times when certain items were stolen or got lost in the community, and if the suspect was a soldier, many of the local leaders did not present the issue to him but took it to another officer who was a native working in Alim.

Personally, I had met him many times in the barracks and at social events, and I wanted to build a relationship of trust with him. On the evening of the attack of October 10, I remember that at the end of the day, I went with a social worker, Mr. Lakwo, and the area representative in the district council/state senate, Mrs. Rose Latoo, to acknowledge his effort and those of the soldiers under him who had defended and protected the town from falling into the hands of the LRA. We found that he had a slight cut on his arm from a bullet that hit it during the dawn attack. He was very gracious to us and greatly appreciated our solidarity with him and his troops. Because of my constant efforts to be in touch with him, he had developed a sincere relationship with me and was no longer afraid to talk freely. In a war zone, there is very little faith in each other, and people are constantly suspicious of others' intentions. I wanted him to know me as a real person, and I hoped that with the human relationship I had developed with him he could see my good intentions and in case of any looming dangers to the community he would feel comfortable enough to alert us.

When I visited the captain, I asked him if he was aware of the fact that most of the people were deserting the place. He told me that he had full knowledge of what was happening, but there was not much that he could do. I reminded him of how much the soldiers had done to protect the people in the last attack, but the challenge now was the need for more confidence building in the community. I told him that he or some of his officers needed to address the people in a rally since previous army commanders who had served in the place did the same in times of great crises.

I could see from his facial expression that he really appreciated the fact that I wanted a solution to the problem. Because of this he asked me a direct question that I did not expect: "Father, do you want to help me?" And I answered, "Yes, I do." Then, he went on to tell me that his rank was low in the army since he was only a captain. If he were to ask for reinforcements from the high-ranking officers at Acol-Pii, where the headquarters of the army in Pader District was located, they would instead admonish him and accuse him of panicking unnecessarily. He advised me that the best way I could help in this situation was to convene a meeting of all the local leaders in the two sub-counties and write a letter to the chairman of security in the district and send copies to the army leadership at Acol-Pii and our elected representatives in the parliament of Uganda describing the dire security situation. This suggestion profoundly excited me. I felt that God had opened a door for us, and this was something concrete that was within our power to execute. I could convene a meeting of all the leaders with great ease since I had a personal relationship with each one of them.

As soon as I reached my office, I wrote a letter inviting all the political leaders to the parish for an emergency meeting. I underlined in my invitation that all of them needed to come since I knew otherwise some of them would not show up because they did not want to meet with their political foes. We were also fortunate to have in our midst a freelance journalist, Mr. Oray. He had no formal training, but the national newspapers relied on him through their local weekly papers to get information on what was happening since it was too risky for them to assign any of their seasoned journalists to Pajule. This reporter was a great asset to our meeting because he had with him data and statistics on the attacks and deaths since the resumption of the conflict in 2002. The parish attendant hand delivered my letter to each one of them, and within an hour, all the local leaders had assembled in the parish.When I brought up the idea of writing a letter to the assembly, it was unanimously supported. We addressed the letter to the head of security in the district and copied it to all the relevant persons. In it, we talked about the latest attack on Pajule: the number of people who were injured or killed, the fear the attack had generated, the fact that many had abandoned the town, the real possibility that Pajule might be deserted, and above all the rebels' threat to return on October 25. As suggested by the captain, we stressed in the letter the need for more soldiers to be deployed in Pajule to give the people confidence, and if it were possible we asked that military tanks be assigned to the place because the rebels fought using light weapons and always avoided taking on army units with heavy weaponry.

Even though communicating with those outside Pajule was difficult, we were able to begin distributing this letter within hours to the intended parties. We tasked some from among us to hand deliver the letters to the recipients as soon as possible. I personally hand delivered the one addressed to the chairman of security, who was the deputy resident district commissioner at the time. After this, we waited for the political and military authorities to respond. And in fact, they were very understanding. They took the date that the rebels had threatened to return very seriously. On October 20, we saw about five hundred government soldiers who belonged to a mobile unit—that is, the military unit that constantly pursued the LRA in the bushes—arrive and camp in Pajule to wait for the deadline the LRA had set to return. There were so many soldiers in the place that the local market ran out of items for them to buy.

Two days later, on October 22, two military tanks arrived in Pajule midmorning. We could hear the sound of their engines as they advanced and there was huge sigh of relief from the people. The residents came out of their houses and lined the streets like they were welcoming a dignitary to the place. At particular hours of the day, the two tanks were driven through the town, and seeing these tanks was psychologically very comforting. Many who had not had any real rest since October 10 could now get a full night's sleep once again.

October 25 came and passed without incident. If the rebels had kept their promise to return this time, they would have sustained more casualties. The government soldiers had the weapons they needed, and their numbers were high. This team effort between the local political leaders and the army commander to beef up security strengthened the relationship between the army and the people. The two for the first time felt that they all had a common interest in working together and promoting peace.

Above all it made me develop a personal philosophy that as a Church leader I needed to develop constructive relationships with all community leaders. I needed to recognize what they do for people and that there is so much power in a community when it speaks with one voice through its political, cultural, and religious leaders. I believe that good politicians and Church leaders who care can serve people without being at loggerheads all the time.

The community also experienced the wisdom and truth in one of its cultural sayings: in unity, there is strength. Through its leaders, the community spoke with one voice, putting aside its differences to compel the military and political leaders to act on the plight of the people.

Personally, I felt vindicated as well, since some people, including fellow priests, constantly questioned the wisdom of my continuing to expose myself to so much risk in Pajule. What I was able to do with the community leaders demonstrated that even if my pastoral activities were now very limited in scope, my presence alone was still very important since I could speak for the people and ensure that they were represented and protected.

This experience of working together with the local leaders to provide security to the community was one of the best moments in my life. In our little way, we were able to bring some hope and relief to the people that we led. At the same time, it became a gold standard for me of how to use authority and power. I believe that Church authority is at its best when it is exercised with humility, not arrogance, and sees itself as part of a team effort to make a positive difference in people's lives. And it is at its worst when those wielding power and influence are indifferent to the plight of the suffering and only use it as a means of control over others, and for accumulating material wealth, advancing selfish interests, and fighting personal wars.

I remember my very first encounter with a person from Pajule after I had been at school for three years in America. I met the local news reporter, Mr. Oray, and on seeing me he said, "Father, I am so happy to see you again; do you still remember our times together in Pajule? Pajule town would have been deserted during the war if we had not worked together." I could see the pride and joy in him that at one moment in our lives we did something that had made a positive impact on the lives of so many people.

154

The need for security for the people also brought me into contact with politicians and let me see how they worked and what their interests were. I was able to see that there were some who had a heart for the people. I remember a member of Parliament called Santa who was very dedicated to their plight. Whenever she heard that there was a security problem, she was quick to respond and would often take the risk to come physically to assess the situation. Santa played a big role in ensuring that Pajule got the reinforcements it needed.

I also encountered politicians who were good for nothing. They were good at talking and making powerful speeches, but when we needed them to actually use some of their influence and power they were nowhere to be found. Their influence and office were used for personal benefit only. Further, it made me discover how politics and voters are unfair. For example, after two years, when the general election was held, Santa, who had sacrificed so much for the people, was soundly defeated when she stood for reelection; and yet was the only member of Parliament who really had a heart for people.

Finally, I was also able to see the similarity between my vocation to the priesthood and political life. They are all about the welfare of people, the management of society, human relations, building contacts and networking, the common good, and the mutual acknowledgment and support of one another. All in all, to be an effective priest one needs some political skills.

My Visit to Jimmy

At the end of October 2003, I left for Gulu, mainly to visit Jimmy, who had been injured in the attack of October 10, since he was like a brother to me. My plan was to meet him at Gulu barracks where the army had an area designated as a military hospital. It was my first trip to the barracks. The soldiers at the gate demanded that I identity myself, which I did, and they eventually allowed me to enter. Gulu barracks is a huge place, and I did not know anyone there. I wanted my visit with Jimmy to be brief since I had other commitments. But I did not find Jimmy in the military hospital since he had been transferred to Lacor Hospital for better treatment.

However, I noticed how most of the soldiers were puzzled and surprised to see me. Non–family members rarely came to visit, but here I was from the battlefront of Pajule to visit Jimmy, who was one of their own. A greater challenge for these soldiers, who were mainly Southerners, was that they could tell that I was a Northerner, yet I had taken the time and risk to travel from Pajule.

Since Lacor Hospital was about thirty minutes away from the barracks, I was able to meet Jimmy within a very short time. It was really exciting for me to see him in person even if he had a deep wound in his right hand where a bullet had torn through it. We were grateful to God that we had survived the attack and that both of us were alive. His injury was serious, but he was getting good care and apart from the scar he would have on his hand, he was going to heal completely and be able to fully use his right arm again. Then, Jimmy told me how the attack started in the barracks and that the very first bullet a rebel soldier fired hit him in the hand. He told me that it was his usual practice every morning to wake up at six a.m. and do some physical exercise and lift some heavy weights. On that fateful morning, as he was doing his morning drill, he saw an armed man standing very close to the boundary of the trench and presumed that he was one of their troops. Because there was no need for a government soldier to be standing there at this particular hour, he ordered him to leave and join the rest on patrol in the town. When he shouted at him to leave, he heard a gunshot and felt a sharp pain in his hand. He immediately touched the area, found an open wound, and discovered that he had been shot. He jumped into the trench to command the rest of the soldiers who were still in the barracks when the rebels started to direct a lot of firepower at them in order to dislodge them from their positions. Jimmy told me that he needed to act quickly because some of the government soldiers were not used to heavy firepower and wanted to give up and run away. As he gave orders while running behind them in the trenches, he had to tear his shirt to pieces to wrap around his hand, as it was bleeding profusely.

As he talked about the fighting in the barracks, he expressed how concerned he was for my safety as the battle progressed. He was afraid that shells from the artillery and mortars that the military were firing to repulse the rebels would accidentally fall upon the rectory or the church and the consequence would be fatal. So he had to constantly remind the soldiers firing them to avoid the direction of the parish and the rectory. Jimmy's effort to prevent a shell from falling on the rectory reminded me of how I had climbed into the ceiling of the rectory to hide, placing my life in great danger. Above all, his sharing reminded me of the power of friendship.

I also came to learn about his selflessness, which gave me a deep sense of respect and admiration for him. When he was flown from Pajule to Gulu barracks with the army informant Omaya, who had a deep head injury, the few medical personnel wanted to attend to him first, Jimmy being an army officer; but he told them that Omaya's condition was more urgent than his own. So, they all attended to Omaya first. Unfortunately, Omaya later died from the brain injuries that he sustained in the attack.

After three months, Jimmy's hand was fully healed, and he returned to Pajule. We were excited to have him back, but his return was short-lived since he was reassigned as an instructor at the army school because he was a teacher by training. He was a soldier who had a heart for the people. I developed a relationship with him because he impressed me. As a government soldier, he always toed the official line, but at the same time, he was very objective in his approach to the issues that came his way.

Once in a while I shared a meal with Jimmy. In Acoli culture, sharing a meal with a person has a profound meaning of being totally accepted and embraced. Culturally, whenever a stranger or foreigner came to a village, if a family gave him or her water or food, this stranger automatically became part of that family and this family had the responsibility to look after him or her as one of their own. In fact, Jimmy was a family member to us, the residents of Pajule.

These are the boda bodas that received the deputy of the bishop. They usually transported people, and once in a while acted as an advance team to welcome guests. This time they have the handles of their bicycles adorned with leaves called 'oboke olwedo' that the Acoli people singularly use for blessing. The leaves symbolize a prayer and a wish that this visit to Pajule be blessed.

As the entourage of the deputy of the bishop approach the gates of the rectory a man drums as a sign of welcome to Pajule parish.

157

Pajule always made a big impression on those who came to see us. The task for any visitor was how to reach it safely. The deputy of the bishop thanks those who had warmly received him into the parish.

I am being cross examined by the deputy of the bishop who is on my right before becoming pastor. He asked me if I would love, take care of and be a good shepherd to the flock in Pajule. To all the questions, I answered yes. I had no doubt how I felt about my parishioners.

These men blow horns in jubilation as soon as it was announced that I was now the new pastor. My installation gave them something to celebrate. In a warzone there is a short supply of good news.

When I was asked to take a seat as a sign that it was now official that I was the new pastor the youth were ecstatic, they rushed to me and lifted me up into the air because they were so happy to see one looking as young as them now in charge.

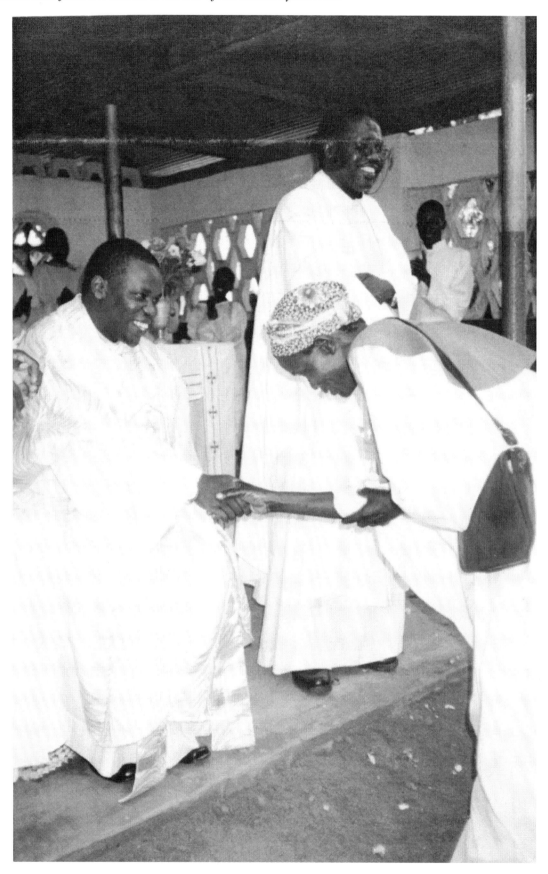

A devout parishioner and a member of the lay apostolate movement congratulating me on being installed as pastor of Pajule parish. I could see her face beaming with joy.

These women bring the offertory gifts in winnowers at the Mass of my installation. They walk in such a way that they balance so perfectly that there is no need to hold them with their hands.

These were the young ladies who performed a liturgical dance at the Mass of my installation. Their skirts are decorated in the colors of our national flag: black, yellow and red. They brought beauty, culture and youthful energy to our celebration.

The Bwola dance is a traditional dance of the Acoli people performed on special occasions. It is a royal and prestigious dance. I was honored to have it performed at my installation.

Pontiano on the right. A man who genuinely loved the Church and always sacrificed for it. He lived and practiced a very simple faith, that if he were good to the Church God would also be kind to him.

Ogan chapel on their day of making bricks. They place the mud into molds before laying them out in the hot sun to dry. Making bricks helped us to get to know each other on a more personal level and enabled me to become a better leader.

Chapter Thirty-Three

My Installation as Pastor

I was appointed pastor in August but my installation did not come until almost three months later on November 16, 2003. The roads were not safe, and because of it we could not immediately invite the bishop or his representative to come to officiate over the occasion. However, we used this time period to prepare for the function.

One thing that I asked of the organizing committee was to be more diverse and inclusive in the preparations. To me this would signal the direction of my administration as pastor. Most of the organizing committee members tended to be people who had belonged to the parish for a long time, which was good since they knew what to do. Unfortunately most of them were women getting advanced in age who had similar sets of skills. I felt the parish needed to tap the creativity and energies of the younger generation. I also wanted a committee that reflected the composition of Pajule parish and the community as a whole, that is, the youth, children, businesspeople, medical personnel, security forces, teachers and local politicians. I was convinced that this would make people feel that whatever took place in the parish, everybody had a stake in it. At the same time it would increase our financial base. I was happy that the steering committee followed my wish. They included people in their ranks who represented different sections of the community. Some of them were not regular churchgoers and were not familiar with the way things are done in the parish, but I was pleased with their inclusion since this was a way for them to begin developing a relationship with the Church and God.

Further, to be all-embracing made the larger point to the community that in the house of God, all are welcome. In this way they could all look at the Church as their home. Since I did have a clear vision of what I wanted the parish to be, one of the very first confrontations that I had was with the status quo, that is, those who had power and influence in the parish. They felt their grip and influence was under threat from the new people, since some of them were more gifted than they were. Others felt that the changes I advocated were too radical for the parish. There were some who were upset with my plans and could not help but express disdain for them. I remember hearing a parishioner who resented the transitions and my appointment say, "You see, this is the disadvantage of the bishop appointing someone so young to be our pastor; if things do not change, this young boy will destroy our parish." However, I knew that if I were to lead, I had to make tough decisions in the best interests of the parish and community, and I could not be a leader if I just wanted to be a beloved figure. To those who were critical of our inclusive approach, I would often push back that it is the character and intrinsic nature of the Church to welcome everybody because a Church that excludes some people is a Church that lacks the spirit of God. In fact, such a Church does not deserve to call itself a Church. Even if I considered it basic knowledge for my parishioners that the Church by its very nature is inclusive, I had to emphasize this several times because it was not totally accepted by some of them. My argument was strengthened by the fact that many of those we were inviting to take charge were the children of those who were afraid of losing influence. This made it possible for me to make the case that it was time for them to pass the torch of leadership to their children since they had passed the faith on to them and now it was their turn to lead. Instead of seeing them as rivals, they should be joyful since this was an indication that God had blessed their own faith and Christian life. It is important to note that the ideas to be more inclusive in the parish were embraced by a large number of people, in particular those who did not have a say in the parish before or felt marginalized. Those who had longed for change in the parish for many years welcomed it wholeheartedly.

I remember one among them was Mr. Lyandro, who was a young boy at the time the parish was started and had been an active member since its inception and at the moment was serving on the land board. When there was a lot of resistance from the old timers about change in the parish, he was very firm in arguing that things change and the parish needed new ideas and ways of doing things to move forward. Since men were underrepresented in the parish administration compared to women, most of them supported the changes that I proposed. And the youth and the children were also pleased because it made them more engaged in the Church.

One of the immediate challenges that I faced as I tried to reorganize the parish administration and implement my vision was the demonization of politics and politicians in general. For long within the Church and Ugandan society as a whole, politics has been considered a dirty game. These societal misconceptions have been reinforced by the confusion and suffering that bad politics has caused. Many of my parishioners have witnessed the extent to which politicians have politicized issues in the Church and manufactured confusion leading to irreconcilable differences. They were genuinely concerned and afraid of my leadership style since I involved all people, including politicians, in the different administrative structures of the parish. Personally I was comfortable with this since I had been working with them on issues that pertained to the whole community. Even if one was a politician so long as he/she did not come to the Church with an identifiable agenda he/she was welcome. To many in my congregation who saw politicians as bad people, involving them in the Church was akin to sacrilege. I would often rhetorically answer some of these critics in this way: If politics is evil why do you vote? Who are these politicians? Aren't they our sons and daughters? Don't politicians have souls that we need to save? Through the questions I raised I was able to begin to point out to them the false notions they had about politics and politicians. I was also able to make them realize that in every profession, including politics, there are bad as well as good people.

The fact that we were able to select an organizing committee that reflected the diversity and the different constituencies in the parish made our mobilization easy and successful. We were able to reach all the different groups in the parish and therefore had plenty of resources and manpower for our use. Because of this, the parish raised four times the amount of money that it normally raised for functions. We were able to buy two bulls to be slaughtered for this celebration. After we put in place all the organizational structures and raised all the resources, we gave the community a period of one month to prepare for the social and cultural aspects of the day.

The Day of my Installation

The day of my installation as pastor of Pajule was November 16, 2003. As the day approached, there was a lot of excitement in the air. People were happy that they actually had something to celebrate because for close to two years much of their lives had been tainted by violence, fear, pain, and loss.

The person who was coming to preside over my installation was the deputy of the bishop, a native priest of the archdiocese of Gulu. He had a gentle, warm personality that made him greatly loved in Pajule parish. He was someone very charismatic, eloquent, convincing, and an excellent storyteller in the local culture and language. The advance information given to the parishioners that he was coming to preside over the function created a good feeling and a sense of anticipation.

On the day the deputy of the bishop was to travel to Pajule, he was to be accompanied by the director of CARITAS who occasionally came to Pajule since it hosted the reception center. They were to arrive a day before on the afternoon of November 15 around three p.m. On the afternoon they arrived, a large group of people on "Boda Bodas" went to receive them at Lanyatido, where we had a chapel five miles away from the parish center along Pajule-Lira Road. Fortunately, in the past few days there had been no rebel attacks in the area. The welcome group traveled in a convoy with our guests into the center of the town. In the town itself, there was a group of traditional dancers waiting to welcome and receive them with the *bwola* dance, a traditional royal dance. These *bwola* dancers led the convoy for one mile into the parish with hundreds of people lined up on both sides of the road. From the church to the rectory were hundreds of children. It was a magnificent sight to watch.

This was a great surprise to me; I did not anticipate how fast the people could turn away their thoughts from the fear and insecurity to the joyful and celebratory. It felt like the war and the insecurity had suddenly come to an end. When the deputy of the bishop arrived at the rectory, I welcomed him and his delegation, and everyone assembled. The deputy of the bishop appeared visibly elated and touched and thanked all the people who had come to greet him and his entourage. He made some brief remarks and blessed the people who had assembled, and then we dispersed to prepare ourselves for the Mass that evening at five p.m. since we had about fifty children to baptize.

The following day, which was a Sunday, thousands of people turned up for my installation as pastor, and I could feel the joy and enthusiasm in the air. I was a little bit nervous since I was going to be the focal point of the installation. The procession at the beginning of the Mass was about five hundred meters long, starting at the rectory and stretching into the shade where we were to celebrate Mass. We were to have an open-air Mass since the church was too small to accommodate such a large number of people—close to 3500.

At the beginning of the function, I heard several women ululate, a gesture that is part and parcel of a celebratory event, saying, "This is Pajule parish, protected by Mary and Joseph, a place of love." The words of these women were very moving to me. I experienced them as very affirming of my work and intentions because it meant that for the short time I had been their spiritual leader they were connecting with my passion and vision for the Church.

Thousands of parishioners and non-parishioners had come for the occasion. Although the roads were insecure, a number of representatives and personal friends from the district headquarters of Pader came to witness my installation. Among them was Billy, whom I had come to know when I was in Pajule only a few days. Even though the turnout for the function was really large, I was at peace and felt confident in our preparations since the people had taken full charge of every aspect of the function and did not need my supervision.

At the very beginning of Mass, I welcomed the deputy of the bishop and all the participants. The Mass started at exactly nine a.m. In his opening remarks, the deputy of the bishop acknowledged with pride and joy the large number of people who had come, in particular the youth, who were almost half the congregation and were the bulk of the choir that day. The deputy of the bishop is a man who is humorous and exceptional at making people feel good about themselves, and he asked the congregation to look at the youth very intently to see how beautiful and handsome they were. His comment was not only unexpected and funny but created a good feeling at the beginning of the Mass since he went on to recognize all the different categories of people and age groups that had come.

He went on to tell the congregation that in ancient times, because of the beauty of Acoli women and their expertise in preparing a traditional dish called *malakwang*, a prime vegetable dish that has a sweet and sour taste, men from the neighboring tribe of Bunyoro used to come to marry them. This sent the congregation into wild laughter since his complementary and generous words touched their unique cultural identity and tapped into their ethnic pride.

In his homily he talked about the role and responsibility of the prophets in biblical times, and that the prophets talked about hope and trust in God even when the situation was terribly bad. He invited the congregation to find solace and comfort in their words today. He compared the suffering of the people in Acoliland to that of the Israelites who were held as slaves in Egypt till God liberated them, and assured those assembled that however long it took, their sufferings would also come to an end. He was confident that this liberation would come at an appropriate time since God neither forgets about His people nor abandons them.

After the homily came the actual ceremony of my installation as pastor. I was cross-examined by the deputy of the bishop before the congregation. The questions were a good reminder to me as a pastor since they were about my commitment to be a servant of the people, to love my parishioners, and to be a shepherd to each one of them. What an excellent teaching at the very beginning of my pastorate! After the cross-examination, I was asked to sit on a chair as a sign that the power and authority of a pastor had been passed on to me.

As I sat in the chair as the new pastor of Pajule, there was so much excitement and commotion in the congregation that the youth ran toward me and lifted me in the air for about five minutes. This was a great surprise to me because I had never seen it happen at an installation. Then those in the congregation who wanted to congratulate me came forward. As I sat I felt so much joy and peace inside.

First, I could tell that the parish had come a long way. They had felt so much pain seeing the missionaries leave almost two years ago. Now they embraced the change to the native clergy and loved it.

Second, my installation was finally some good news for them amid the many hardships that defined their lives. I felt that they were inspired by it and that it brought out the best in them. And this made me confident that whatever the hardships I would endure as a pastor, we were going to be in this together.

After Mass, we had lunch followed by plays and traditional dances interspersed with speeches from the civil, political, and traditional leaders. The celebration lasted a full day. I remember that in my speech, I thanked the bishop for the trust that he had shown in me since Pajule was a tough place to lead because of the unrest. I told the congregants that as their pastor I was going to have two major objectives.

First, I was planning to celebrate the Golden Jubilee Year of the parish. One day when I was looking at the old annual files of the parish, I found that the parish had not celebrated her fiftieth anniversary of existence, which was supposed to have been in 1998, nor had it celebrated her Silver Jubilee Year in 1973. I believed that this celebration would be a driving force for many of the things I wanted to achieve during my pastorate, such as calling the community to action and bringing about Christian renewal in the parish through different activities geared toward the spiritual and material renewal in the parish, as well as thanking God for His blessings to the community in spite of the many hardships.

I also wanted my time as pastor of Pajule to be defined by something more positive than war, violence, and bad news on a daily basis—instead, hope, Christian renewal, and the promise of the Christian faith. I was convinced that I would be the pastor for a minimum of five years and be able to implement these plans and ideas that were generated in the course of the celebration of the Jubilee Year.

Second, I was going to focus on renovating the physical structures of the parish. The deputy of the bishop on behalf of the diocesan bishop congratulated me on becoming pastor, encouraged the people to remain faithful even if the times were a great challenge to their faith, and informed them that the diocese was donating a truck for the activities of the parish.

The following Monday after the celebration of Mass, the deputy of the bishop met the returnees at the reception center and urged them to thank God for what he had done in their lives because their escape from captivity represented an extraordinary sign of divine intervention. Because of this, they needed to remember to keep a close relationship with Him from now on. Later in the day, he left for Gulu, and so I began the first day of my short pastorate of Pajule parish.

After the deputy of the bishop had returned to Gulu, there was still much excitement in Pajule. Many people who were not present on the day of my installation and others who wished to see me individually came to the parish to congratulate me. I remember an elder called Major Ocan, who was in his late sixties or early seventies, told me, "Father, I grew up in Pajule, lived here most of my life, and have seen a lot of things, but your installation as pastor was one of the greatest honors to this community and me." Even as I walked in town whenever I met people who were in a group or a small gathering, they would change the subject of their conversation and talk about my installation. Others wished to introduce me to their friends and people I had never met.

However, unlike my predecessors, who were most of the time called pastors or parish priests, I was called pastor for only a very short time. Instead, the people gave me a new title, *parewa*, meaning "our priest" And this was my title throughout my time in Pajule and up to today.

After a week, I left for Kampala to begin some networking with friends and people who hailed from Pajule since I needed their participation in the parish activities. I spent one week in the capital city and returned to Pajule via Gulu. While in Gulu, I picked up the truck that had been donated to the parish. Indeed the truck was a great help, as I could transport large amounts of supplies for the parish and people for parish activities if there was a need.

The morning I was to travel back to Pajule from Gulu, I felt tense and not at ease. I worried about my safety on the road. I decided against traveling through Atanga to Pajule, the shorter route, because I considered many spots along the road to be unsafe. Instead, I used the Gulu-Lira Road. Since I was not at peace, I decided to take it easy, drive slowly, and stop along the way wherever possible to rest, eat, chat, and ask questions about the safety of the area and the roads.

As I left for Lira from Gulu, I stopped at a place called Aboke in the Lango region. I visited one of our senior priests, Father Afric, and had a great time with him. If one wanted to know what was happening on the ground inside or outside the Church in the region, he was the right person to talk to. He was a contemporary of my father in the seminary high school in the 1960s. After about one hour of conversation with him, I was surprised to get a call on my cell phone from my mother in Kitgum, and fortunately, the Aboke area had network coverage. She immediately asked me a specific question: "Father Robert, where are you?" I did not expect it, because she rarely asks about my location whenever I talk to her. I told her where I was and informed her that I was on my way to Pajule through Lira.

I noticed in her voice that my response troubled her, but she did not make any comment. I guess she must have said to herself that her grown-up son knew what he was doing and the risk he was taking. Around this time, there were a lot of tribal tensions between the Acoli and Lango communities in Lira and the Lango region because of the atrocities being perpetrated by the LRA, and I believe that the question of my safety must have been on her mind.

I talked with her for about fifteen minutes, then said good-bye to Father Afric and continued my journey. I traveled safely to Lira and reached Puranga, where I saw a man dressed in a military uniform waving at me to stop. Even though I was speeding, I slowed down and stopped. He asked me to give him a lift to the next township along the road called Rackoko. I told him that I could not because he was dressed in his uniform. I was afraid that since my truck was green like that of the army commanders in the area, transporting a soldier in uniform would make it appear as if I were carrying an army officer, and that would be a magnet for rebels. And since there was no way for this soldier to put on any other clothing, I left him by the roadside and continued with my journey.

After about twelve minutes, I reached Rackoko, where I met my former pastor, who had just finished celebrating Mass. We chatted for a short while, but since I was tense, I quickly said good-bye and continued with my journey. It was a great feeling driving the parish truck for the first time. It had plenty of space for me in the front seat, unlike the Suzuki I had used before and it was fast, firm, and comfortable on the road despite the many bumps and potholes.

As I drove into Pajule, I increased my speed, since there were unsafe spots along the stretch to town. Because the town was on a slope, I saw several town dwellers standing on both sides of the road looking in the direction I was coming from, and I immediately thought that they were wondering whose vehicle was traveling so fast since my truck was stirring up so much dust. When I reached their location, I stopped and got out of the truck, and they were surprised to see that I was the driver. They were happy to see the new parish truck, but at the same time most of them were glad to see that I arrived safely because a passenger vehicle that had arrived twenty minutes ago had been fired at by the rebels. Fortunately, it was traveling at a very high speed and passed through the volley of gunshots. This incident had occurred between Puranga and Rackoko. When I heard this I felt a sharp pain in my heart, and I was certain that if I had not spent almost seventy-five minutes talking with Father Afric and my mother, mostly likely I would have preceded the passenger vehicle and been the one shot at.

Before going to bed in the evening, the thought of nearly entering an ambush once again kept lingering in my mind. I kept on questioning myself and asking God what kind of life we lived in Pajule where there was so much danger, uncertainty, and death all the time. I also wondered how the parish would have responded to the news if I had entered an ambush on my return and lost the truck, was wounded or killed less than three weeks after my installation. Once again, I told myself: "I will not worry about these near misses. It is God who is in charge of my safety. So long as He sees that I have a role in Pajule, He will always keep harm away from me."

Chapter Thirty-Four
Spiritual Activities in the Jubilee Year

At the end of November 2003, I asked my bishop to write a letter to all the parishes and institutions in the archdiocese of Gulu informing them that Pajule parish was going to be celebrating her Golden Jubilee Year beginning on December 8, 2003, with the official conclusion on December 8, 2004, with a Eucharistic celebration led by him. We also wanted all diocesan institutions and parishes in the archdiocese of Gulu to pray for the success and the intentions of our parish Jubilee Year. Pajule parish had given birth to two other neighboring parishes in the Archdiocese, Puranga parish and Atanga parish. We wanted to give advance notice to all people of goodwill to prepare to join us on the final day of our Jubilee Year celebration.

On December 8, 2003, at a gathering of the parish leaders and after an evening prayer service, we inaugurated our parish Jubilee Year, and I explained to those gathered its concept. Its focus was going to be giving thanks to God and promoting Christian renewal in the parish. I also announced my intention to form a new parish pastoral council (leadership body) since the current one had been in office for the last twenty years. Apart from expressing my desire to get new blood into the parish administration, I also stated that it needed to be more inclusive and representative. That is, the membership of the new parish pastoral council should reflect the composition of the parish community, and children needed to be represented since they made up almost half of the total parish population.

Since I wanted this parish Jubilee Year celebration to be a moment for the parish to reconnect with its past and to acknowledge the contributions of our predecessors, I wrote a letter to all who had worked in the parish at different times, most of whom were Italian missionaries who had retired and returned to their home country. I informed them that Pajule parish was celebrating its Golden Jubilee Year. First, I asked them to pray for the success of the parish Jubilee Year, and second, I indicated to them that at some point we might need some financial assistance from them since we had plans to renovate the buildings. The response to my letter addressed to the Italian missionaries was the most surprising and interesting of all: "Father Robert, we do not understand you and in particular your motivation to organize a Jubilee Year celebration at this time, for we are aware that the security situation in Pajule is now worse than it was at the time we served the parish. You need to give a second thought to what you intend to do."

As I read their letter, some questions came to my mind since if felt like a lot had been left unsaid: "What does this young man know?" "We lived and worked in the place for many years and could not celebrate any Jubilee Year of the parish because of the insecurity." "Is the young man living in a dreamland?" "Could it be that he is so full of zeal and imagination that he cannot see the reality around him anymore?" Their concerns were appropriate. The security situation was really bad. So I gave myself some time to reflect on how to reply to them. I needed to address the subject of the insecurity directly with them since I wanted to have them on board in whatever activities we carried out as part of the parish Jubilee Year.

After a period of about two weeks, I thought that I had an answer to give the retired missionaries. I wrote them a letter that challenged them and above all appealed to their own faith. I wrote: "I personally understand a parish Jubilee Year celebration to be a time for Christian renewal. For a parish Jubilee celebration is not essentially a social event that is characterized by eating and drinking, but its primary focus is to give people the opportunity to examine and renew their relationship with God." I went on to state that as Christians, even if there is so much chaos and insecurity, we are an eternally hopeful people, and this is the message that we always celebrate at every Easter event. We should not surrender or despair when faced with tragedies in life. Our people need to hear that even in the present circumstances God continues to love and care for them. That is why it would be very meaningful and important to have the celebration now. As I posted my letter, I felt that I had explained myself very well, and when they received my letter, they were surprised by the extent to which it was laden with faith and concluded that we knew what we were doing. They wrote back asking me to keep them updated about what would be taking place in the parish and expressed their willingness to support us in any way possible when we had a clear sense of what we would expect of them.

As part of the observance of the Parish Jubilee Year celebration, we agreed to have two sets of activities, spiritual and material. The purpose of the spiritual activities was to revitalize the faith life of the parish. I also found spiritual activities easy to manage because I was confident I would be able to conduct them if facilitators could not travel to us because of the insecure roads.

One of the very first things we initiated was to have a regular day of prayer in the parish. Every last Saturday of the month, we invited all the members to observe a day of prayer and recollection. This would begin at around nine a.m. and end at one p.m. On this day of recollection, I would give two talks based on a gospel passage that I had selected for the day. After the two talks, we would have the Blessed Sacrament exposed for adoration, and as some adored the Blessed Sacrament, others came for confession. The turnout for this day of prayer was always very good. Most of those who came were in their forties and older.

In a Jubilee Year celebration retracing one's history or life journey is an important element. As part of this, on the last Sunday of the month we celebrated Mass in Pajule market. This market was very significant in the life of the parish and faith community. It was at this spot that Mass was first celebrated when the first missionary arrived in the area in 1947. At that time, there were hardly any roads and the place was sparsely populated. There were no buildings under which he could conduct Mass, so he said the Mass with a few people under a mango tree. Today, this mango tree, which once was in the center of farmlands and hunting fields, is surrounded by shops on all sides. It is now one of the tallest and largest trees in the whole of Pajule. From that very first day, this spot became the place at which worship was held in the Pajule area until the current church, which is a mile away, was built in the early fifties.

The idea of going to celebrate Mass in the market was one of the most unexpected ventures that we embarked on. This is because an African market is a chaotic place, and the spirit that hovers over it is not one of worship or tranquility. On a normal market day, it is not only busy but noisy, windy, dusty, and full of commotion. Some customers would be haggling over prices on the one end, and on the other end others would be cutting fresh meat with axes since the abattoir is within the same market. There would also be some people drinking, tipsy, shouting, dancing, or staggering as they walked in the market. To a person with a sound mind, it was inconceivable that Mass could ever be celebrated in such a context.

However, what surprised us most were the reverence, respect, and cooperation that we got from the traders, regular customers, and the dwellers of the town. They suspended all their trading activities till we had finished celebrating the Mass.

To the people who were older, praying under the mango tree brought about feelings of nostalgia. I could see that they were visibly moved, and some were even tearful. They talked about how praying in the market brought back good memories of when they were little children, since it was the place in which some of them were baptized and confirmed.

Whenever the last Sunday of the month approached, I always wrote a letter to the mayor of Pajule asking him to allow us to use the space in the market. He always very punctually gave his consent to worship in the place. On the Sundays when we celebrated Mass in the market, hundreds of people from

Pajule turned up to be part of the occasion. Many who were not churchgoers came to see and find out what took place. The Mass started at eight a.m. and lasted for three hours. After the Mass, I could hear some say with admiration how beautiful and pleasing the experience was for them. This made me feel like we were taking God to those who never came to church. In short, we were evangelizing them. Others who had fallen away from the Church recognized how much the worship had changed, since it now incorporated a variety of cultural and emotional expressions including traditional dances, ululations, and body movements in the worship.

At the conclusion of the Mass, I expected the congregation to go straight to their homes since most of them lived within the town and near the market. Instead it was like a burning flame of faith had been lit at the market and an energetic spirit of worship emerged, and the congregation would begin to sing songs of praise thanking God for the parish Jubilee Year while accompanying me on foot back to the parish church, where some remained singing for an additional thirty minutes or more.

Chapter Thirty-Five

Pilgrimages in the Jubilee Year

Kitgum Mission

As part of the spiritual activities for the parish Jubilee Year, we also arranged pilgrimages. The first was to Kitgum mission in the middle of May 2004, and the second was to Gulu cathedral in the middle of June of the same year. These two places were very significant in the life of Pajule parish. Kitgum mission was the parish that gave birth to Pajule parish. The priests who opened Pajule parish were based there. Gulu cathedral was the parish that gave birth to all the parishes in the archdiocese of Gulu. We saw the pilgrimages in which we were to participate as a way to retrace our faith.

As the day for the first pilgrimage to Kitgum Mission came near, tension built up within the pilgrims since there was a real possibility that we could fall into an LRA ambush. Some members of the choir proposed that if we kept singing religious songs for the length of the journey, the rebels would hear and be respectful of our intent and allow us to pass without any interference.

Others challenged the idea of the choir singing continually while on the road by saying that this could be the very reason the rebels attacked us. First, the loud sounds of singing voices would draw the rebels to the roadside. Second, the LRA rebels would connect any singing to a celebration, and it was well known that they resented seeing people happy and joyous since they considered themselves to be suffering in the bush. It was practical to sing while traveling to Kitgum mission, which was a drive of about forty-five minutes. But it was doubtful that the choir would be able to keep singing till we reached Gulu cathedral since it was a drive of about two hours. We were committed to go to both places even if the roads were not safe, because we wanted to make the Jubilee Year celebration a profound experience and so we placed the question of our safety in God's hands. Even if these two trips were filled with danger, taking risks had already become very much a part of our lives.

Our concerns were also heightened by the fact that a large number of people would have to travel in the same vehicle. We needed to use trucks that could transport about one hundred people in a single trip since they were the only means available. If we entered an ambush, it would be catastrophic because all the victims of an attack would be from the same parish and even some from the same family. Getting a means of transport was also a challenge for us. In the first place, we had to find the owner of a truck who was willing to allow his vehicle to travel over risky roads, and second, the parish had very limited financial resources so if the owner of the lorry were to charge exorbitantly it would thwart all our plans.

Fortunately many in the parish had an appreciation for the message and spirit of the Jubilee Year celebration in which we encouraged people to begin to see the parish as their own by putting in their time and sacrificing their resources for its activities. So Pontiano made a generous offer and provided his truck to transport the pilgrims to all the destinations; he asked us only to buy the fuel for the journey, and he would take care of other costs and expenses along the way. Fortunately, a single trip was sufficient to transport all the pilgrims to their destinations. However, since he used his truck for commercial purposes, it meant that we had to plan our schedule around the truck's work schedule and be willing to put up with additional inconveniences like long delays when the truck failed to arrive on time.

For our first pilgrimage we hoped to travel to Kitgum mission on a Friday afternoon. By two p.m. all the pilgrims had assembled in the parish waiting for the truck to pick them up. At four p.m. when the truck had not arrived, we called the owner to find out what was causing the delay and learned that he had forgotten about the arrangement. It was understandable that he could have forgotten since most arrangements in our society are not written down; most people tried to commit them to memory. So when it happened that the owner of the vehicle had forgotten about the arrangements, we made the best of the situation. We learned that the truck was on its way transporting goods and passengers from Lira to Kitgum at that very moment and was going to pass through Pajule town in about one hour's time. So we rushed to the center of Pajule town, taking the children who were to be a part of the pilgrimage to find and occupy any available space. These were the altar boys and the liturgical dancers. Children were an important pillar of my ministry and were represented in all parish activities. If we were able to send them the day before, the following day we could use smaller trucks to transport the adults. We were confident that the nuns at Kitgum Mission would take good care of them.

Because we could not all leave for Kitgum mission on Friday evening, our Saturday morning activities were going to be interrupted, as we had planned to spend a large part of the time in prayer and reflection. Kitgum mission was not far, but the government soldiers would only allow us to begin traveling at eleven a.m. We were able to travel to Kitgum mission midmorning on Saturday using smaller trucks and arrived at different times in the afternoon. When my group reached Kitgum mission, we entered the church and knelt before the Blessed Sacrament and sang songs praising God for His inexhaustible blessings upon us, since it was from this church and parish that the message of salvation by Jesus Christ was taken to the people of Pajule.

Kitgum mission had another linkage with Pajule. It was the home parish of Father Cesario Odida, the first native African priest in the whole of the Kitgum Vicariate who was ordained in 1945. After his ordination, he was posted to Pajule parish and worked there for several years, and the pilgrims in their midfifties and above who were young boys and girls at the time still remembered him. As a young boy in 1983, I remember seeing this priest saying his rosary inside the parish church the first time I toured it with my mother, since this was the parish where he came to retire. At that time he looked frail and weak and his body shook most of the time; as I look back I guess that he might have been suffering from Parkinson's disease.

At six p.m., we assembled in the church and were welcomed by the parish priest, who talked about our schedule in which we would celebrate Mass together with the parishioners of Kitgum mission the following morning. I was going to be the main preacher and speak about the common bond between Pajule parish and Kitgum mission because of the Christian faith. After the Sunday Mass, all the pilgrims would leave immediately in a truck for Pajule parish.

After our welcome, we left the church to recite the rosary and thank God for the safe travel from Pajule. We also wanted to entrust all the activities of the following day into God's hands. In front of the church on the right-hand side, there is a burial spot for some of the priests who died while serving in Kitgum vicariate; among them was Father Odida. We felt that this was the best place for us to recite the rosary. Praying at his gravesite renewed the bond that Pajule parish had with him. At a personal level, I felt that I was continuing with the work that he had done in the parish.

And this was also a great honor for us since we were able to pray with and thank a founding member of the parish in concrete terms. I was convinced that this evening of prayer was going to have a significant spiritual impact on Pajule parish and my parishioners were going to experience the love and presence of God in their lives because of their prayer.

Father Odida died in 1989 after a long illness. On his tombstone is one of the most striking writings that I have ever seen, which made me conclude that he was a holy man. The words are as follows: "Dear people of Kitgum, the time for me to go to Heaven has arrived. I would like to wish you well and I will always be praying for you. I hope and know that one day we will meet in eternal life." I have not often read such faith-filled words on gravestones. I sincerely believe that his many years of illness after serving the Church for close to five decades had prepared him for the life to come.

After the rosary, we had dinner, and two representatives of the pilgrims came to me. They proposed that we change the plan to return to Pajule immediately after Mass on Sunday. Their main reason was that there were many pilgrims who wanted to spend Sunday evening in Kitgum town since they had people they wished to visit and other personal things they could do. We called the owner of the truck on his cell phone to get his consent. He was of the firm opinion that the truck had to take us back to Pajule directly after Sunday Mass because it had to be available for work on Monday morning. However, the two ladies who represented the pilgrims stuck to their guns, arguing that the truck could take the people to Pajule on Monday morning and then it could do anything the owner desired. Since the two sides were at a stalemate, I intervened in order to provide a way forward. I told the two ladies who were representing the pilgrims and the owner of the lorry that I was for the idea of returning to Pajule immediately after Mass on Sunday, and my reason was simple: it was our original plan. All of them accepted it without any debate. Because of the insecurity I practiced the belief that if I had specific plans it was better to stick to them.

So on Sunday after we had a great celebration of the Mass with the parishioners of Kitgum mission, most of us immediately left for Pajule. Some had decided to stay and made plans to return the following day. We were all pleased that our plans had worked out so well. The choir sang throughout the journey, and we arrived at the parish without any incident on the way and concluded our pilgrimage with a thanksgiving prayer.

The following day, Monday, around eleven a.m., I went to do something at the center of town and heard that a vehicle coming from Kitgum going to Lira on its way through Pajule had been attacked by LRA rebels and four people had been killed. This was a shock to me because we had considered changing our travel plans to Monday morning, and I later learned that the truck we were to travel in narrowly missed the ambush since it was preceded by the one that was actually attacked. In fact, the truck that we were to travel in returned the dead bodies and the injured to Kitgum.

Within an hour, some of the members of Pajule parish who had traveled on Monday morning arrived. All were in a terrible state of shock and wished they had returned with us on Sunday afternoon. We were really lucky, for if we had changed our travel plans our vehicle would most likely have been the one attacked by the rebels. Unlike other travelers we were all assembled in one place and as soon as we had boarded the lorry we would have immediately left for Pajule ahead of all the other vehicles.

When the people in Kitgum town heard of the news, many who had celebrated the Mass with us on Sunday had one comment: "God has spared and protected the pilgrims from Pajule parish." Personally, I believe that this was the first miracle that Father Cesario did for the pilgrims of Pajule.

The Wednesday morning after we had returned from our pilgrimage to Kitgum mission, a rumor began to spread in the community that hundreds of LRA rebels were coming toward Pajule and their intentions were not clear; a few of the townspeople thought they were coming to surrender, but most were of the opinion that they were coming to attack the place.

At seven fifteen a.m., while I was celebrating Mass, from the altar I started to see hundreds of people running from the camps on foot toward the church. But as they reached the church compound, they ran through to the neighboring bushes to hide. Once again the church compound was not safe enough for most of them.

I had a small group of people celebrating Mass with me, and the commotion outside the church put us under a lot of stress because we were afraid that an attack on the town was imminent. Because of the commotion outside the church, I made eye contact with one of the three nuns signaling that she should find out what was happening, and she went out and reported to me that people were on the run because they suspected that the rebels were coming to attack the town.

I had paused during the celebration of the Mass to listen to her attentively and realized that there was nothing new in what she told me, so I proceeded with the Mass. I did not make any comment to her or the congregation about the information she passed to me. I believed those who were celebrating Mass with me trusted that if the situation were really bad, I would have informed them accordingly. I was also convinced that if the town were to come under attack, I would decide what instructions to give the congregation.

However, as we were coming to the end of Mass, before the final blessing, a soldier entered the church. He came directly to me at the altar to inform me about what was happening and to apologize for the commotion that had been generated since dawn in the community. This is what he said: *"There are rebels coming on foot to surrender, and for their safety the military kept this information secret. In fact, we were afraid that other rebels who still wanted to fight might interfere with their plans to surrender."*

Hearing this, I felt a sudden peace and calm within me, and I immediately passed this information to the congregation. I reassured them that there was no danger and no need to panic, and that those who were interested could go and wait for the former rebels as they entered the barracks.

When I later reflected on this morning in which close to seventy LRA rebels surrendered, I came to the conclusion that this was the second miracle that Pajule parish experienced through the intercession of Father Odida.

Gulu Cathedral

The second place that we went for a pilgrimage was the archdiocesan cathedral named after Saint Joseph in the middle of June 2004. This cathedral was the first church that the Comboni missionaries started in the whole of the archdiocese of Gulu, and it gave birth to all the parishes in the archdiocese. We wanted to thank God for this church that had spread the Christian faith to all corners of the archdiocese. However, our journey to Gulu was again plagued with transportation problems. The truck only arrived to pick us up at around three p.m., and when we started to leave for Gulu it was nearly four thirty p.m. This time I drove my truck. To travel to Gulu would take us about three hours; however, it was late since at four p.m. the soldiers protecting the roads returned to the barracks. There was also the possibility that the soldiers in Pajule would not allow us to leave the town.

I left Pajule for Gulu ahead of the lorry with the altar boys and liturgical dancers in my truck; I was under a lot of pressure and driving very fast. As I drove past Acolibur, which was about twenty-five minutes away from Pajule, government soldiers who were now leaving the roadside and returning to their barracks kept on pointing their guns at me; in fact, they were warning me of the risk I was taking. Because I was speeding and since they were leaving the road side, the risk of me entering an ambush was much higher. Because of these warnings we spent the night at a Catholic parish called Atanga along the way; this was a neighboring parish to Pajule and had been carved out of it. There was no priest living in it, and it looked like an abandoned place. Most of its members had either left or were living in camps.

At the parish young boys of the same age as my altar boys came around and when they saw my altar boys, they said they wanted to compete in a soccer match. What a coincidence, I found myself refereeing a Jubilee Year soccer match between the altar boys of Pajule parish and those of Atanga parish.

After an hour, the truck that was transporting the rest of the pilgrims arrived, and I told them that we could not go to Gulu that evening because it was getting late. They had to spend the night in a place called Lacekocot, which was about fifteen minutes away, because Atanga parish had very few soldiers to protect such a large number of people. I spent a quiet evening in Atanga with my altar boys and liturgical dancers, and then in the early morning we left to join the larger group.

We reached Gulu Saturday morning at ten a.m. without incident and were again warmly received by the pastor and parish community. We were able to do some of the activities planned, including an afternoon of prayer and recollection in the cathedral. In the evening we went to visit the archdiocesan seminary high school. The head of the seminary, the deputy of the bishop, who had installed me as the pastor of Pajule, was very welcoming and complimentary of our efforts to celebrate a parish Jubilee Year in such an insecure environment. He had kind words for each one of us in the delegation and about my leadership as the pastor of Pajule. After the speech and welcome by the deputy of the bishop in the seminary chapel, we got out and some of the parishioners had the chance to informally greet the seminarians and encourage them in their calling to the priesthood. I felt this was a great experience for the seminarians since they were meeting the people they would be serving in a few years. After the informal session with the seminarians some of the youth came to me and said that that they were hearing a lot of good things being said about me that made them concerned and disturbed. I asked them why they felt that way; they told me that I could be transferred to come to work in Gulu instead of Pajule. I laughed off any thoughts of ever leaving Pajule and told them that any credit or praise I got as a pastor was because of them.

On Sunday, we celebrated Mass in the cathedral. My parishioners were all excited to be part of the occasion and be at the center of the activities. The first reading of the Mass was acted, and one person played the part of God. He spoke from one of the domes of the cathedral, and the echo made his voice sound deep and supernatural. The worship led by Pajule parish was vivid, lively, and full of creativity. Part of this was because I gave my parishioners plenty of latitude to be themselves in their worship and to bring their talents to it.

To me the most moving experience of this day was the impact on the altar boys and the girls who were the liturgical dancers. The church in Pajule had a capacity of about 450 to 600 people, but today they were serving Mass and doing liturgical dancing in a church that had a capacity of almost 2000 people. They appeared nervous and tense at first, but I assured them that the major difference was the size of the place. They should carry on as if the worship was going on in Pajule, and above all I was with them. I believe that this day left a lasting impression upon them because they talked about this visit very often when we returned to Pajule. In their words they felt like the cathedral swallowed them up since they felt very little in it.

After the Mass we presented a goat as our gift to the main celebrant who was the head of the Gulu vicariate. Culturally a gift of a goat is considered a substantial gift. Then we immediately left for Pajule. Our visit to Gulu was covered in the local news stations, which made many in Pajule feel honored and proud. This was something I had not anticipated: that celebrating the Jubilee Year of the parish was going to raise the self-esteem of its members.

When I reached the parish, I felt exhausted and began thinking of taking a vacation for two weeks.

Chapter Thirty-Six
Material Activities in the Jubilee Year

As part of the celebration of the Jubilee Year, we made sure that material activities were also planned since one of our goals was to deepen the sense of stewardship in the parish. My message to the Christian community was that the church in Pajule came into existence because of the hard work and sacrifices of the earlier generations, and that it was our turn to do something representing the contributions of our own generation. I also saw this as a way that the current generation could express its appreciation for what their predecessors had done.

The rectory in which I lived was not safe because whenever the rebels attacked, it was among their three primary targets: the barracks, the town, and the parish. We did have a brick wall around the rectory but it was only about three feet high and was easy to climb over. We needed to raise the wall to about nine feet high to prevent anyone from scaling it or stray bullets from hitting anyone inside the compound. If we succeeded in raising the wall around the rectory, it would make it more difficult for the rebels to climb over. A high wall would force the rebels to enter and leave the compound strictly through the main gate, and if they were being pressed by government soldiers it would make them reluctant to enter. Raising the wall was a big project requiring thousands of burnt bricks since the wall around the rectory was about four hundred meters wide. Pajule parish had very limited financial resources, but the community was always very generous with its time and energy when it came to parish activities.

We organized ourselves according to the different chapels that had been displaced in the parish. Each of these chapels had a set date for coming to bake bricks in the parish. They would begin from the very first stages of brickmaking by digging up the sandy red soil and on another day mix the soil with water while stepping on it with their bare feet and placing it in molds made of wood that gave shape to the eventual brick. They would then lay the wet brick out in the sun to dry, and if there were any signs that it might rain in the evening or at night, they covered the bricks with a huge pile of grass so that the rainwater would not damage their shape. After the bricks were dried, they placed them in a kiln in the shape of a barn for storage. A single stack would contain seven thousand bricks.

I provided those baking the bricks with twenty liters of the local brew to drink for relaxation and to keep them awake for the night. The bricks in the kiln took thirteen hours to bake lasting from six p.m. till seven a.m. the following day. By this time the whole kiln from bottom to top would be red-hot, and the grass on top of it would also be in flames indicating all the bricks had been baked. What struck me most was that the materials used for baking the bricks were fresh tree branches. The "brick barns" were so hot that fresh trees placed in them caught fire immediately. Dry wood was not used since within less than fifteen minutes it was totally consumed.

Many times I joined the different chapels when it was their turn to make bricks. In bare feet I joined them to step on the soil and mix it with water, and even participated when it came time for the actual baking. I did this because I wanted to communicate the message that we were in this together. However, my active participation was also an encouragement to the lazy ones to try to come to work when it was their chapel's turn. I really enjoyed the experience of making bricks with my parishioners. The collaboration and joint efforts strengthened the sense of community in the parish. It was the first time I had participated in such a venture. It was physically demanding, but full of fun, too. We laughed, joked, and told stories. I came to know my parishioners much better since we spent many hours working together under the hot sun. I was able to see each one of them as their true selves because it was impossible to keep one's real character and inner personality and thoughts from the group. I believe this knowledge made me a better pastor because I came to learn their challenges and their psychology as well.

Through this collective effort we made about eighty thousand bricks. Some of the parishioners who were builders volunteered to raise the wall, and my own father gave us his tractor to help with the transportation of the materials. The bishop gave us money to buy cement for the construction. In this project, I once again experienced the wisdom in the African saying that <u>in unity there is strength</u>. We were able to accomplish such a big project because we were willing to work as a team. Our time, energies, and cooperation were the main resources we had.

When we had finished baking the bricks and I was watching the building of the wall, a nun from Pajule parish convent who had been a religious for over thirty years came and stood beside me. She could sense that I was being fulfilled by what was going on. She told me: "Father, before this wall is completed you will be asked to leave Pajule to go somewhere else." This was strange to me. I had no plans to leave Pajule and was certain that she did not have any contacts or connections with my superiors, but she did have long experience as a nun in being moved to different places. This disturbed me, but I ignored it and continued with what I was doing. Later I asked myself if it could be that God was the one speaking to me through this nun.

One of the highlights of the parish Jubilee Year celebration for me was the building of the grotto of our Mother, Mary. Mary, help of Christians, was the patroness of the parish, but the parish community did not have any concrete symbol showing the spiritual significance of Mary in our life. We resolved to build a grotto because we wanted to thank her for the protection that many of us had experienced through her intercession in the community and to create a sacred space where members of the parish could always go to meet her in prayer and feel her constant presence.

When we knew what we wanted to accomplish, one of the very first challenges we had was the funding. We needed close to three thousand dollars for the work. Trusting in providence once again, I invited a sculptor who was a blood relative to come from Gulu to Pajule, and I took care of the cost of his transport and upkeep. He remained with me for three days.

While in Pajule, I explained to the sculptor what we intended to do. I showed him where we wanted the grotto to be built and the size of the statue of Mary, and then asked him to make a statue of St. Joseph that we would place in the church. As he was returning to Gulu, I gave him two hundred dollars from my personal savings to begin the work and promised him that if I got additional money, I would send it to him. I felt deeply within myself that if we were doing God's work, God would open a way for us to get the money for this project as long as we got it rolling.

One morning an idea came to my mind, and I went to town and began sharing it with a few friends who were mostly businesspeople. I reminded them that Mary was the spiritual mother of the community and had been our protector throughout the war, and it was time for us to do something for her. These businesspeople were mainly non-churchgoers. Many of them had fallen away from the Church for various reasons, some because of laziness and indifference and others because they had become polygamists so the Church became an uncomfortable environment for them. And a few of them never made any attempt to join any Christian Church. These non-churchgoers responded very generously to my request. While they may not have been practicing Christians, they believed that if they had some success at business it was because God had blessed them and continued to protect them as they constantly traveled on the risky roads. A few of them who had not set foot on the parish compound for years asked me to give them a lift to the parish to show them what we intended to do and then donated generously to our cause. From these businesspeople we had a donation of thirty-five bags of cement. Some of them paid for the building stones and others for the costs of transporting the building items to the site of the grotto. I could see so much joy in them, first, because they were being recognized as important to the Church, and second, they were being given the chance to do something for the Church even if they were not active members in it.

However, our request for their active participation tapped into the long-standing belief of most Africans: that there is a higher power in charge of their destiny even if they do not belong to any organized faith group. It is a rare phenomenon to find an African who says he or she is an atheist. Since most of these businesspersons did not come to church for one reason or another, I often joked with them that "even if you have more important duties to perform on Sundays than worship, the Christian community will always pray for your well-being and intention to make more money." It was an exciting moment for us to see non-churchgoers energized about activities going on in the parish.

As part of the parish Jubilee Year activities, within six months we built a protective wall around the rectory, made a grotto to the Blessed Virgin Mary, replaced the roof of the church, got a new statue of Joseph and Mary, transferred the tabernacle and placed it immediately behind the altar to make it convenient for those who wanted to adore and show reverence to the Blessed Sacrament, and finally had pilgrimages to Kitgum mission and Gulu cathedral. We had very little financial resources to do the things that we accomplished, and we relied on the participation and the goodwill of the community members. This whole experience of being able to do so much in material terms yet with very little resources confirmed and strengthened my belief in divine providence.

Chapter Thirty-Seven

Unsung Heroes in the War Zone

The months of December 2003 and January 2004 were relatively peaceful in Pajule even though we continued to get reports of abductions and attacks on travelers. But on February 11, 2004, a major incident took place. In January 2004, CARITAS had employed another accountant to be the financial controller of the Pader branch office. This accountant was a personable, gentle, and humble man. He was named Mr. Lagulu. Previously, he had been an accountant in one of the church institutions. He was well trained and aware of the risks he was taking in accepting his new job. He needed it to support his young family. And he was strongly inspired by the desire to do something for the victims of war.

When I met him, I was impressed by his personality because he exuded calm and peace. Most of us in the community usually acted out of stress. Surprisingly, he knew a lot about me since he saw me visit the seminary in which he was employed on a couple of occasions, and yet I did not ever remember seeing or meeting him.

One Sunday after I had celebrated three Masses in the parish, I felt very bad. I did not feel happy; I was bored and had no appetite for my lunch at all. Normally, when the place was relatively peaceful after I had celebrated two Masses, I would go to celebrate an additional Mass at one of the twenty-five chapels in the parish. But in the month of February 2004, most of the chapels were still closed, and there was no way for me to ascertain if it was safe enough to travel because there were very few people on the roads on Sunday.

What I often did after saying Mass was have my lunch and immediately take a siesta. Sometimes I slept very deeply since I found it safer to fall asleep during the day than at night. I thought that maybe I was tired and needed a rest. So instead of eating lunch I went to bed. After sleeping for three hours, I woke up at around five p.m. and still felt bored and restless; my mood was as bad as before. I began to think that I was falling ill since I often lost my appetite as an initial sign of a fever. I tried to eat once again, but the food was tasteless in my mouth. Since I was feeling down, I drove to Pajule to spend some time with friends. I was thinking that if I spent some time with them, I would feel better. Culturally, a good and successful day for my community is not judged by the amount of work one has done but by the good conversations and the company one has had.

In the whole town we had one social joint and drinking place where most of the opinion leaders, in particular the men, met in the evenings and shared their experiences of the day. It was also the place where the only satellite television in the town was located. I frequented the place since it made me feel connected to what was happening in the rest of the world. We often watched news programs carried by cable networks like CNN, Sky News, and the South African Broadcasting Corporation (SABC). Watching things other than violence reminded us of what we missed in the community and the peaceful times that we were longing to have once again.

When seven p.m. came, it was time for me to return to the parish. I had met many people and talked about the events of the day, but my spirit continued to be low. Even the glass of beer that I once in a while enjoyed tasted like bitter herbs in my mouth. Back in the parish, I opted to take a cup full of warm milk and go to bed at seven thirty p.m. While in bed, I felt mentally and physically exhausted and yet I could not fall asleep. I kept on endlessly turning in my bed.

I woke up early and celebrated Mass in the parish at seven a.m. Immediately after the Mass a social worker who was a trained catechist and a close friend came to see if I was sick since he thought I looked tired, demoralized, and exhausted at the altar. I told him that I was fine but I had not had a good rest the previous night. He understood since it was common for us to spend sleepless nights.

On weekdays after I celebrated Mass in the morning, my regular routine was to immediately check on my pigs, and then I would eat breakfast. It was only after I had my morning breakfast that I would begin to see people in the parish office. It was a rule for me to eat first before embarking on office work because if I did not I wouldn't have another chance. I often joked that I always woke up fresh and happy in the mornings, but it was the people with their issues who disturbed my day since they brought all sorts of matters for me to handle and some of them were beyond my comprehension. This was because I was everything to them: spiritual leader, security analyst, economic adviser, medical doctor, and transporter.

This particular morning, just like many other mornings when I felt unwell after Mass, I went back to bed. Whenever I did this, the parish attendants automatically concluded that I was feeling sickly that day. After two hours, I got out of bed to call the headquarters of the archdiocese in Gulu and make arrangements to have the color of the parish truck repainted from green to golden because green was considered the color of the military. I did not want to be shot at because of mistaken identity.

At about ten forty-five a.m., I took my cell phone from my bedroom, met the cook in the dining room, and told him that I was going to call the diocesan headquarters and would return in an hour's time. As soon as I got out of the house, I met one of the social workers running into the compound of the rectory shouting, "Father, Father, Father, the accountant is dead." Hearing this was like being rudely woken up from a deep sleep. At once I recognized that the restlessness, the lack of peace I had was the spirit of a death hovering in the place. With this terrible and shocking news, my restlessness came to an end since I knew that this was what my body had been trying to communicate to me for almost twenty-four hours.

Instinctively I realized that I needed to be calm and cool since I needed to take charge of the whole situation. I rushed to the vehicle with the body of the victim that had just parked minutes before under the mango tree in front of the parish office, but I did not know which accountant I would find dead since CARITAS at the time had two. At first what came to my mind was that it was the accountant of the Pajule Reception Center because he often traveled the same routes in the same vehicle. I was fond of him since we had been together in Pajule for a longer time; the parish cook, Ojok, had nicknamed him Akunta, a name that we used because many in the parish found it hard to pronounce his job title of accountant.

As I approached the vehicle that had been attacked to view the dead body, I saw Akunta and the chauffeur of the Pader branch office get out, their clothing soaked in blood. At once, it dawned on me that he had survived, and it was the accountant of the Pader branch office that had been killed. On reaching the car, I found that the front and back windshields of the car had been shattered by bullets. The accountant sat lifeless, still occupying the middle front seat in the truck, his head leaning toward the left-hand side of the windscreen. There was still plenty of blood gushing out of his head and his mouth was wide open. The bullet had hit him in the back of his head. Four days ago I had met him at the Pader branch office, and the previous day he came for Sunday Mass. Now he was dead.

The sight of his lifeless body made something like a cold chill enter me. I could feel so much weight on me: my head, heart, and legs. A day that had started like all other days suddenly turned dark. I could not feel anything except pain and uncertainty. Even though his body was before me, he seemed to be very far from me and in a different world completely. Death had violently snatched him away from us.

The CARITAS truck that entered the ambush was carrying three social workers: the two accountants, one for the Pader branch office and the other for Pajule Reception Center, and the chauffeur. They left Pader at around ten twenty a.m. after breakfast. The drive to Pajule under normal circumstances was about fifteen minutes. As the vehicle reached a spot within Paiula, the occupants of the vehicle heard loud sounds and blasts. At first, they thought that one of the car tires had burst, but surprisingly the truck continued moving normally. Then, they saw seven men jump from the bushes onto the road, line up on both sides within a distance of one hundred meters, and begin firing directly at them.

At this moment, because the vehicle was moving very fast, it passed through and nobody was hit. But the rebels ran into the center of the road and fired bullets at the vehicle as it passed. This was when the accountant was hit in the back of his head. When blood splashed inside the vehicle, the other accountant held the hands of his colleague and, finding that they were cold, concluded that he was dead.

With this brutal killing, our bright morning was taken away from us. Instead of going to call about work being done on my truck, I went now with one of the social workers, Mr. Sam, to inform the diocesan authorities of what had happened in the area of my jurisdiction. When we reached Oguta we found the army commander in the area communicating from the spot. He was aware of what had happened and told us that we ought to be quick and leave as soon as we were finished since there were suspected rebel movements in the area. Sam and I communicated to the deputy of the bishop and the director of CARITAS what had happened.

When we returned to the parish, we found that it had calmed down and the body had been removed from the car, cleaned, and was now in the house. I was impressed by the civil and political leaders, for as soon as they heard of this unfortunate incident they all came to give us moral support. We were determined to take the corpse to Gulu, and from there it would be delivered to his family. However, the major problem we faced was that there was no road we considered safe enough to use. After considering all the options possible, we realized that we could not agree on how to proceed because every option was laden with serious risks. We then asked the chauffeur who was to transport the body to Gulu what he felt. He was not the one who was involved in the ambush, for he and his vehicle were specifically assigned to Pajule Reception Center. He told us that deep in his gut he felt that if we took the shorter route to Gulu via Atanga, even if it was riskier, we would arrive safely. So a convoy of vehicles left for Gulu using Atanga Road.

After about one hour, those of us who remained in Pajule called and were able to confirm that they had arrived without any incident along the way, and this was a big relief to all of us. The following day, Mass was conducted at Saint Joseph's Cathedral in Gulu before the body was taken to Kiryandongo for burial. Those of us who were left in Pajule followed the whole event on the local FM station called Radio Mega.

It was sad that this gentle man died before even receiving his first monthly paycheck since he had been at his new job less than a month. His wife, parents, and relatives were devastated. But what impressed most people at the burial was the spirit of his family. While they were very sad, they were not filled with rage or vengeance. They saw their loss and pain in the context of the losses and pains that many families were going through because of the war. It was absolutely within their rights to pursue compensation from the authorities of the archdiocese of Gulu since their son was employed in a Church organization, but they did not wish to.

I personally consider Mr. Lagulu, the accountant of Pader branch office, as one of the heroes of this war. He was like so many husbands and wives, men and women, who were willing to take extreme risks because of the love and the sense of responsibility they felt to their families to put food on the table and meet their needs. And many times, they woke up in the morning to go about their daily routine and never returned in the same way that they had left home.

Chapter Thirty-Eight

The Rhino and the Elephant Cannot Always Walk on Eggshells.

A day after my installation as pastor of Pajule, the mayor brought a little girl, who was about ten years old, to meet the deputy of the bishop. He wanted to bring to his attention the unhealthy tribal dimension that the LRA war was increasingly taking. Both of this girl's parents had been killed in a place called Oyam in the Lango region. They had gone shopping in the local market, and since they spoke the Luo language with an Acoli dialect, someone falsely accused them of being LRA spies. They were both physically attacked and clobbered to death. Even though it was almost one month since the death of her parents, the little girl could hardly talk and was still in a state of shock. She remembered that when her parents were killed, some of the neighbors came and took her home and hid her for several days till they felt that it was safe to put her in a passenger vehicle and take her to Pajule, the home of her deceased parents.

The Lango region also suffered greatly from the LRA war. Most of the LRA attacks were intended to create terror, abduct new recruits, obtain supplies, and break the resolve of the people to resist them, but what we shall never know is if the motivation behind the attacks had a tribal component to it. Although the LRA committed crimes in both northern and eastern Uganda, the reality of the situation is that it created bad blood and resurrected old tribal tensions between the Acoli and Lango tribes because Kony and the majority of his fighters were Acoli. The perceptions of the two communities were diametrically opposed as well, for while the Acoli people looked at themselves as victims of the Kony war, the Langi (people), with the exception of some intellectuals and the business community, saw themselves as victims of the aggression perpetrated by the Acoli people through the participation of their sons and daughters in the LRA.

Since the resumption of the LRA war in 2002, we constantly received reports from sources such as eyewitnesses, army intelligence, and former LRA abductees that there was a great deal of hostility to the Acoli people in the Lango region due to the LRA attacks. Some of the returnees who surrendered in the Lango region and returned home to Pajule shared stories about how close they came to being stoned or beaten to death by villagers because of their background, and their lives were only spared through the intervention of the army, since the local leaders stood by and watched, unable or unwilling to protect them from the hostile crowds.

Because of these constant reports of hostility, there was a popular view in Pajule and Acoliland in general that the Lango region had become completely unsafe for the Acoli. At a certain point, there were even attempts by the business communities from the districts of Kitgum and Pader to boycott shopping in Lira and go to Gulu instead because of the tribal attacks.

The many atrocities committed by the LRA in the Lango region, especially at the beginning of the month of February 2004, put the spotlight on the Acoli and Lango communities and in particular their response to the events. One morning in Lira, demonstrations were organized to protest the failure of the government to protect the people, but they soon got out of control and became violent. The Acoli people became targets; two were killed, and many more lives could have been lost had the military not intervened. And in Gulu that very evening, irate youths who had heard of the attacks on the Acoli people that morning in Lira town went on a rampage searching for the Langi in passenger vehicles. Fortunately, they were unable to identify anyone of Lango origin, and measures were taken by the government in both the Lango and Acoli regions to make sure that there were no more tribal killings.

As tensions caused by the LRA war between the two tribes mounted, other Ugandan tribes could not understand why the two tribes whom they saw as victims of the war were turning on each other. They questioned if the Kony war was really the cause of the tension or if there was something deeper because they have so much in common socially, culturally, and even historically. For most of the history of Uganda as an independent country, they have shared the good and bad times together.

In the month of April 2004, the tribal tensions came to Pajule. I was suddenly awakened from my afternoon siesta by the sound of cries from the parish compound. I immediately went out of the house and was told, "Father, the Amuka (Lango people) have killed some of our people today, and among them is Mr. Akaj." In fact, Akaj's vehicle was parked in the parish compound. The previous day he had gone to Lira to buy some spare parts for his truck. His relatives were trying to force open the door since they could not locate its key, and they wanted to drive it home.

I knew Akaj well, since every evening he parked his truck at the parish. He was almost seven feet tall, gentle, and if he were in a crowd, you could barely hear his voice. His life revolved around his passenger truck, which was old and constantly in need of repair. I am convinced that if he had not been a mechanic himself, the vehicle would have stopped running long ago. He had been killed together with six other residents of Pajule.

As part of the effort to fight the LRA in the Lango region, the government set up and recruited a militia called the Amuka to fight the LRA and to protect the people in the camps. The word *amuka* means "rhinoceros." This is the cultural symbol of the Lango people. For the Acoli people, it is the elephant. The choice of the name of the militia explicitly stated that its purpose was to protect the Lango tribe. And because of this, the Amuka embodied the cultural attitudes and dynamics of the two communities regarding the war. When doing their morning drills, they would sing songs saying things like "We shall push the LRA back to their birthplace; we will reclaim our ancestral land and the new boundary line between the two tribes will be at Pajule." Because of such statements and the prevailing negative attitude toward the Acoli people resulting from the LRA attacks, traveling for many Acoli people through the Lango region in places where the "Amuka" were deployed became a nightmare.

Most ambushes were attributed to the LRA, and few investigations were conducted since the LRA usually disappeared into the bushes. But the circumstances regarding the one in which Mr. Akaj and the others were killed was very suspicious. It occurred just after a place called Agweng on the Lango side of the road that was thought to be safe and was close to a temporary barracks of the Amuka militia. The amateurish manner in which the attackers tried to burn the vehicle raised more questions. Usually, the LRA successfully set a vehicle ablaze if that was their intention because they knew how to do it and only failed when the military intervened. They would use a stalk of tall dry grass shaped like a piece of corn but longer, set its top on fire with a match stick, and then push the burning torch directly into the fuel tank; instantly the vehicle would burst into flames. What was most surprising about this ambush was that the attackers did not seem to know this; after they set the dry grass on fire, they placed it under the gas pedal, but the vehicle did not catch fire because the hard board would not burn. This made many speculate that the Amuka must have heard that the LRA set vehicles ablaze in this manner and wanted to do something similar but did not know exactly how.

Seeing the anger and the tension at the parish among the relatives of Akaj, I immediately left on foot for town. I was afraid that in the heat of the moment, the people and the families of the deceased would begin to attack any Langi in our midst since some lived and worked in the place or were married to people in the community. Fortunately, when I reached the center of the town, I was relieved to find that my worst fears were not taking place. As soon as the bodies of the deceased were delivered, the Langi in public places immediately went home and locked themselves in their houses out of fear.

I then embarked on what I call the "apostolate and ministry of presence" for the families affected. I had done it many times in the past, especially when people had been killed in LRA ambushes. I would spend about fifteen to twenty minutes with the family that had suffered a loss and any mourners present. Most of the time I sat down or stood quietly, later prayed silently, and then left. If it was possible for me to talk to a member of the family, I offered my sympathies, spiritual and emotional support, and concluded with a prayer and blessing; but most times, I could not do this because there were too many people present. But this time, the spirit and the air around the deaths were full of anger, revenge, and violence since these were suspected to be tribal killings.

According to Acoli custom, when a person passes away, the corpse is put in the house, covered, and treated with dignity. But since the dead were suspected to have been the victims of tribal killings, the relatives were firmly of the view that consolation for them and the spirits of the deceased would only come if these killings were avenged. So as an expression of their anger, they did not take the corpses into their houses but left them in the yard with much of the bodies uncovered and the bullet wounds open to the view of the mourners. The more the people looked at the corpses, the more anger it generated in them. And when it began to rain, the mourners left, and the family members of the deceased went inside their houses and left the corpses to be soaked by the rain.

By the time I got to the last family, it was still raining heavily. I entered the mud hut where they were gathered. After I had expressed my sympathies, I asked them why they left the dead body out in the rain, as it was the first time I witnessed this tribal custom. They told me: "Father, according to Acoli culture and tradition, when people die by tribal violence, their deaths call for the blood of the attackers to be shed." I listened to them without comment, as I knew quite well they were aware I did not approve of what they were advocating, and at the same time, I considered it inappropriate for me to enter into an argument with them.

What surprised me most was the age of the men explaining the cultural practice to me; they were in their late twenties and early thirties. I did not expect them to be aware of such things and above all, to be their custodians. They were discussing practices that I believe were only actually done by their ancestors when ethnic wars were a reality. And above all, they were born to Catholic families and grew up as practicing Christians.

In the hut, I felt like a stranger and to some extent rejected. It was like they were telling me: "Father, this is what we truly believe in and where our real identity and loyalty is. Today, we are just being true to ourselves. Christianity, the religion brought by the white missionaries that you represent in our midst, does not speak to or address this moment and time in our lives. But our African culture and tradition does."

After about twenty minutes, it was coming on eight p.m. and was now dark. I walked back to the parish as it continued to rain heavily. And I kept asking myself numerous questions. "What do my people really believe in? Have they really been converted to Christianity? Why do they think that Christianity does not speak to them at this particular moment of loss and pain?"

The following day, the burials were conducted. Fortunately, there were no incitements against the Langi, and Pajule began to calm down. But the tribal bitterness and anger expressed on the day the corpses were brought hung over the community. As I was still thinking about my next actions, what I found most gratifying was that many in the community were also concerned about the same thing: they did not want any revenge killings or for the Langi in our midst to live in fear. Within days, individuals, neighbors, and local leaders began to discuss the way forward. They reached out to families who had lost loved ones and urged them not to entertain thoughts of revenge, and in fact, they found most of them to be very receptive. To make all the Langi families feel safe, they were invited to a meeting and reassured that the community would never carry out any revenge killings against them.

The initial response of my community to the ambush laden with feelings of hate, violence, and revenge, I believe, tapped into the complicated, underlying, and unresolved issues at the heart of the relationship between the Acoli and Lango tribes. These two tribes have been neighbors for several generations. They have lived and worked together peacefully, and they have fought for political dominance, land, and hunting grounds, especially before the creation of the modern state of Uganda.

The most recent conflict was the overthrow of the government of Milton Obote, a son of the Lango region, by some Acoli army officers. And in past bitter conflicts, several lives were lost and feelings deeply wounded causing long-term resentments, biases, and feelings of contempt and mistrust between the two tribes, most of which exist to the present day.

The conflicts that took place several generations ago produced statements that both tribes consider culturally offensive and radioactive. For example: "You are cowards, you have no brains, you are stupid, we grabbed your land, and we torched you." If an Acoli says any of these straight to the face of a Lango person or a Lango does the same to an Acoli, however educated and civil they may seem to be, a brawl may literally break out. And this is the main problem that the two tribes face, that most things are read through the prism of tragic events that occurred in their past. This is the primary means through which they view one another and interpret the actions of the other. As a result, their relationship with the other is often defined by mutual mistrust, suspicion, and at times, contempt.

Today, for the most part, these two tribes maintain a cordial relationship in their dealings with each other. But a lot of this has been motivated by a fear that any apparent disagreement or criticism may reopen old wounds. There is the constant fear that the matter at hand might spiral out of control and no one would know how to address it. In short, it is a delicate relationship, because it is like trying to walk on eggshells all the time.

As the LRA war was increasingly being viewed through an ethnic dimension, there were some meetings organized by the cultural and religious leaders of the two communities in Gulu and Lira, and joint visits to the areas that had been affected by the killings. But there was no persistent and concerted effort on the part of the cultural and religious leaders to boldly provide leadership on the subject. On most occasions they could not even agree on the realities of the situation or acknowledge that some lives could have been lost because the Kony war was becoming tribalized. For the most part it was left to the military and political leadership to handle as if it were a law-and-order issue because there was too much suspicion, lack of trust, and unease between the cultural and religious leaders of the two communities to have a frank discussion on anything. And above all, no attempt was made to address the underlying issues at the heart of the differences between the two tribes. And yet, I am convinced that it was and it is still within their power to call for and organize a historic reconciliation between the two tribes that would put an end to several generations of mistrust, resentment, and suspicion.

Further, I am of the opinion that the religious leaders in the two ethnic groups need to be actively involved in reconciling the two tribes that are almost 90 percent Christian. Without this, the conversion of their flock is cosmetic and only skin deep, and it makes Christianity seem impotent since it is incapable of transforming and converting certain aspects of the lives of the two communities—which I do not believe is the case. And if it is not addressed, the two tribes will continue to live with social and cultural "minefields" that remain potential sources for future violence on a mass scale. This also points to the broader challenge that Christianity faces in many parts of the world: while it has an enthusiastic following, it has had a minimal impact on changing the negative stereotypes and cultural attitudes that the tribes had toward one another before they embraced it.

The issues between the two tribes can be used as a template for understanding the many violent tribal and cultural conflicts in Africa and other parts of the world. Most of these conflicts are not about the issues of today but unresolved past issues, and the current troubles only serve to reignite them. Most of the time, these conflicts never really died but continued to be fought in other ways than through violence.

All in all, I believe there is no place for tribal conflicts in the modern society. The boundaries and separation it tries to create among people is superficial and artificial. Human beings today are so interconnected. There are no pure tribes anymore. The Acoli and Langi are much better off in all sectors of life when they put their past behind them and pursue their common interests together. That is why I believe it is time for the elephant and the rhino to reconcile through cultural means, hug each other, and stop walking on eggshells.

Chapter Thirty-Nine

Mato Opwut: The Way Forward

I believe that in reading through the previous chapters of this book, one of the questions that you must be asking yourself is: *"If a society has gone through so much violence, pain, and suffering, how will it ever put its past behind it and lead a normal life?"* To me, the way to bring healing and closure to the many pains and hurts that the ordinary people of Acoli and neighboring communities have gone through is in the cultural ritual practice of the people called Mato Opwut, which literally means "the drinking of bitter herbs." This ritual has worked in the past and even today continues to realize positive results whenever it is implemented. The basis and foundations of this cultural ceremony are reconciliation, forgiveness, love, and conversion.

Mato Opwut is an Acoli cultural ritual ceremony in which two parties, one representing the victim and the other representing the perpetrator of a crime, drink the roots of a bitter herbal tree called *opwut*. What often precipitates the exercise of this ritual is an unfortunate incident, like the killing or murder of an innocent, which has strained relationships and created tension in the community among relatives or clan members. To move past this unfortunate incident, the society as a whole embarks on a journey of reconciliation and forgiveness to restore harmony among its members through a ritual ceremony.

This is an effective ritual for healing and reconciliation among the Acoli because it has the following characteristics: it is expressive, formal, traditional, and authoritative; it is public, social, and collective; and it embodies and transmits vital cultural information and processes, meanings, values, and categories with the primary intent of achieving social cohesion.

There are several operative elements. The first is a meeting between the elders on the side of the victim and the side of the perpetrator of the crime. In this meeting, there is the active participation by all the elders present. The two sides examine the circumstances under which the incident occurred and discuss its negative consequences on existing relationships and bonds in the community.

Further, they place blame where it is due and condemn any crime that was committed against a member of the community; then they urge the two sides to forgive and reconcile so as to live harmoniously. They deliberate on an appropriate fine or reparation depending on the circumstances. If they determine that a crime was intentionally committed, the fine or reparation charged is higher; if it was accidental, the fine or reparation is lower. The reparation is often paid in terms of animals (bulls or cows), and if the family of the perpetrator cannot afford to pay it on its own, its whole clan comes in to assist because of the value that the society attaches to reconciliation and healing among its members

The second operative element in the ritual is the drinking of the bitter herbs. This is done after the reconciliatory discussions have been concluded. Culturally it is believed to be curative and medicinal. The elders in the meeting drink the bitter herbs on behalf of both sides because there is a sociocultural belief that an offence causes hurts, wounds, bitterness, and pain. Bitter herbs are drunk symbolically to bring about healing to the individuals involved and society as a whole.

The third operative element is the social celebration and dancing. The elders and the two sides now come together to eat, drink, and dance, marking the end of the ritual, forgiveness, reconciliation, and a new beginning.

Fundamentally, the cultural ritual Mato Opwut is significant because those who participate in it believe that they are participating in a sacred action. It is shrouded in mystical powers, and there is a strong cultural belief that going against the commitments and pledges made in the ritual ceremony will anger a higher power that watches and expects the two sides to faithfully implement its resolutions. This is because once the ritual has been performed, there is no looking back, and the matter is closed for good. And the whole community believes in its effectiveness; no matter how bitter, angry, or contentious the past may have been, with the completion of this ritual total trust and reconciliation is achieved and restored.

Culturally there is the spiritual conviction that once the ritual has been completed, human transformation and conversion is realized, and peace between the two sides is permanently restored. The offender is forgiven of the crime and is reconciled to the community once and for all, a free person from that moment. If this person would like to continue living in that same community, he or she is free to do so, but if not that is acceptable as well.

I personally believe that this traditional means of reconciliation is the best way to bring about justice and healing for the people in the Acoliland and northern Uganda in general. First, it has been proven effective; second, it is rooted in the spiritual value systems of the people, which are forgiveness, reconciliation, and love. All in all, Mato Opwut as a ritual may be unique to the people of Acoli, but the cultural values that it embodies are shared widely by other Ugandan cultural groupings and tribes.

My Bone of Contention with the International Criminal Court

In the year 2003, the Ugandan government invited the International Criminal Court (ICC) to study the LRA war for the atrocities committed against humanity in northern Uganda. After reviewing the case, the ICC opened an investigation in northern Uganda in 2004. And in July 2005, the ICC issued arrest warrants for Joseph Kony, the leader of the LRA and four of his key military commanders: Raska Lukwiya, Okot Odhiambo, Dominic Ongwen, and Vincent Otti. Even if there were real grounds for the invitation of the ICC to get involved, I am critical of the role of the International Criminal Court for a number of reasons:

First, the mandate of the ICC to investigate only the LRA is unfair to the victims of the war in northern Uganda. I believe that if the ICC is fully committed to the cause of justice for all the victims of the war in northern Uganda, it should investigate all parties in the conflict in northern Uganda, both the government soldiers and the LRA rebels, since these have been the primary adversaries.

Second, the mandate of the ICC is too limited in its scope, which is only to investigate crimes committed by the LRA rebels after July 1, 2002—that is, from the time period when the tribunal investigating war crimes in northern Uganda was put in place—and yet the war between the LRA and the government of Uganda started as far back as 1988. The ICC, in my opinion, cannot conduct a credible investigation and later prosecution of war crimes in northern Uganda while ignoring the years between 1988 and 2002 since there are several cases of abuses of human rights committed by government soldiers and LRA rebels that have been documented by the civil society in northern Uganda. I feel very strongly that an investigation of war crimes based on terms that are convenient to the Ugandan government is unacceptable and cannot bring justice to the people of northern Uganda. This makes the ICC appear like a tool of the Ugandan government.

Third, the involvement of the ICC denies the victims of the war in northern Uganda the final say on what should be done to those who have committed atrocities against them because the legal system that is at the basis of the ICC is that of retributive justice that is Western, European, and foreign. And yet for the people of northern Uganda, true justice for crimes committed is based on a restorative system of justice in which one comes face to face with the perpetrator of a crime against one, and after going through a cultural ritual process, forgiveness takes place. Most people of northern Uganda believe that it is only through the forgiveness of past atrocities that closure can be achieved and the past put behind them; then society can begin to heal. Hurling insults during court sentencing and passing death sentences, hangings, or long periods of incarcerations as in other cultures do not meet the benchmarks of true justice for the people of northern Uganda.

Personally I believe that the involvement of the ICC in Uganda was counterproductive because it served only to provide ammunition for the government of Uganda to sabotage the dialogue that it was reluctantly engaging in with the rebels, since it could now argue that it could not negotiate with indicted war criminals and the LRA rebels could not be part of any political arrangement if a peace agreement were reached. I believe this also had a negative impact on the commitment of the LRA to the peace process since they saw that they had no future for themselves in the political system even if they put down their weapons.

Further, the indictments of the LRA rebels by the International Criminal Court had a negative impact on the dialogue since they were outside the control of the government of Uganda and its people. The LRA rebels constantly raised this as the remaining obstacle that had to be addressed if they were to commit themselves to any final peace agreement.

All in all, the involvement of the ICC made the government of Uganda succeed in her scheme against dialogue. At the same time, it was a major disappointment to many people in Acoliland and the region, as it complicated the dialogue that was going on and left war as the only means to resolve the conflict. It also disrupted any cultural or traditional process to bring justice and closure to the people. And the ICC has not been able to execute her own indictments by arresting any of the indicted rebel commanders.

Chapter Forty
My Abrupt Departure

The news that I would leave Pajule to come to the United States of America was most shocking to me. In late June 2004, as I was returning from my vacation in Tororo archdiocese, the deputy of the bishop called me and informed me that the bishop had something important to discuss with me. So I postponed my return to Pajule to go to Gulu to find out what the bishop wanted to talk to me about. I did not know what to expect, but I thought that maybe he wanted to advise me against the many Jubilee Year events that made us travel out of the parish in large numbers placing our lives in danger on the roads, or that someone in the parish had raised a complaint against me.

However, when I reached Gulu, I found that the bishop had left the day before. In the evening after dinner the deputy of the bishop invited me to his living room and presented to me the prospectus of a university. He broke the news that the bishop had gotten a scholarship and wanted me to study at Walsh University in Canton, Ohio. When I heard this, I was shocked; I did not know how to respond since I did not have any plans to go to school at the moment. And the deputy of the bishop went on to say that the bishop was well aware that Pajule parish was celebrating her Jubilee Year, but he had made up his mind that I go to graduate school in the United States of America within two months. When he had presented me with the documents that he had and all the communications, I thanked him and told him that I needed to pray about it, promising him that I would also seek an audience with the bishop in the coming days.

My selection by the bishop to take this scholarship troubled me in several ways. First, I did not expect it, because all along I had hoped and planned to work in Pajule parish for a period of five years before considering any opportunities for further studies. Further, it was my hope that if I were to leave the place it would be in the month of August 2006, almost two years after completing the celebration of the parish Jubilee Year. This would have given me ample time to see that some of my plans for the place as pastor were implemented and realized.

However much Pajule parish was insecure and life full of risks, I found my work fulfilling since it gave meaning to my vocation as a priest. Because of this I considered working in it as the most important thing in my life at the time, and I was willing to forego other opportunities that might come my way. I was also concerned about the damage that would be caused to the morale of my parishioners by my abrupt departure, because even if they carried out most of the Jubilee Year activities independently, my presence and leadership galvanized them to tap into their potential.

Further, I had also built a strong relationship with the community. I could not imagine how I would begin to tell my parishioners that I was suddenly leaving and going to school in the middle of the celebration of the parish Jubilee Year, which had brought us much closer together than ever before. This strong bond and vibrant spiritual life in the parish made it possible for us to add two additional Sunday Masses to the Mass schedule. The Masses for the youth and children were the new additions at seven and eleven a.m. respectively.

My Days of Agony in Pajule

Because the bishop was not around, I returned to Pajule hoping to come back later to see him. While in Pajule, I felt confused. I was also physically, emotionally, and mentally drained. With all these things going on in my mind, I felt sick to my stomach. I did not know what to do. I felt lost. In fact, I needed some quiet time to process what I had heard and my thoughts about the situation.

At the parish, the community did sense something was going on inside me even if I had not told any of them. I could hear some of them ask themselves questions like "Our priest these days looks very low spirited and depressed; what is happening to him?" When others would come and ask to find out if I was OK, I would constantly reassure them that I was fine.

During this time, once in a while, I considered the possibility of accepting the offer. The question that always came to my mind was "What is the United States of America like?" I had seen movies made in Hollywood and some of them were about life in the USA, but I was certain that most of them were fictional and did not reflect real life in the USA. I had no idea at all what the place was like, and because of this it became more difficult for me to come to terms with the decision that I had to make. This kept me constantly restless and sleepless. Even when I allowed myself to think wildly, my imagination came up empty.

Sometimes, I would ask myself this question: "If I am to go to school in the United States, what theological discipline would I study?" I always believed that academic studies in the United States were more secular and liberal, and yet my interests were in historical theology. Other times, I wondered what student life would be like again: staying awake for long hours in the night to complete assignments, a tiny space to live in, and sitting in class for many hours listening to professors, who might be boring and not add anything of value to my life.

Pajule was a hard place, but I knew how to live and survive in it. It was a big parish with about sixty thousand people under my authority. To be entrusted with such a significant responsibility after being a priest for only three years was a big achievement. If I were to go to school, I had to give it up.

Even though I had all these misgivings about the timing of my going to school in the United States, I had always admired certain things about the United States of America as a country. First, the political system that periodically allows citizens to choose new leaders freely and fairly, and the fact that those who hold political office most of the time reflect the popular will. The institutions of the country serve the interests of citizens other than those who are in power. In short, the feelings and the desires of the citizens matter in the way the country is governed. And real political power is in the hands of the people and not the military. Second, the fact that the citizens are free to speak on all subjects including security and threats to their country without being intimidated by any of the security organs of the state.

The Elephant in the Room

After two weeks in Pajule, I returned to Gulu to meet the bishop. I still had mixed feelings about leaving Pajule to go to school in the United States of America. But I was now leaning toward accepting the offer and beginning to think more and more that it was what God wanted me to do. I also felt that it would be beneficial to my future ministry as a priest, even if it would mark the end of my ministry in Pajule since there was no guarantee I would ever return.

I wanted to ask the bishop to allow me report to school in January of 2005 instead of August 2004 since this would allow me to serve in the parish till the end of the year and to celebrate the Parish Jubilee day on December 8, 2004. I presented my case, which I thought was reasonable, to the bishop. He listened to it attentively but did not engage in any discussion with me on the subject, and only reaffirmed his earlier decision. And he informed me that the university was expecting me at the end of August

2004. I was left with less than two months before I reported. His response to my plea was a disappointment to me.

I felt like I had confronted an elephant in the room that both of us could not talk about. That is, respecting my promise of obedience to him as a priest. I saw that the merits of my arguments seemed not to matter to him. On my part I believed that I had grounds to say no to his decision to send me to school since less than a year ago he had appointed me pastor; by the virtue of the office that I was holding, the laws of the Church would have required him to consult with me and get my consent. However, I chose to obey him and trust in his judgment.

My bishop had been my rector for the three years in which I studied philosophy in the seminary. At the end of my third year, he was appointed to be the first bishop of a neighboring diocese called Nebbi, and I believe that as he took up this new role he left many things still in progress. After three years, he was sent back to my diocese when it was elevated to an archdiocese. Reflecting on what my bishop had gone through made me now accept going to school, and I requested that he designate my successor as soon as possible so that I could begin the orderly transfer of power to him. In fact, before the end of the day, I got a letter from him thanking me for my time of service in Pajule and communicating to the significant people in his administration that I was to travel to America to attend school.

The following day I left Gulu knowing that I needed to set up structures for the Jubilee Year celebration in the parish so it could function independently of me or the priest who would take over the parish administration. I put in place the committees for publicity and fundraising since I considered these to be absolutely necessary in the coming months.

Even as I worked on these, I could not communicate to the parishioners that I was leaving the place because I was afraid that it would have given rise to many questions I had no answers for. In fact, I had no information to give to my parishioners about who would succeed me in the parish except for some rumors I had heard that a deacon who was not yet ordained a priest would be assigned as an associate pastor in Pajule. Above all, I did not want my imminent departure from the place to become a distraction from what we were doing or to interfere with the smooth handover and transition.

Visa Issues: A Game of Cat and Mouse

Since I had decided to accept the bishop's offer, during the week I had to drive to Kampala to process my visa. The drive took almost six hours because of the poor road situation. And yet, I couldn't stay until the issue was resolved because I had to return to the parish to lead Mass over the weekend.

Before going for my visa appointment at the embassy, I had in my possession a number of documents from several sources including letters from my bishop, the schools that I had attended, and the secretary general of the Uganda Episcopal Conference. With these documents, including the university admission to the United States I felt confident that I would easily be granted the visa.

At the American embassy, the practice at the time was first come, first serve, which meant that if I were to secure a visa appointment I had to be there very early in the morning. For each and every visa appointment at the embassy, whether it was successful or unsuccessful, one had to pay one hundred dollars. The first time that I went for an appointment, there were close to four hundred people waiting at the gates. Since I arrived early and had all my documents in order I was allowed in for a face-to-face interview. When my turn came, a lady sitting behind tinted windows asked for my documents, which I showed her. She glanced at them and told me that they were not granting me the visa because even if my documents indicated that I had a scholarship, it did not specify that I had room and board. I left the embassy very disappointed because I had put so much work and time into preparing for the appointment. However, I was confident that if I got assurances and clarification from the university, things would be fine. So, I immediately sent them an e-mail asking them to send me a fax confirming that my scholarship covered room and board that I could take to the embassy. Then, as the weekend was drawing near, I left for Pajule.

I returned to Kampala on Tuesday since the university faxed their confirmation letter over the weekend. The following morning I went to the American embassy, and this time I was certain that I would be granted the visa. Because it was a second and separate visit, I presented one hundred dollars once again for the visa interview. When my turn came, I presented the documents that I had and the fax message from the university indicating that I had room and board. This was a different lady from the first visit, and she cursorily looked at my documents and the fax message and then asked for my grade-school certificate, which in Uganda is the primary leaving exam certificate. This request was strange because rarely do we present a grade-school certificate for anything unless it is the only certificate that a person has, and I was going to graduate school. I felt that the visa application process was like a game of cat and mouse, since with each and every visit the rules changed. It was focused more on finding a reason to deny giving a visa to someone to travel to the United States. Indeed, if they had wanted my grade-school certificate, they should have informed me about it when they declined to grant me the visa the first time. Then I would have brought it with me to my second appointment.

I once again returned to Pajule and called my bishop, telling him that I needed his intervention. A man with little standing like me needed him to use some of his influence and power. The second visit to the embassy had left me stressed, drained, demoralized, and devastated. I felt that I had enough problems in Pajule because of the insecurity. The emotional pains that I was going through at the embassy were self-inflicted; if I canceled the idea of going to school in the United States, I would be spared these troubles. As I was returning to Pajule, I made up my mind that if my bishop had not talked to the people at the embassy and gotten assurances that I had a possibility of getting a visa, I would not return to the embassy again and would cancel the idea of going to school altogether.

Before returning to Pajule, a friend advised me to call the public relations officer at the American embassy and register my complaint, which I did. I passed the cell phone number to my bishop, who called him after two days and had a discussion with him about my plight.

A week later the public relations officer at the American embassy called me and told me that the status of my application had been reviewed and my chances were good. I needed to bring all my supportive documents, and they were not going to charge me any new visa fees for this appointment. This made me leave all that I was doing in Pajule and hurry to Kampala since my third appointment at the embassy was scheduled the next day at 12:30 p.m. I reached Kampala at midnight the night before my appointment.

As I entered the US embassy from the side gate, I found everyone nice and friendly to me this time, though in my heart I wondered if they were not trying to make up for the pains I had been suffering at their hands. This time I met a much older man, who looked at my documents and cross-examined me; he wanted to know where I came from and what I did and why I was choosing to go to school in United States. He asked me more details about the school, its ownership, scholarship policy, etc. I could answer some of the questions but not all since I did not know how the university system operated in the United States, but he appeared satisfied with my answers and told me to return to pick up my visa the following day at three p.m. When I heard this, I was really excited and relieved. I felt like running out of the embassy and calling friends to tell them that I had been granted the visa. I returned the following day, picked up my visa, and was among the nine people in total whose application had been approved out of hundreds. I was happy that I had been granted the visa, and at the same time I was filled with pity for those who could not get one. I belonged to a big institution, the Church, within which I had someone to speak for me; yet there were many people who had credible and legitimate reasons to travel but were not connected like me.

As I returned to Pajule parish with my visa, there was still no word of who was to succeed me. But I felt that it was important to communicate to my close collaborators that I was soon to leave and that it was important that they begin to prepare themselves for a change of administration. I had to reassure them that even without my physical presence everything was going to be fine.

The Official Announcement to Leave Pajule

When I had two weeks remaining before leaving Pajule, I invited the Episcopal vicar of Kitgum vicariate to officially inform the people that it was time for me to leave. He was happy to come to Pajule because it had been almost two years since he had visited the place. After he had celebrated Mass with my parishioners, he made the announcement before the final blessing. He was certain that the news of me leaving was going to be greeted with great disbelief and noticeable disappointment.

However, he spoke skillfully to the people. He thanked them for their faith and what they were doing in their parish with regard to their parish Jubilee Year celebration. He said that the Church in the archdiocese of Gulu was proud of them and because of this the bishop would be appointing a second priest to Pajule parish. He was referring to a newly ordained priest who would be the associate pastor of the parish. He went on to say that the bishop was also pleased with their collaboration with the priests, and because of this he was sending their parish priest (meaning me) to the United States to acquire more knowledge to serve them. When the people heard this, I could sense a certain degree of confusion and disbelief as they tried to digest what they had heard. It was exciting for a few, because they saw it as if it were their own achievement, since they took me to be one of their own. But most of them loudly complained and grumbled, "If our priest is to go to study in the United States, it means that he will be leaving us and will not to be present in our midst, and this is not a good idea."

Then the vicar went on to tell the congregation that my former pastor would be in charge of the parish while the newly ordained priest was going to be resident in Pajule, and would handle the day-to-day affairs of the parish till the bishop had identified my replacement. When the people heard this, the murmurs became even louder, and I did not know what to make of it. After Mass, I noticed that the spirit of my congregation had become so low that they looked like deflated tires. I heard many of them wonder aloud, "What shall we do without our priest? What about our Jubilee Year celebration? Will the spirit of volunteerism in the parish be kept alive? Will the parish still continue to be a welcoming place? Will the parish be the same?"

In the evening, I visited town and met some of my friends who were not churchgoers but had helped us to raise the money to build the grotto of the Blessed Virgin Mary. Many of them were in a state of shock when they learned that I would soon be leaving them. A few of them were happy for me to have the chance to go to school and at the same time disappointed that my time among them was coming to an end. Others talked about how I made them feel loved by God even if they were considered public sinners in the community because they were polygamists.

After this I went to Gulu, making sure that I returned with the newly ordained priest who was going to be resident in Pajule. I knew him quite well since we had been students of theology at the same seminary, except that he was three years behind me. We'd had a good relationship there, and I knew him as someone who always spoke his mind. Personality-wise, we had some similarities since we were both quiet and reflective. This was one of the factors considered in his choice as my replacement. But in our leadership style, we were very different for he came across as stricter and followed up things to the minutest detail, while on my part I was more relaxed and interested in seeing the big picture.

When we arrived, the youth in the parish were waiting for us, and we immediately entered the church to celebrate a Thanksgiving Mass for the arrival of the new priest in their parish. The Mass was well attended. After Mass the youth came to sing welcoming and farewell songs at the rectory; the songs were meaningful, but in them one could feel a deep sense of sadness that I was leaving. I could also see that the newly ordained priest was overwhelmed. In the first place, Pajule parish was still very insecure; I had lived and worked in it because I had come to the resolution that perseverance was what God wanted from me at this particular moment of my life. He had soon to decide if this was the place God was calling him to work in as well. Second, he was going to be at the helm of the organization of the parish Jubilee Year celebration, and yet, he needed some time to develop self-confidence in his new role and build the necessary relationships in the community. Third, Pajule parish had real financial problems: our expenditures exceeded our income, most of the time our parish account was in the red, and he was taking over at a time when the parish needed more financial resources because of the Jubilee Year celebration.

Personally, I survived on providence and faith. But the trust in the invisible or intangible things I could not pass on to him. He had been a priest for less than two months and I believe that his appointment to run the day to day affairs of the parish put him into a situation where he would have too many unknowns to deal with.

I was with him for five days. During this time, I showed him around and answered some of the questions he had with regard to the finances of the parish, admitting that we were definitely in poor shape. But I assured him that the resources the parish had were sufficient to allow him to always have food on the table; it was when he would want to do a big project that resources were always limited. I also encouraged him that the former pastor would be with him in the transition process even if he was committed at the moment to his parish.

I also wanted to take this time to say farewell to the members of the chapels of Pader and Acolibur since I had written to them that I was leaving but I was just too afraid to travel. I felt that since I had already said farewell to those at the parish church I had at least to make sure that I got out of the place safely and reached my destination in the United States of America.

Day of Departure

The morning I was to leave the parish, I had Mass in the parish church to say farewell. Close to one hundred people attended. I was impressed and pleased that so many came to the Mass on a weekday. This morning was particularly striking in its personal nature; those who attended had accepted me as a member of their family.

In this Mass, I told the congregation that even if I was going to a distant land as a student, they would always be in my thoughts and prayers. I promised them that I was going to approach my education with the same commitment and determination I had when things were difficult among them. After the Mass, when we were outside the church, I had the chance to say good-bye to each one of them individually. In fact, this morning provided me with an occasion to feel their affection and warmth for a final time.

After most people had left, about fifteen couples came to meet me in my office and shared things that I had not expected. They talked about how my three years working among them had touched and transformed them as couples and individuals. Others described the positive changes my leadership had brought into the lives of their children.

When it was almost time to leave, at midday, the altar boys and liturgical dancers that had celebrated Mass with me for the last three years came running to see me off on their class break. This was one of the hardest moments for me. Leaving Pajule was not an idea anymore; it was a reality now. I found this time to be very painful and felt a profound sense of separation like one caused by a death, since I was not sure if I would ever return to work among them as their priest or even to visit. I loosely quoted Ecclesiastes 3:1–8, saying that three years ago was the time for me to come to work in Pajule as a newly ordained priest, and it was now time for me to leave as well. I went on to say to those assembled that I was thankful for my time among them, and even though I wasn't sure what was ahead in the coming few years, I knew that God would continue to guide me and lead me as He had for the time I worked among them.

As I finished my farewell speech, I saw my altar boys, liturgical dancers, and parish staff struggle to hold back tears. Seeing this made me emotional. I shook the hands of all present and boarded the vehicle to begin my journey to Kitgum. As I drove out of the parish going through town, many stood by the roadside to say good-bye; once again I saw a lot of sadness in their faces, and some even stopped the vehicle for me to give them a final hug.

I remember one woman, who had a son called Tony and was always referred to as the mother of Tony, stopped me and said, "Father, it is a sad day that you are leaving, but we put everything in God's hands." This whole experience made me understand how painful it was to leave a place I enjoyed working in. As I reflect on this experience, I hope and pray that I have very few of these painful departures in the years to come.

When I reached Kitgum, I met up with many old friends. Most of them were very happy that I was going to school in the United States. They had heard the news the previous Sunday in Kitgum Christ the King Church. Some of these people were social workers who worked in Pajule at the peak of the war. Seeing them reminded me of my farewell speech stating that there was a time for everything. They had worked in Pajule and their time had come to an end, too. In fact, the moment I had with them made me truly realize that my time to leave had come as well.

I spent about three days in Kitgum saying farewell to my family and close friends before leaving for Kampala for my flight. Both of my parents were excited about my going to school in the United States but for different reasons. My father saw it as an opportunity to get more knowledge and broaden my perspective on life, but my mother was happy because I was getting out of the conflict zone in Pajule. Whenever she heard of any attack on a vehicle or a parish, she was always afraid that I could have been involved in it.

Chapter Forty-One

Arrival in the USA

After three days in Kitgum, I drove to the headquarters of the diocese in Gulu, where I spent a night on my way to the capital city. On reaching Kampala I spent another night. I was exhausted since I did not have any real time to relax. I looked forward to having some sleep in the course of the long flight that would almost take twenty-four hours.

On September 29, 2004, I flew to the United States six weeks after school had begun, since I had failed to get my visa on time. It was my first truly long-distance trip alone, but my bishop encouraged me to seek help from the airport officials whenever I needed it. As soon as the plane took off from the runway in Entebbe at midnight, I fell asleep only to wake up at Brussels. I remember at the beginning of the flight the waitress wanted me to eat since we were starting a long flight, but I declined since I was too tired. As the plane traveled further away from the continent of Africa, I felt like I was physically being separated from my own people and thrust into a foreign land. At the same time, the further we traveled, the more composition of the passengers changed: as we boarded the plane in Entebbe most of us were black, but as we approached the United States, most of the passengers were now white.

I found my trip from Europe to the United States extremely long, and the different entertainments on the plane did little to take away the sense of boredom as we flew over the ocean. At times it felt like an endless trip, which once again gave me a moment of introspection. I began to ask myself: "Why do I have to travel such a long distance away from home?" Once in a while I would remind myself that I must be going for some really serious business in the United States.

When I was lost in thought, I heard the air hostess make an announcement that we were flying over the state of Maine and that in less than an hour we would be landing in Newark. This was a great relief for me, but I still had to take a connecting flight from Newark to John Hopkins International Airport in Cleveland, Ohio.

When we landed and I got out of the plane, my level of anxiety rose immediately. First, the size of Newark was intimidating to me. Second, I had to change flights and make sure that my luggage was placed on the next flight. I was worried that I would not be able to identify my luggage and transfer it to the next flight. Fortunately, I was able to check my things on the flight to Cleveland. Third, the physical shock of the environment, coming from a country that is almost 99.9 percent black, was like being thrown into a sea of white people since all around I was the only black person among them. All the men and women looked alike in my eyes. They were polite, but they spoke too fast. However, I was fortunate that I came from an English-speaking country and was able to communicate even though I could see those around me strain their ears to understand me.

At the airport, I could hear the televisions broadcasting an address by Senator John Kerry on CNN, as I had arrived at the height of the 2004 presidential campaign. I rushed to the gate to board the flight for Cleveland and got lost a couple of times, but some people directed me. As soon as I entered the plane, its door was closed immediately, and I was the last person to board it before it took off.

First Impressions

When I reached Cleveland, I expected to take a taxi to Walsh University, but surprisingly, there was a student priest from my diocese waiting for me. It was exciting to meet him, as we had not seen each other for almost two years. He had come to the United States when we were at the height of the insecurity in Pajule. We had been contemporaries in the seminary, but he was four years ahead of me. As soon as we picked up my things, we headed to the airport parking lot, which was one of the first big surprises for me. It was the first time I had seen such a large parking lot with several levels and above all with very many cars, since in Uganda most cars park on the side of the street.

When we began to drive out of the airport, another surprise for me was the amount of space and the sizes of things. The road signs appeared really big to me, and the highways were also extremely wide. The many roads leading to different destinations were striking, too. This was the first time I had seen two or three lanes of cars moving in the same direction and two or three more going in the opposite direction. The number of cars and above all the high speed at which they traveled was also a big shock to me. As we continued, I kept wondering how each car could keep within its own lane, and most of the time I was afraid that the car behind us would smash into our car since they all drove very fast. The roads in Pajule were dirt, narrow, single lane. When two vehicles came from different directions, one vehicle, usually the smaller one, had to go to the side of the road and wait for the bigger one to pass.

The priest who had picked me up was filled with happiness to see me. He had just bought a car and he was learning his way around. In the excitement, he gave me his road map and asked me to read it and guide him as we drove to Canton, Ohio. Can you imagine a person from Pajule who has spent less than two hours in the United States being asked to guide a driver to an unknown destination? I looked at the map for a few minutes, and it did not make sense at all. It made me feel more tired and exhausted than ever before. I closed my eyes and wanted to sleep. In fact in the years to come, I often joked with the priest about how he had traumatized me by asking me to read the map.

Before going to Walsh University, he drove me to the Catholic parish of Our Lady of Perpetual Help in Aurora, Ohio, where he lived as a priest in residence at the time. We entered the church and prayed and thanked God for my safe trip to the United States. I loved the church, which was not the traditional rectangular church but round, brightly lit, and with plenty of space. The cleanliness was remarkable, and I questioned myself how it was kept so clean. I could not see dust at all on anything. The grass on the compound was cut and level. Being September the skies were clear and bright and the air was cool.

He later took me to Walsh University in Canton, Ohio, where I was welcomed by the Brothers of Christian Instruction since I was to live with them. My arrival in the United States marked not only the end of my ministry in Pajule but also the conclusion of a significant phase of my life. At the same time it marked the beginning of a new ministry as a priest and a student in the United States.

Epilogue

Life can be so hard and yet fulfilling as well. This was the nature of my priestly ministry in Pajule parish. Most of the days were full of risks, but not on any single day did I ever feel that it was not worth it. Deep inside me, I was convinced that this was what God wanted me to do as His priest. Even today, after almost eight years of being away from Pajule, whenever I talk about my ministry there, I get filled with so much energy, passion, and joy that I cannot compare it to anything else I have ever been a part of.

What is more gratifying to me today is the relationship I have maintained with the many friends I met there. In most friendships, as the years go by, people cut off contact with each other and move on with their lives. This has not been the case for me, as a significant number of people who became my friends in Pajule have kept in contact with me through cell phone and now e-mail. Most of them have asked me when I would finish my studies and ministry in the United States and return to work in Pajule. Some of them who have been transferred away from Pajule and are now employed in other places have promised that when they hear I am back, they will ask their employer to transfer them back to Pajule.

Even though I was exposed to many life-threatening situations as a young man and priest, I now look at my service in Pajule as a great privilege from God. In my limited ways I had the opportunity to alleviate the sufferings of my people and the chance to gain a profound understanding of the negative consequences of war on the lives of individuals and communities. It is from this background and experience that I urge advocates for peace today to give the utmost importance to the sufferings of communities and the thousands of people who live in inhuman and degrading conditions in war zones, rather than focusing on figures and statistics like the number of lives lost, the amount of money spent, the length of time the war has lasted, and the property damaged. These are important but in my view insufficient.

I would like to recognize the fact that my ministry in Pajule made me grow in my faith. I am more than ever convinced that God has a purpose for me. It is this same God who led me from Pajule to the United States and has sustained me throughout my graduate studies and ministry in this country. This is because, during my ministry in Pajule, I often ate, drank, and chatted with a person who was killed the next day. The question I always asked myself was this: "Why do some of the members of my community get killed, and though I have taken the same risks as they did, I keep on surviving?" This made me come to the conclusion that if I am still alive today, God must have a purpose and a mission for me to accomplish.

Further, it is a fact that the many years that have passed have created some distance between me and the raw feelings and trauma caused by the war. And yet I know that the impact of the war will live with me for the rest of my life, and there will even be times when I find it difficult to articulate it. I remember in my first days as a student at Walsh University in 2004, a fire truck drove onto the university in the middle of the night and honked its horns very loudly. When I heard the loud sounds in the middle of my sleep, I was gripped with fear and wanted to run out of my bedroom, thinking that the LRA were breaking into the place. Minutes later I realized that I was now in the United States—the bedroom where I lay was smaller, cramped, and brightly lit compared to my previous one in Pajule, which was more spacious and darker, since power outages were common. In fact, it took me almost two years to be healed from the fright of any loud sounds and bangs. Even after spending almost eight years in the United States, the blasts and the sounds of fireworks for Independence Day celebrations on July 4 every year bring back the memories and tensions of a rebel attack. Whenever Independence Day is approaching, I always worry about how I will pass the day.

While most of my time in the United States has been spent going to school, I have had the unique opportunity to meet many people and learn from them about their culture. I am today much more attentive to cultural similarities and differences. At the same time, this has made me more appreciative of the uniquely distinct values of my own Acoli culture. For example, I have come to the realization that while all people may desire justice, we achieve the same goal differently. In my Acoli culture, true justice is restorative justice, and this cultural perspective needs to be explained to other cultures so they can develop respect for it and accept it as good.

All in all, I did not expect to come to the United States to go to school. But I am glad things happened the way they did. It gave me a break and allowed me to step out of the center of violence. I have also had the time to reflect and write down my recollections. Through my graduate studies, I have acquired knowledge that I believe has made me more insightful, self-confident, and a better writer. It is my hope that my education and priestly ministry in the United States will one day enrich my service in Uganda and in particular the archdiocese of Gulu when the time comes for me to return home and again work among my people.

Acknowledgements

I am happy that this project has come to an end. It has taken me three years to complete it, and it has been a great learning experience for me. In the first place, I came to learn that with any good work that gets completed, there are several people who commit themselves to see it through to the end. Second, each one of us has unique talents and gifts. I experienced this in the course of the writing, as all my proofreaders brought a new perspective to the work. Third, I came to learn that openness to critique is key to any good piece of writing.

I would like to specifically thank these people that worked with me throughout this project, beginning with Reverend Father Doctor Jino Okech Mwaka for his encouragement. When I first shared with him my desire to write a book, he was very enthusiastic about it and was a great source of inspiration throughout the process. I also appreciate his feedback and his pointing out small but significant details that I often overlooked in the course of the writing of this book.

To Reverend Father Doctor Alex Ojacor, a contemporary at the St. Pius X Seminary High School in the archdiocese of Tororo, I am grateful for his insights and insistence that the work ought to have a logical flow and be internally organized. Father Alex is a busy man and spends a lot of his time spreading God's Kingdom, and I am thankful that he could devote some of his precious time to this work.

I am also grateful to Reverend Grace Aciro, a member of the religious congregation of The Little Sisters of Mary Immaculate of Gulu, for taking time from her many school administrative responsibilities to read through this work, which benefited from the variety of words and expressions she recommended in the course of the writing.

I am also thankful to Donna Caputo, who used one of her summer vacations to give me the first comprehensive report on the project. Her overall evaluation pointing out the strengths of the work and its contribution to society was a great impetus to continue with the project. This book also benefited from her pointing out the ideas that I could develop, expand, or where suspense could be employed. I also thank my sister, Monica Ageno, the eighth born in my family and a young fiction writer, for what she brought to the work as she highlighted areas in which creativity and imagination could be used.

I would also like to thank Father Ruffino Ezama, an African Comboni missionary priest from Uganda, for his daily encouragement in the course of the writing and the editing of the work. At the end of an exhausting day of writing, he was someone I could always talk to. His words, "Robert, the work is coming out well and holding its own," served as a constant inspiration to me. I also thank him for introducing to me the computer software program known as Grammerly that we employed at the initial stages of editing. Thanks to Father Olweny Charles for reading through the work and identifying areas in which we could add more detailed information, and to Father Ronald Okello for his availability and help in case we needed to cross-check specific details about particular issues and events on the ground.

I also like to thank Mr. Jerry Spurgeon, a World War II veteran of the US Navy, who served in the South Pacific. Jerry is an avid reader of books on the American Civil War era. I gave him a new name in the course of the writing of this book: Muzeyi, a common word in Ugandan local languages that refers to an elder. This book benefited from his wisdom and counsel. He pointed out concepts and ideas that would be obscure to the audience in the United of States of America, and as a result I had to clarify them or give more detail. Whenever he approved of a chapter, I was confident that it was accessible to the ordinary man or woman.

I also thank my own father, Mr. Andrew P.K. Obol, for the support and encouragement throughout the course of this project, as well as my own sister, Flora Aling, the third born in our family, for selecting and making sure that the photographs we needed to be incorporated in the book were sent to the United States from Uganda on time.

Finally, I thank my editor, William Skoluda, for the enthusiasm and passion he brought to the work. He spent nearly every evening of his life for six consecutive months on this work. It was fascinating for me to learn from him that my book reminded him of his childhood experiences and was connected to the broader human experience even if the context was very different. I will always remember those moments in which we haggled over words and expressions we were to use, since we wanted to communicate to the audience in United States of America and at the same time to the continent of Africa and other parts of the world as well.

To all these people and others whose names have not been mentioned but have contributed in one way or another toward the completion of this book, you have my sincere gratitude and appreciation.

About the Author

Dr. Robert Nyeko Obol was born in December 1971 in Kitgum District. He is the firstborn of the nine children of Mary Tina Obol and Andrew P. K. Obol, and is a priest of the archdiocese of Gulu. Dr. Obol completed his training for the Catholic priesthood in his home country of Uganda and was ordained a priest on August 18, 2001.

He holds a bachelor's degree in Philosophy from Urbaniana University in Rome, a master's of arts degree in education from Walsh University in Canton, Ohio, and a master's of arts degree in theology and a doctorate in ministry from Saint Mary Seminary and Graduate School of Theology in Wickliffe, Ohio. He has also successfully completed a one-year residential training course as a spiritual care provider at the Cleveland Clinic in Ohio.

After his ordination to the priesthood, he was immediately assigned to work in Pajule parish in the archdiocese of Gulu as associate pastor and later pastor. Of the three years he served in the parish before coming to the United States of America, he experienced only five months of peace as a newly ordained priest. The rest was marked by war and violence with the return of the LRA from their bases in South Sudan to wage war in Uganda, and Pajule parish suddenly became the epicenter of the conflict.

The Life and Lessons from a Warzone is a memoir that has taken Dr. Obol three years to write. In it, he discusses the events that occurred almost on a daily basis during the time of unrest in Pajule and northern Uganda in general. Further, he reflects on the role of faith, providence, community, and reconciliation in a warzone. And above all, he shares the enduring lessons that he has learned about life and himself from working in such an environment. Finally, it is his hope that sharing these experiences will educate those who have not had the experience of war about what life is like in a warzone.

Dr. Robert Nyeko Obol resides in Kansas City, Kansas and he is a spiritual care provider to the sick.